All in a Day's Work

A shot rang out. Dottie jumped, though she couldn't tell right away who had fired it. A moment later she saw Tiny holding his bloody forearm. Flesh wound.

"Mom," Brandi said, "have you got these other two covered?"

"I do." Dottie had the Stinger out and aimed at the two fat boys, hands raised.

"Very good," Brandi said. "Now, Tiny, get your sorry ass in front of the headlights unless you want a matching hole in your head."

Tiny, who now understood this was for real, came forward.

"Mom, about that girl inside . . . ?

The trailer door swung open and the naked Lorita, with a rifle in her hands, came out shooting. . . .

THE
HUNTRESS

...

The True Saga of
Dottie and Brandi Thorson,
Modern-Day Bounty Hunters

...

CHRISTOPHER KEANE
with DOTTIE THORSON

A TOM DOHERTY ASSOCIATES BOOK
NEW YORK

THE HUNTRESS

A Forge Book
Published by Tom Doherty Associates, LLC
175 Fifth Avenue
New York, NY 10010

www.tor.com

Forge® is a registered trademark of Tom Doherty Associates, LLC.

ISBN: 0-812-58988-2

First Forge edition: October 2000

Printed in the United States of America

0 9 8 7 6 5 4 3 2 1

For
Ken Barras

Acknowledgments

. . .

Many thanks to the following whose efforts contributed enormously to the work: John McCarthy; David Keller; Don Fine; Jason Poston; Matthew Snyder; Mandy Syers; Margaret Lazarus; Renner Wunderlicht; William Martin; Scott Neister; Rhode Island School of Design Faculty Grant; Martha Frisoli; Connie Biewald; Tracy Winn; the late Gary Provost; and Susan Crawford of The Crawford Literary Agency, with love.

Author's note

■ ■ ■

I have used pseudonyms and altered descriptions of certain characters to protect privacy. The name and identifying characteristics of Q. D. Reese have been changed. The character's internal thought processes were constructed from Dottie and Brandi's observations and recollections, along with file documents, including those from various correctional and psychiatric institutions where Reese was evaluated. Robin Ripley is a composite character based upon women with whom Dottie and Brandi associated over several years and is not intended to be a portrayal of a single individual.

Though this is a work of nonfiction, I have taken certain storytelling liberties, particularly having to do with the timing of events.

—CHRISTOPHER KEANE

Foreword

■ ■ ■

On a hot July afternoon in 1994 the telephone rang. I picked it up and heard a woman's voice say, "Christopher? This is a voice from the past."

A pause. I wasn't sure what to think.

"It's Dottie Thorson, and I have a proposition for you."

And then it all came rushing back.

In the late seventies I wrote a book, *The Hunter*, about Ralph Thorson, a modern-day bounty hunter who lived and worked in Los Angeles. Steve McQueen starred in the movie, McQueen's last, based on the book.

In the biography and the movie, and in Thorson's life, Dottie Thorson, twenty years Thorson's junior, played significant roles: wife; mother to their daughter, Brandi; business partner. Indeed, as a business partner in the bounty-hunting business Dottie often hunted fugitives with Ralph, kept the books, and dealt with an array of criminals, cops, movie stars, convicted killers, bank presidents, high-and-low-lifes who paraded through their North Hollywood, California, home.

On the phone Dottie told me that Ralph had recently passed away. She and Brandi, left with a mountain of debts, had inherited only one thing of value—the family bounty-hunting business.

In this rugged profession, bounty hunters' targets are, with few exceptions, male fugitives who will do literally anything to stay out of jail. Because of the nature of the work, no insurance company will insure bounty hunters. They have to rely on quick wits, contacts in the field, a network of law enforcement officers *and* criminals, and tight-fisted bail-bondsmen for their sustenance.

"How would you like to write our story?" Dottie said. "A mother-daughter bounty-hunting team working out of Los Angeles."

She told me how she and Brandi had been ridiculed, scorned, dismissed for being female, warned against the consequences of their decision; mentally chastised by their peers and physically brutalized by the fugitives they chased, and how still, against these substantial odds, they battled on.

In the months following Dottie's phone call I went to California, where Dottie, Brandi and I rummaged through boxes of documents and questioned scores of people who worked with the family, past and present.

Ralph Thorson's death, the secrets he kept and an old enemy with a score to settle came back to plague his family. The story herein is true. Dottie and Brandi Thorson live as testament to it all.

—CHRISTOPHER KEANE
Cambridge, Massachusetts

The Law

...

TAYLOR VS TAINTOR, 16 WALL 366 (21 LAW ED. 287). In this case the SUPREME COURT OF THE UNITED STATES said:

"When bail is given, the principal is regarded as delivered to the custody of his sureties. Their dominion is a continuance of the original imprisonment. Whenever they choose to do so, they may seize or deliver up in their discharge, and if that cannot be done at once they may imprison him until it can be done. They may exercise their rights in person or by agent. They may pursue him into another state; may arrest him on the Sabbath; and, if necessary, may break and enter his house for that pupose. The seizure is not made by virtue of new process. None is needed." (It should also be noted that this rule is not limited to cases of felony, but is applied to every case where a person is released from legal custody upon the giving of a bail bond or recognizance and includes all cases of misdemeanor and even cases of civil arrest out of a civil action.)

An Opinion

■ ■ ■

Out of state bailbondsmen apparently have greater rights with respect to obtaining custody of a fugitive from justice than does a peace officer from another state.

Although peace officers must go through the courts by way of extradition proceedings to obtain custody of a suspected law violator, under existing law a bailbondsman can gain custody of a fugitive without the necessity of resorting to state court proceedings.

—HON. MARK BRANDLER
JUDGE, SUPERIOR COURT
COUNTY OF LOS ANGELES
STATE OF CALIFORNIA

One

...

STEAM ROSE OFF Otsego Street's blacktop. For twelve days running the temperature had climbed over one hundred degrees. A massive orange sun beat down upon the city. Los Angeles was on rationed water, and in this intense heat the world slowed down, lost a step. Liquor stores tripled their sales, violence broke out like a virus across Southern California. Tempers flared. Bullets flew. A crime wave rode in on the heels of the heat wave and the bodies were piling up.

None of this mattered to Q. D. Reese, who sat dressed in black driving a late-model Jaguar. In his forty-four years Q. D. could not remember waiting for anything with greater anticipation. Even getting out of prison after eight years didn't match the downright glee he felt at this moment.

He had been cruising the neighborhood where Ralph Thorson and his family lived, where he, Q. D. Reese, had once been a welcome guest in Ralph Thorson's home, where he had in fact worked as a bounty hunter in training for *Mr.* Thorson, the most famous of all bounty hunters. Worked for him, that is, until the police came and threw him in prison.

Before his old pal Ralph Thorson had turned him in.

Q. D. had been driving through this neighborhood for nearly three weeks, searching for patterns in the daily movements of the Thorson family—Ralph, Dottie and their daughter Brandi. And he had found one—a work pattern—that suited his purposes. His plan had been laid and now Q. D. was ready to watch the culmination of his efforts. "Ready, Ralph?" he muttered, looking at the Thorson home's front door as he passed. "Today's the day."

Famous Ralph Thorson, big-time bounty hunter, with a book written about him and a movie made on his life. And what a life! The old alcoholic bastard could hardly walk anymore, could hardly breathe, still smoking and drinking, hooked on medication. You reap what you sow, Ralphie, Q. D. thought, and now we'll see what you're made of, how much you've got left. Q. D. had been waiting for this day for a long time. Eight long years.

He checked his watch. Seven A.M. on the nose. Time to pull over and watch the show. Q. D. eased the Jaguar to the curb, squirted washer fluid on the windshield and wiped it dry. Didn't want to miss a thing.

He removed the .22 bullet from his mouth and inspected it, cleaned the saliva off on his shirt sleeve. He inspected the tiny scratch marks his teeth had made on the casing, kissed it, and replaced it in his mouth, shell-tip facing the back of his throat. He ran his tongue over the slug's smooth surface. Old habits never die, eh, Ralph?

7:03. Q. D. leaned back against the seat's fine brown leather and fixed his eyes on the Thorson's front door. Any minute now.

Two

...

DOTTIE THORSON STOOD by the window and looked out at the blistering California morning. Tall, angular, with reddish brown hair and a girlish way about her, she was twenty years younger than her husband. And she was worried about him. About Ralph's diminishing physical condition. During the past few weeks he had been getting noticeably worse.

Down on the street she saw Ralph's Cadillac and her canary-yellow Plymouth, the Banana, hugging the curb. It was also after seven and she was fretting about Brandi being late for work. Strauss's *Rosenkavalier*, to which Ralph awoke every morning, crescendoed from the stereo.

She could hear him ranting in the back bedroom about some problem or other. There had been so many problems lately that Dottie had begun to shut them out. But they were hard to ignore. Ralph, with his codeine addiction and increased drinking, had been more abusive than ever to her and Brandi. Over the years his dependence on the codeine, originally prescribed for a foot infection, had become serious.

The alcohol aggravated his foot condition, for which he took more codeine to calm the pain. He was caught in a vicious cycle, and so were they all.

Dottie spent her waking hours in constant turmoil. Her stomach raged in nervousness, she couldn't sleep. She'd become the referee in the battles between Ralph and Brandi, and when she and Ralph went at it, Brandi refereed.

"I'm driving Brandi to work today," Ralph announced, marching into the living room in his standard uniform: a flowered shirt, shorts and sandals. He had lost a lot of weight, down from 275 to 200, which under normal conditions would be a good thing, but he had lost it all in a little more than a month. Dottie had been trying to get him to see a doctor, but the more weight he lost, the more stubbornly he clung to his infamous hatred for, or fear of, doctors. He was a strong man, but at sixty-eight his immune system was not what it used to be.

"Ralph," Dottie said, looking him over, "I don't mind taking her to work." The usual plan was for Dottie to drive Brandi to work at the restaurant and in the late afternoon when she was done, to pick her up. Ralph hadn't driven her in months. But there was no telling with him these days; sudden inspirations ruled his life.

"I'm never too sick to take my own daughter to work!" he announced. He carried a case file with him, one of the thousands they kept in the small office off the living room where a bank of phones and file cabinets stood. This was the "cockpit" from which they did the preliminary paperwork in tracking down fugitives who had jumped bail, and whom Ralph had been hired by bailbondsmen to bring back, dead or alive.

"Furthermore," he was saying, "I spent most of last night figuring out how we're going to get rich."

"We're never going to get rich, Dad," Brandi said, "haven't you figured that out yet?"

She stood in her bedroom doorway in the blue and white waitress uniform with *The Biscuit and Brandi* stitched in blue over the pocket. She placed her schoolbook on the back of the chair. Tonight at Valley Junior College, where she went to evening classes twice a week, she had a psychology exam.

"Hey, your old dad may be crippled but his brain works just like it always has." He waved the file in the air. "I've spent a lot of years tracking this guy down and I am moving in for the proverbial kill. It's off to the desert, worries over. Life is going to be a helluva lot better around here. Bet on it."

"Yeah, yeah, sure," Brandi said. "I mean, gee, Dad, does this mean I can spend junior year abroad?"

"Why is today's youth so cynical?" Ralph sat at the bar where he had hosted—as "Papa" Thorson—the famous and infamous on both sides of the law for nearly forty-five years. He tapped the file. "In these pages is the answer to our problems. I've already started thinking about the new car."

"What new car?" Brandi said. "And after you answer that one, maybe you can tell me how I'm going to get to work on time."

"Come on then, Brandi," Dottie said, "let's get a move on."

"God damn it!" Ralph shouted, banging his fist on the bar. "I'm trying to tell you how we're going to climb out of this and all you can think about is getting to that greasy spoon."

The violins of *Rosenkavalier* soared through the house.

Dottie crossed her arms in front of her chest, wondering how long this was going to take. "All right," she said, calling on the gods of patience. "Let's hear it."

"Oh, for chrissakes." Ralph snatched the file off the bar and carried it, limping, into the office where Dottie heard the opening and closing of the drawer and Ralph's angry mumblings.

Brandi looked at her mother and rolled her eyes. "Let's see if we can start today without a brawl."

"You ready?" Dottie said softly to Brandi, who nodded and grabbed her psychology book off the back of the chair.

"Not today," Ralph said, coming back into the room. "Today, *I'm* taking her to work. Maybe *she'll* listen to how I've been able to solve our financial problems."

"Ralph, I don't mind—" Dottie said.

"Well, I do, and I will drive my own daughter to work.

Case closed." She watched him moving with determination, and a great deal of pain, across the room and out the door. She went to the window where she could see him at the steps, gripping the rail for support and hobbling down to the street. Much of his suffering he had brought on himself, but that didn't stop her from trying to keep his spirits up. It wasn't easy. As angry as he got, she had to remember when things had been good and in those memories she found strength. He needed her and she was not going to abandon him, though God knew there had been times . . .

"It's okay, Mom," Brandi said. "I'll listen to his big plans. He'll be much easier to live with today."

"Let's hope."

"Just don't aggravate him."

"Why don't *I* go to the restaurant and *you* stay here?"

Brandi leaned over and kissed her on the cheek. "I don't know which is worse."

"I do." Though Dottie knew that Brandi, at nineteen, could take care of herself, she worried constantly about her. "Got your purse?"

"See? I've inherited *some* things from you," Brandi said as she hurried back to her room.

Dottie walked outside where she stood at the top of the steps by the ivy patch, watching Ralph, sour-faced, struggling into the Caddy.

She saw him put the key into the ignition and listened to the engine grind and grind and finally cough and die. Oh, Jesus, she thought, this'll send him into orbit. Ralph coaxed the engine again but the Caddy would do no work for him today.

He climbed out of the car, fuming, and hunkered back to the Banana.

"Keys in it?" he growled.

"Under the mat." Dottie knew how much Ralph loathed the Banana, pile of rust that it was, whose seat would not go back, behind whose steering wheel he had to squeeze his aching body so that he could barely breathe.

Dottie moved down beyond the ivy patch to the small flower garden she had planted, her pride. Their home, a white stucco adobe with a red tile roof, stood on a knoll in their middle-class North Hollywood, California, neighborhood, giving it the highest vantage point of any house on the block. Because of its elevation, the people who had lived and visited here over the years had become known as the Otsego Hill Mob.

As Ralph fumbled with the Banana's keys, Dottie felt something, like a premonition, crawl up her back to her neck. She involuntarily turned her head and stared off down the street, looking for something, not knowing what. The feeling, a creeping sense of dread, burrowed in. Her eyes skipped and darted from windshield to windshield, from car to car parked along the hedgerows, beside the curb, in the shade of the maple trees that lined the block.

Just then Brandi flew out of the front door and hurried down the steps, stopping to give her mother another peck on the cheek.

Behind one windshield belonging to a late-model sports car across the street, Dottie saw a pair of eyes. Weird eyes, sick eyes, she thought, mentally disturbed eyes. She locked onto them. Whatever had been crawling up her back had taken hold, dug its teeth into her flesh. And these eyes behind the windshield of the sports car told her that her premonition should not be taken idly.

She rocked back on her heels. Her sudden impulse was to shout to Ralph. She turned and opened her mouth, but her scream was lost in a blinding flash of light and the roar of an explosion down below.

Out on the street she saw the Banana's front end blow apart, shooting iron and chrome into the air. Flames burst out of the front, throwing Ralph back into the seat. Brandi, arms raised into the air, kept moving, toward the flames and roar, down the steps toward the car.

A second explosion picked her off the ground and hurled her into Dottie. The impact propelled them back into the ivy patch.

Dottie slammed to the ground face first. The shock dulled her, she tasted dirt. Another explosion erupted in her ears, then came the crackling of fire. Ralph's screams mingled with a hot wind carrying the smell of charred flesh. She felt the need to push herself up and run down the steps to the car, to save him. But she was pinned to the earth, as if roots had grown up around her, fastening her there.

Above the sound of the fire, she heard Brandi crying, "Daddy, Daddy . . . !"

Three

∎ ∎ ∎

ONE BY ONE Dottie watched the mourners advance to the pulpit and tell the gathering what a strong yet gentle man Ralph Thorson had been, how the world would miss him. She watched as tears gathered in their eyes. These were Ralph's friends, and hers, some of whom they had known since the beginning.

A heaviness overtook her and she lowered her head. For twenty years she too had been strong and this was no time to falter. Yet she was tired; whatever energy she'd possessed had been drained off. She adjusted her body in the pew and straightened. If not for herself, she needed a show of courage for Brandi, who sat beside her, tears streaking down her face.

Dottie Thorson had her own private feelings about her husband. She loved him, and at times hated him, admired and resented him. Through the years they had changed, grown together, been torn apart and pulled together again. But no matter what else they'd become, they were always a family.

"Ralph Thorson was the last of a breed," Bill Sallie, the Commander of the LAPD Valley Division and their closest friend, said from the pulpit. "He was a man born out of time. His heart and sensibility lived in the ancient code of the West, while his duties belonged in the modern world. Therein lay Ralph's great conflict, one always pulling him away from the other. I loved him like a brother, as many of us have. He shared his extraordinary gifts with his fellow man."

More than a thousand people had come to the service. Army Archerd made note in *Variety* that in Steve McQueen's last film, *The Hunter,* McQueen portrayed the life of Ralph Thorson, modern-day American bounty hunter, last of a breed. Paramount Pictures, who had made *The Hunter,* sent flowers and took out a remembrance ad. The L.A. *Times* and other papers included in their obituary notices a chronicle of Ralph's accomplishments.

In the pews Dottie recognized ex-cons whom Ralph had put in prison and for whom he later found jobs, along with police officers, bailbondsmen, and mafiosi he had befriended over the years. All had come to pay their respects.

Long-time neighbor Jimmy Doohan, Scottie in "Star Trek," delivered one of the eulogies. Presidents of banks, movie producers, people who had drunk at Ralph's living-room bar, "baby" bounty hunters in training who had camped in the house for months on end, learning the trade; they were all here.

Each whispered a word of condolence to Dottie and Brandi or gave them a nod as they passed.

Dottie suffered through a flood of memories, one of which carried her back to the first time she had met Ralph. In a bar near the L.A. County Courthouse she had gone looking for a bondsman to find her check-kiting boyfriend who had jumped bail and left her holding the bag. The bondsman introduced her to his investigator, Ralph Thorson. At the time, newly off a bus from Iowa, Dottie was living in the Evangeline Home for Working Women. Two months after meeting Ralph she moved in with him. They set up house behind Grauman's Chinese Theater, in a neighborhood of struggling film people who ate cheap Mexican food and spent long nights on back porches trading stories. How glorious and new it all had been for her, and how she had loved him.

"Dottie," the voice said. "It's time." Bill Sallie stood above her, extending his hand.

"Ready, sweetheart?" she said to Brandi, who plucked the last Kleenex from the box and blew her nose into it.

Brandi stood. Dottie suddenly realized how tall Brandi had become, since when? Dark-haired, with Ralph's strong features and her own slim angular figure, Brandi wiped the tears from her pale blue eyes and followed her mother into the aisle.

On the way to the rear of the church, Dottie searched the faces she passed and saw their sympathy. Many of them knew how her life with Ralph had disintegrated; she felt momentary guilt for not having made peace with him before he died.

Before he'd been murdered.

In the small garden behind the chapel, she heard someone say, "Doesn't Dottie realize that explosion was probably meant for her?" A chill raced through her.

She looked at the speaker, one of Ralph's baby bounty hunters who quickly realized his mistake and turned away. The thought had occurred to her that the dynamite had been in the Banana, her car—but who, she wondered, would want her dead?

The other part of the puzzle frightened her even more. The question haunted her: if Ralph hadn't insisted upon driving Brandi to work that morning, neither one of them would be alive.

That she and Brandi had been the bomber's targets was lost on nobody. As a precaution, Bill Sallie had assigned a plainclothes officer to watch the house from an unmarked car.

The mourners formed a line outside the church to shake her hand and kiss her cheek and mutter words of condolence. When the crowd had cleared out and she and Brandi were left alone, instead of going straight home they decided to take a drive.

"What are you thinking about?" Dottie said.

"Nothing."

"No, come on."

Brandi had taken off her shoes and put her feet up on the dash. "This lump in my chest or pain in my chest, or whatever it is. I don't think I have any more tears left. You?"

"Cried out."

"I can't help thinking about Dad. I mean, you know, he's not *here* any more. Not *here,* ever again. We're never going to see him again. Isn't that *weird?* Never see him, gone."

Dottie wished she could say or do something but nothing seemed right. "We have each other," she finally said, "that's something." She noticed two fresh rivers rolling down Brandi's cheeks.

"Each other," Brandi muttered.

"It's something you shouldn't dwell on. There's nothing we can do except play the cards we're dealt." Dottie realized she was starting to sound like a condolence card, so she stopped.

"There you go again, Mom, not facing reality. You have to face the fact that he's gone, confront it."

"Why should I when I have you to face reality for me?"

"Are we being sarcastic?"

When Dottie said nothing Brandi grunted and looked at the trees passing by outside the car window. After a while she said, "I'm losing it, Mom, but I guess that's sort of natural under the circumstances, right?"

"Right."

Dottie wanted to tell her it wouldn't be long before the feelings of loss went away—hours or days, even weeks or months, or maybe even as long as a year—but secretly she believed it would probably take years, maybe forever; but you lived with these things, didn't you, while other things crowded in to take their place.

Four

...

Q. D. REESE, WORKING actor, ex-con, man about town, sat on the deck of his hideaway up on Mulholland Drive, smoking cigarettes, drinking tequila out of a bottle, swallowing the worm, chewing on his bullet.

With the city below him, feeling strong and vital, he remembered with relish the moment just before the explosion when he had looked through the windshield of his Jaguar and seen Dottie on the steps outside her front door staring into his eyes like some arrogant queen. They should have been Ralph's eyes. Dottie and Brandi should have been in that car. They should have been blown to shreds.

When he'd seen the screw-up happening before him he hadn't been so pleased with himself. He had driven out of their neighborhood back up here, sickened by the mistake. His chance to watch Ralph Thorson's reaction to the death of his wife and daughter had been stolen from him.

Q. D. assuaged his disappointment with the memory of Brandi's lithe figure hopping like a young rabbit down the stairs towards her Daddy. And then, in the explosion's impact, her body being hurled back against her mother's, and the two of them sprawling into the ivy bed. Birds of paradise among the stinkweed.

Then there had been the funeral. Pathetic. Teary-eyed friends mourning. Actually, Q. D. had been surprised by the size of the crowd, especially since Ralph Thorson had fucked up so many lives, including his own. Including *my* own, Q. D. thought bitterly.

Q. D. had been in the back pew taking it all in.

Now up at his house, on his deck overlooking the city of angels, he felt more content. He carried the bottle of tequila back inside to his makeup table and got to work. First he worked on his eyes, then his hair color—a little white, a little blond—and deepened the wrinkles in his face and hands. Never forget the hands; they're a dead giveaway. He chose his wardrobe: floppy hat, canvas shoes, loose-fitting shirt and trousers. He fashioned a limp. He put *The Wild Bunch* tape in the VCR and watched William Holden hobble around for a while until he got it right.

Q. D.'s dog, a Yorkie that had belonged to his former roommate Bill Porter, the owner of the house, wiggled up to his makeup table like a whore in a heat, wagging its tail. Ugly little shit. Watching all this eager canine enthusiasm, Q. D. felt a momentary guilt at what he had planned for the little rodent.

He spent the next half hour putting the finishing touches on his makeup job and could actually *feel* the years growing on him.

By noon he had perfected his character to the point where he was ready to introduce him to the public.

Five

■ ■ ■

IT WAS EARLY morning and Dottie couldn't sleep. Since five she'd been roaming around the house, which felt like a tomb, silent in Ralph's absence, the ghost of him everywhere. Truth was, while his spirit had remained, the physical part of him—the walking, shouting, grumbling part of him that took up so much space—was gone, leaving behind a terrible emptiness. She looked in on Brandi, all tangled up in her sheets, and promised herself to take extra care with her, to fill her days with opportunity, and to keep the pain of her father's death at bay.

By eight Brandi was up and sluggishly wandering around, visiting the refrigerator, roaming aimlessly through the house in her underwear, listening to Dottie's offers of going out somewhere.

"Where, exactly?"

Dottie couldn't think of anywhere specific. "Just out. Let's make it an adventure. We'll get in the Caddy and drive."

Brandi grunted, returned to her bedroom and closed the door. Dottie couldn't help but think about all the teenage suicides she'd read about in the paper, from depression, or hopelessness, or loss.

"Leave your door open a crack, please," she said to Brandi. "Have to keep the air circulating."

"Don't worry, Mom, for God's sake. I just want privacy." They looked at each other through the bedroom's dull light.

Condolence messages clogged the answering machine. Bailbondsmen, for whom death was just another aspect of business, called routinely to inform whoever answered that the dates on some cases were about to expire. And Myrna Factor, one of Dottie's oldest friends, left a teary-eyed message that Dottie could barely understand through the nose-blowing. "I wanted to go to the funeral, Dottie, honestly I did, but you wouldn't have wanted me ruining a lovely— what am I saying, lovely—what I mean to say is that I just couldn't . . ." Dottie punched *Erase* and Myrna vanished.

An hour passed, two. Dottie looked outside and saw an old man walking his dog. At three in the afternoon Brandi emerged from her room and they ate roast beef sandwiches at the kitchen table. Dottie tried to take a nap. She read two pages of a mystery novel and put it down. Brandi took out her paints and easel and twenty minutes later put them away.

They jumped when the phone rang, screened messages, returned none of them. At five o'clock Dottie went outside to water the ivy and saw the same old man walking his Yor-kie, said hello to him. The poor old guy was bent over in pain and Dottie wondered if she would end up like that, a depressing thought.

She noticed a blue unmarked car parking halfway down the block, with a guy behind the wheel—Bill Sallie's plain-clothes surveillance.

Later she and Brandi sat on the floor of Ralph's office surrounded by case files, financial records, overdue bills, bank and credit card statements. Gloom had settled in at last.

"We're fucked," said Dottie.

"Don't swear, Mom, will you?"

"We're broke, more broke than I realized."

"You did the books, how could this be?"

"Ralph spent and didn't get receipts."

"He spent and didn't have the money to spend, you mean."

"Both."

"How bad is it?" Brandi said. "I don't want to know, do I?"

"No."

"Tell me anyway."

Dottie picked up a sheet of paper. "From what I can gather your father took out a mortgage on the house."

Brandi waited.

"Somehow he convinced a mortgage company to part with ten thousand dollars."

"Ten thousand? Okay . . ."

"Everything would be okay if I could find it. Which I can't."

Brandi's brow-wrinkled. "When did he do this?"

"Three months ago."

"And there's no record of it? What about a savings account?"

Dottie would have laughed if she didn't feel so glum. "What use would your father have for a savings account?"

"He had to spend the money somewhere."

"Sweetie, he probably drank it away, or loaned it to somebody, paid off a debt . . . who knows?"

They sat for a while until Dottie announced she was ready for a nap and went off to bed. At midnight she climbed out of bed and returned to the living room, where she collapsed on the couch.

Brandi came out of her own room and joined her. "Mom," she said, "this is not working."

"What's that, Pumpkin?"

"That dynamite was meant for us, wasn't it?"

"For me."

"*Us*," Brandi insisted. "Whoever did this knew you drove me to work every morning."

"Let's not dwell on it."

"Somebody tried to blow us up. Which means they'll try again."

"We don't know that."

"Mom, get real!"

"I'm not going to get pulled into an argument with you, especially about this."

Brandi threw herself back against the cushions and pouted. Long dark hair fell over her sour expression. Her pearl-colored skin—Ralph's skin—and pale eyes made her look surreal in the dim light: tough, determined, stubborn, almost Oriental in the way she refused to betray emotion. Another mirror of Ralph. Dottie tried hard to appreciate these traits Brandi had inherited from him; the best she could do for the moment was to accept them.

"You don't face things, Mom," Brandi said, getting to her feet. "You avoid them."

"I face them in my own way. What do you want me to do, walk around bearing a cross? I wish I had your ability to grasp things so easily, but I don't. Some things take me a long time."

When Brandi went back to her room Dottie wandered into the office, which lay buried under an avalanche of paper. She knew that a lot of Ralph's money had gone to bar tabs. She had seen the credit card bills, the ATM withdrawals, the checks Ralph had written to this grill and that pub.

Ralph was lonely and needed the company of men. Up and down the California coast he and his pals had sat on bar stools, reliving great moments from the past or scamming cases or reinterpreting law. At the end of each night, full of whiskey, Ralph would call for the check and plunk the money down. That's just the way he was.

She also knew he had used liquor to medicate his pain. His foot problem caused him great suffering and hindered his ability to work—which was why, after four or five hours on the job, he started drinking by early afternoon. But he had worked and was paid for it.

That source of income was now gone. She and Brandi literally had no money except for what Brandi brought in from her waitress job at The Biscuit, and whatever Dottie could cajole out of tight-fisted bailbondsmen. When bondsmen found out about Ralph's death they refused to honor his back pay. Death, as their credo went, satisfies all debts.

She heard Brandi call her from her room.

Dottie left the office and hurried down the hall. In the bedroom she saw Brandi's paintings on the wall, along with a bold sign: FOR SALE: Original Characters from THE HUNTER!

"What are you doing?" Dottie said.

"Selling my portraits. Not that I can get a lot for them, but what do you think?"

These were Brandi's rogue's gallery portraits of the men and women who had frequented the house over the years. From the time she was twelve and started to draw, she asked regulars to pose for her and she would capture their likenesses in oils. She had become quite good.

"You don't want to sell them," Dottie said.

"Not good enough, huh?"

"I think they're *very* good, Brandi. It's just . . ." Dottie felt the tears gather behind her eyes. The memories started pouring out.

Brandi came over and wrapped her arms around her. "It's your turn, Mom," she said, "let 'em rip."

They stood in the center of the room, surrounded by Brandi's gallery peering at them from their canvases, and cried until they were raw and dry and the salt had caked on their skin. Then, cried out, they went back through the living room into the office, where they sat cross-legged on the floor, facing each other, surrounded by the flurry of bills.

"Money. Living expenses. Day-to-day loose change." Dottie reeled off the items while Brandi made a list. "What do we have and what do we owe?"

"Expenses." Brandi wrote the word at the top of the page.

"Food. Mortgage. Car payment. Kitchen plumbing."

The list grew. They found places to scrimp, they agreed to reduce their fast-food intake. House payments came first, but the bold truth was they were not going to make the mortgage payments and pay the bills, too. They had $700 in the bank and, for starters, owed $3,000, most of it overdue.

"I'm too old to turn tricks," Dottie said with resignation.

"And I'm too young to die from some virus. So what else?"

"No one will loan us money. *I* wouldn't loan us money."

"We don't take charity anyway."

They sat in silence.

"Do they need anybody else at the restaurant?" Dottie said.

"Not like you, they don't."

"What's that supposed to mean?"

"Not like you, not like me. They already have me, who tells the customers to take a hike if they get out of hand. They don't want the *mother* of somebody like me working for them. Plus it's a rotten job. You'd hate it."

"We have to live. But I get the picture."

"Yeah, well, don't go feeling sorry for yourself and start smoking pot."

"I smoke pot once a month. And what's with you, on a pack of Camels a day, telling *me* not to smoke."

"Mom. I'm telling you. There'll be no pot smoking in this house. I will not have another addict living here."

"I am not an addict."

"Go ahead. Try me. One more whiff of that crap and I'm out of here."

"Now you're threatening to leave."

"You're forcing me to go."

"We've had enough rules and regulations for one lifetime around here."

"You smoke pot, I'm leaving."

"Fine."

"I mean it."

"Too bad, Ralph, cause I'm doing it anyway!"

"What?"

"Too bad, *Ralph*, because I'm smoking pot when I feel like it. Get the picture, *Ralph*?"

Brandi dropped her head and Dottie listened to her intakes of breath. She poked Brandi's arm with her index finger. "I'm sorry, Brandikins, I got out of hand."

"I sound just like him, don't I?"

". . . on rare occasion."

"Dictatorial, overbearing, wanting my own way . . ."

"That about sums it up, but I wouldn't worry about it too much. You balance it with all the wonderful aspects you inherited from me."

Brandi's head shot up. She wore a big grin.

"Now," Dottie said, "where were we?"

"Destitution," Brandi said, "heading for debtor's prison."

They pushed the bills aside and started, almost unconsciously, to pick through the outstanding case files. These files represented fugitives who had jumped bail and had not been found and brought to justice. In the hundreds of times Dottie had had to explain to the uninitiated about how Ralph made his living, she had put it this way: In California a bail-jumper—someone who fails to show up for his or her court date—must be returned to court within 180 days of his failure to appear. Otherwise, whoever puts up the bail—cash, a home, a business—forfeits it.

The LAPD Fugitive Detail did not have the manpower to go after every bailjumper. That's where Ralph's bounty-hunting talents came into play. When traditional methods to locate a fugitive failed, and the 180-day time period closed in, whoever put up the bail—the fugitive's husband, wife, uncle or friend—not wanting to lose everything, hired a bounty hunter through the bailbondsman to make one last-ditch effort to find the fugitive and bring him back. Dottie estimated that she had explained this procedure a dozen times a month during her twenty years in the business.

She and Brandi sifted through more files. Husbands who had run off with their kids, hookers who vanished into the woodwork, crack dealers who jumped bail and were now hiding in Mexico or lay buried in a Southern California oil field. It took Dottie mere seconds to decide how much attention, if any, each case deserved.

"What exactly are we doing with these files, Mom?" Brandi asked. "Why are we going through these?"

"I'm just thinking," Dottie said. "I can't think unless I'm busy."

For twenty years with Ralph she'd been chasing after fugitives and bringing them back. That is, on *paper* she'd chased after them, she'd find them, Ralph would bring them in. She would go with Ralph if they were after a woman, who more often than not would cry rape to beat the rap. With Dottie as matron, that option was eliminated.

Dottie remembered the first night she and Ralph had gone on a pickup. To work off the $200 fee Ralph charged Dottie for tracking down her check-kiting boyfriend, he had suggested that she help bring in three female fugitives at $50 a head.

Dottie agreed and off they went. That night they chased down a wealthy multi-offense female drunk driver from Bel Air, a $20,000 hit-and-run violator, and an Asian dominatrix who had hacked up one of her tricks. By the end of the evening Dottie had begun to fall in love with Ralph Thorson. Within two months she had moved in with him and started taking care of the books. Eight years later Brandi was born. Six months after that Ralph hit her for the first time, a shot to the back of her head for, as he put it, disagreeing with him in public.

In the years that followed, Ralph, through drinking and an assortment of physical ailments, had become a broken man whose will to live was replaced, however unsatisfactorily, by his strict refusal to die. God knew he had been trying to kill himself by drinking (while on insulin for diabetes), smoking two packs of cigarettes a day and popping codeine like aspirin. For twenty years Ralph had vented his anger on a daily basis, and Dottie, except for a handful of short-term escapes, had endured it.

"Mom, hey, Mom. Wake up." Brandi held up a case file. "You keep drifting off. What about this Benito Cruz guy?"

It took Dottie a second a shake off the memories. "What about him?" she said.

"A hundred fifty thousand bail. We could make, what, fifteen, twenty thousand if we brought him back?"

"We'd never get to spend it. Benny Cruz killed his own brother. We'd be like gnats to him. Ralph and ten thousand other guys have been trying to grab Benny Cruz for years."

"It says here that he's in Mexicali," Brandi said, "right over the border."

"Protected by a dozen banditos and the Mexicali chief of police, who owes Cruz his job. Cruz especially hates Ralph, who was the only one ever to bring him in, who put Cruz in Vacaville for five years. Do you have any idea what he'd do if he found out that we, Ralph's wife and daughter, were after him?"

They moved on to other cases, some having passed the bail statute of limitations, others too small to warrant the time and effort. Dottie was getting the nagging sensation they were going in a direction they shouldn't, but they were being pulled by a force called survival.

"What about this guy here Daddy was after," Brandi said, holding up a fat file. "Tiny Bellows."

"Add a few inches to Tiny, put him on a Harley-Davidson, add a couple of tattoos of naked women, wrap an American flag around him and he's another version of Cruz. Cool it on this line of thinking, Brandi. We are *not* going into the business. End of story." She didn't sound as determined to herself as she had an hour ago.

"You're such a naysayer, Mom. So negative. I bet we could get this guy. Easy. According to this—"

"Forget Tiny Bellows. Forget all of it!" Dottie pushed the files aside and went into the living room.

"Forget eating, forget living," Brandi said, following her. "Forget breathing."

"Go back to bed."

"Go back to bed! One more standard answer from the wisdom of Mom. I've *been* to bed. I spent all day in bed wondering what we were going to do. This is what I came up with."

"Well, do some more thinking, sweetheart."

"I did all the thinking I'm capable of and it keeps coming back to this."

"No. That's my final word."

"You can say no for yourself," Brandi said, folding her arms across her chest. "I'm of age."

"To do what?"

"Whatever I want."

"That's what you think."

Brandi smirked. "I have plans," she announced.

"Good for you."

"And they include you, Mother dear."

There was something about the tone of her voice that made Dottie look up sharply, but all she saw was Brandi strutting off toward her bedroom, upright, proud, certain. Oh, Lord, she thought, another Ralph.

Six

■ ■ ■

AT SEVEN THE next morning Q. D. Reese, dressed as an older professorial type walking his dog, ambled down Otsego through the Thorson neighborhood. Q. D. had bought a *Variety* and noticed with some irritation that in his column Army Archerd gave mention to the passing of Ralph Thorson, on whose life Steve McQueen had made his final movie. What a crock. The movie was a joke. Bad action, bad acting. Q. D. could have played that role himself, the way it *should* have been played, in that special way he knew Ralph. He could have blended into the role, becoming Ralph, being invisible himself in the role.

It was like being invisible in these disguises of his. Walked right by the plainclothes cop in his blue car, the remains of a McDonald's saturated fat breakfast plunked on the dashboard. A guy in a plain Ford, doing nothing. Who did they think they were kidding?

The thought of Ralph Thorson in his grave gave Q. D. comfort. As he thought about it, this explosion gone wrong might have been the handiwork of fate. It was true that Ralph was not around to witness the demise of his women, but so what? It was a signal that he, Q. D., should use his imagination in new, creative ways.

When he thought about it he really hadn't needed Ralph to see Dottie and Brandi's death. He, Q. D. Reese, had to be his own witness. For eight long years he had suffered in prison, waiting for his satisfaction, and in an odd turn of events he had not been denied. He had, after all, eliminated the source of his original pain.

He stopped while the mutt peed on a bush, then he lifted his face to the sun and bathed in its mellow light, inhaling the sweet air. With his eyelids half closed, he could almost smell Brandi's soft fragrance. Just then the front door opened and out she walked, in jeans and bare midriff, and reached into the ivy bed for the morning paper.

She had grown so much over the past few years. She was a woman now, he noted. Strong, vital. She raised her head and looked at him with those pale blue eyes, Ralph's eyes. He froze at the sight of her.

Finally, back in character, he hoisted his arm into the air. "Good morning, young lady! Lovely day."

She raised the newspaper a couple of inches and went back inside.

Q. D. had suffered a momentary shock at the sight of her. A shock of what, sexual passion, he thought? Why not? In a daze, he limped back down Otsego to the Jaguar and sat behind the wheel.

He'd begun sweating though his clothes. His hands shook. His breath came in short ragged bursts. Calm down, he told himself, gripping the steering wheel, staring out through the windshield, hoping for a final glimpse of her.

He didn't like this new feeling; it was interfering with his intentions here. Can't have that. He took a deep hollow breath and squeezed his eyes shut.

Seven

. . .

DOTTIE, STANDING IN the kitchen, saw Brandi outside the front door, squinting into the sunlight. Down below on the street an old man walked his dog. A splitting headache had bunched up behind her right eye and curled around her ear: a stress ache. No wonder, she thought, with all the emotional clogging going on.

Dottie saw Brandi raise the newspaper a couple of inches in a half-hearted salutation to the old guy. Then Brandi came inside. "I had a thought," Dottie said.

"This early? Better sit down, Mom, before you hurt yourself."

"Funny." Dottie collapsed into a kitchen chair and wedged her head between her hands. "Stealing your Dad's lines already?"

"And before he's even cold."

Dottie gave her a look. "I wonder about you sometimes."

"Somebody's got to thaw out around here. Things are depressing enough. So . . . this thought you had?"

"I'm going to look for work."

"Didn't we beat that one to death yesterday?"

"I've decided to call some bondsmen."

"Uh-huh."

"Go out on pickups. Nothing heavy, maybe some hookers or traffic no-shows, light stuff."

"And they're going to hire us—two women?"

"Hey, yesterday you were gung-ho."

Brandi snorted. "There's no money in the light stuff."

"Considering our present situation, I think it's worth a shot."

"I make more waitressing. Now, if you're talking about going after bad guys, we could do that. You used to go with Dad lots of times."

"Not after the real bad ones."

"Stayed in the car and did your nails?"

Dottie gave her a look. "Boy, are you bitchy this morning!"

Brandi took the orange juice container from the fridge and carried it back to the table. "Convince me."

"Things have changed," Dottie said. "It's much worse out there now than it was a few years ago. Meaner, more dangerous. Not a place—"

"For women? Come on, Mom, you know the business as well as anybody," Brandi said. "You solved the Billy Rivers case, and what about that coke dealer you tracked down, and the . . ."

"I never actually went after those guys."

Brandi reminded her that when she was a baby her father had used her as a decoy on surveillance jobs.

"Dammit, Brandi, I don't want you packing a gun. For what, to pay the mortgage? We won't need to pay the mortgage from the cemetery."

"That'd be one more worry off our backs," Brandi said defiantly. "We could do it together, Mom. I know we could."

"I should be thinking like you, not like a forty-eight-year-old woman who wants to keep her daughter around for a while."

"Mom, we're broke and we're going to lose what we have unless we do something." She let out a sigh and folded her arms on the table, laying her head on them. "You know we could."

"Forget it."

"At least *I* could. Daddy drilled it into me. How many times did he say that by using your brain, you cut the risk in half."

"He never wanted you in the business."

"Yeah, but he's gone and we need to eat, I can use a gun, I know the procedures, and I know how to think like these creeps."

Dottie lowered her eyes while she thought. It seemed insane, but Brandi was right about one thing. They needed to work. To eat. And to do something to take their minds off Ralph's death.

"Mom?"

But going after Benny Cruz and Tiny Bellows? Dottie knew that the bondsmen who had these cases would never go for it—even though there wasn't anybody more qualified than the two of them to find these guys. On the phone, combing through files, she could trace fugitives with the best of them, had the contacts, knew the moves—and, as Brandi said, they could think like these guys, anticipate their moves. Ralph had taught them.

"Mom!"

"Let me make some calls," Dottie said, remembering that this is how the conversation had begun. "See what I can do."

THROUGHOUT THE AFTERNOON Brandi sat at the kitchen table watching her mother on the phone. This was what her mother did best. Dad used to say that Dottie worked the phone like a lover, could get anything out of anybody. Sweet talk the panties off a nun, or whatever the expression was.

Brandi tried to keep her mind busy, away from thoughts of her father, even though every second one had him in the middle of it—a memory, an expression he'd used, the way he used to pick her up and swing her around when she was a kid, when he taught her how to shoot or took her out with him to bars.

She kept looking at the front door, half expecting him to march through it with a couple of his buddies. The certainty that he wouldn't ever again made her want to cry. But Jesus, she wasn't kidding when she told her mother she didn't think she had any more tears left. She had never felt like this before; all she wanted was to climb into a big hole and pull the lid over her head.

She had to admit that she really didn't fancy going after killers to pay the mortgage. Part of her enthusiasm was a show for Mom, to let her know she wasn't afraid. If her mother ever got taken out by one of these guys, Brandi didn't know what she'd do. Actually, she knew exactly what she'd do—she would not *let* Mom be taken out, period.

She looked at her mother on the phone. Work, work, work. Mom's key word. Mom the workaholic. Brandi remembered as a kid getting sick at the sound of the click, snap, clank of her typewriter till all hours of the night, working on case files, sending out bills or excuses for not paying on time, writing reports.

Her mother never took a break, then got bitchy because she was tired all the time. After which came the criticism in the name of parental guidance. "You drink too much, you smoke too much, you don't eat enough, you sleep too late . . ." What it came down to was that her mother was a worry-wart. She didn't know how to leave things alone.

Brandi took in a breath through the mouth and let out the air slowly through her nose, one of her father's calming techniques. To Brandi's way of thinking, her mother had worked way too hard on things, especially on her marriage, which as far as Brandi could tell was always on the rocks. As far back as she could remember, she had wanted them to get divorced. Instead, they buried themselves in work, as if the business was a glue designed to mend everything. So with both of them working and fighting and fighting and working they never did get around to where the real mending should have taken place, inside.

*   *   *

". . . DANTE, HOW MANY times have Ralph and I bailed you out of a tough situation?" Dottie said into the receiver. "How many times have we gone after somebody and saved you money? A lot of money, as I recall."

"Dottie, Dottie, Dottie, whaddya think the world will think of Dante Cicollo if he sends a woman to do a man's job? They ridicule me, they laugh, they think Dante's gone crazy. I would help, but not in this way. Anything else, you name it."

"This is what I want, Dante."

"And this is the only thing I cannot give you. We reach an impasse, *cara mia*."

Dottie resisted slamming the receiver in his ear. This was the tenth bondsman—or was it the two hundred and tenth?—who had said no. Same answer each time: "You're a woman! A woman can't cut it. Buy a computer, learn to type. It's the modern age, push an electric broom. Blah blah blah."

Dante was a friend so she thanked him for his time, replaced the receiver and screamed, "Bastards!"

"Don't swear, Mom. Remember your blood pressure."

Brandi was at her easel in the middle of the living room. Now that her father wasn't around to complain, she had moved her studio out here. A half finished canvas of Dottie's oldest L.A. friend, Myrna Factor, stood before her. "I've been thinking," Brandi said. "Maybe if we approached this from another angle."

"For instance?" Dottie said, carrying a stack of files over to the bar. The bar was long and crafted out of polished mahogany, a real showpiece Ralph had been given by a Bank of America executive whose no-good son-in-law Ralph had brought back to justice. On the bar, Dottie divided the files into three stacks: active, passive, dead.

"These old-time bondsmen, Mom, they're all chauvinist pigs. They'll never send us after their fugitives."

"I'm beginning to believe that."

"Believe what?" At the sound of the voice they both turned and in the doorway saw Myrna Factor in all her flamboyant glory. Voluptuous at thirty-five (she said), with jet black hair, in tight black Spandex pants, a loose halter and three-inch spikes, Myrna had the kind of porno-sexy look over which certain men salivated. A sometime heroin addict who was always trying to kick it, Myrna was up for anything, as long as it was spontaneous. Dottie had spent twenty years getting into terrible scrapes because of Myrna. Dozens of people had wondered out loud why Dottie tolerated her. It had nothing to do with tolerance. Beneath the wild surface, Myrna had always been there for her, no matter what. She cared, she had a heart. And if sometimes she went overboard, how many true friends do you find in a lifetime?

An heiress to the Max Factor cosmetic empire, Myrna had become a little too nuts, as far as the estate executors were concerned. Myrna, who had always longed to be a mobster's girl, made monthly calls to the executors, threatening to send gangsters if they didn't cough up more money, which was already in the vicinity of $5,000 per month, tax-free, for life. They had also thrown in a lovely home in the Pacific Palisades. Ralph always said that money saved Myrna. Without it she would have been crazy. With it, she was eccentric.

Azure eyes and long, drooping lashes made Myrna look as if she were always on the verge of tears. "Babies," she exclaimed, and hurried across the room, throwing her arms around each of them. "I'm so sorry, so sorry, even though, as you know, in recent years I had never been one of Ralph's greatest fans, knowing the way he treated you, the bum. But I can't think about that now. It's you, you poor darlings. What can Myrna do for you?"

"Sit down and have some coffee," Dottie said.

Myrna plunked herself on a bar stool and crossed her long legs. She sighed heavily and folded her hands over her chest. "Is there anything I can do?"

"No," Brandi said. "We're talking business."

"Business?" Myrna said, "I can tell you something about business, specifically about one particular businessman I have recently met."

Dottie looked at Brandi, knowing they would have to table their future while Myrna had the floor.

"I've just come from being with him," Myrna said. "Howard. Quite rich, not as old as the last one. Howard doesn't drink either, or do much else for that matter—or so I thought. I went to Marin County with him for a few days, stayed in a suite with a Jacuzzi, drank champagne. It was all so wonderful, until . . ." Her expression turned sour.

"This ought to be good," Brandi said.

Myrna turned away in mock embarrassment. "I don't know if I can bear to tell you."

"If you'd rather not . . ." Dottie said, Myrna's cue to begin.

"I'm down on men. They'll fool you every time. Howard . . . has a fetish."

"Should we be surprised?" said Brandi.

"You know I'm not a prude." Myrna yanked on the Spandex. "God knows I've been a freewheeler in my day."

"Do we really want to hear this?" Brandi said. Myrna was an amusing storyteller, but her exploits were sometimes disgusting.

"Howard has . . . mother love."

"Mother love," Dottie repeated.

"He wanted to dress me up as his mother."

"You're kidding me," said Brandi.

"Clothes, makeup, accessories. Even had a photo of her to go by, taped it on the bathroom mirror."

"Where do you find these people?" Brandi wondered.

"He made me up to look exactly like her. Only then would he take me to bed."

"Is that sick or what!" Brandi shouted.

"He wouldn't take me out to eat unless I went dressed as her, as his mother."

"Oh, brother," Brandi said, got up and left the room.

"It really wasn't so bad. Nobody would have known it was me, not in that awful flowered dress."

"Get some help, Myrna!" Brandi called from her bedroom.

"That must be it, mustn't it? I must like this kind of abuse. Dottie, we're all human beings with likes and dislikes, aren't we, and mine are, well . . ."

"Maybe we ought to drop it," Dottie suggested. "It's a little strange."

"Maybe I'm just telling you all this because I feel guilty about not being here for you."

Myrna moaned and Brandi, feeling sorry for her, returned to the living room. She understood Myrna's need to dominate conversation and occupy the center of everything, recounting in lavish detail her terrible plight with men. Myrna made embellishment a high art. In each version her men grew more brutal while she became more victimized. Brandi was less intrigued by Myrna's new stories than by how she decorated the old ones. For Myrna, fact and fiction wore the same clothes.

From the kitchen Dottie brought out tuna fish sandwiches and iced tea in tall glasses.

"If you can't trust men," Myrna was saying, "you have to rely on women. Women are supportive, caring, smarter, really, than men."

"That's it," Dottie said.

"What's it, Mom?"

"How we can pay the mortgage."

Dottie hurried to the office and plucked a card from the Rolodex file. She cradled the phone in her shoulder and dialed.

"Who are you calling?" Brandi said.

"Patti Ashbury."

"Yes!" Brandi exclaimed. "Now you're cooking."

"What's going on?" Myrna said, frowning. "I was in the middle of explaining something to you."

"We'll get back to it," Brandi assured her.

Patti Ashbury, one of the few bondswomen in the business, worked out of her North Hollywood office.

"It's Dottie Thorson, Patti. I have a problem that you might be able to help Brandi and me with." Dottie knew not to beat around the bush with Patti, who had no tolerance for small talk.

"I'm very sorry about Ralph," she said. Dottie could hear the silent *Next?* in her voice.

"Thank you. The problem is there's no money left and Brandi and I need to live. You know how involved in the business I am. I have the contacts, can expedite." She shifted her weight and inhaled, blowing the air out slowly. "Have you got any non- or semi-violent fugitives you want brought in, any women?"

Without missing a beat, Patti said, "Robin Ripley. Nineteen, white female, fled California on a robbery charge. Picked up in Chicago by the Cook County Sheriff's, for soliciting. Called her pimp Henry Fowler, here in L.A., for bail money. Henry wants nothing to do with her except to use her as an example to the other girls in his stable of what happens to somebody who screws him over."

"What did she do?" Dottie asked.

"Tried to jack up the price on one of Henry's well-heeled clients. When the john balked, she stole his wallet. The john yelled thief, the cops arrived and found Robin a block from the motel with the john's wallet in her purse and no explanation as to how it got there. A big no-no when you're one of Henry's girls."

Henry, Patti told her, had posted Robin's bail and was waiting to teach her a lesson when she came out of the L.A. lockup. Robin had given him the slip and flown off to Chicago.

Dottie calculated. The bondsman's fee in cases like this was normally ten percent of the bail, which in Robin's case was $20,000, making Dottie's cut $2,000 upon delivery of the fugitive. The closer the case got to the 180-day limit, the higher the percentage. With ten days or less before the deadline, Ralph got as much as 35 percent for hard-case cocaine dealers or fugitives with class A felony priors on their rap sheets. Robin Ripley was a mere hooker-thief.

"A thousand," Patti said.

"I've got my daughter working with me. We're sort of taking over for Ralph."

"Twelve hundred," Patti said. "Remember, I'm doing you a favor."

"I'm using Ralph's and my contacts, I can do this in no time. We're doing each other a favor."

"I can't go higher, Dottie. Don't forget, I have to contend with Henry."

Dottie waited for Patti to change her mind, which she

probably wouldn't. Dottie knew other bounty hunters who would do it for less, so she held her breath when she said, "I can't do it for less than two thousand. Thanks anyway."

Just before replacing the receiver she heard Patti say, "All right. Fifteen hundred."

"Done," Dottie said and began writing down the details. After she hung up, she said to Brandi, "We got it."

"We eat!"

"Way to go, Dot," Myrna said. "You were awesome."

Dottie called the number Patti had given her for Henry Fowler, who answered on the first ring. After listening to Dottie explain that Patti Ashbury had hired her to bring Robin Ripley back to court, he said, "You don't know how much I want that bitch."

"I'll do what I can, Henry," she assured him, though she was already having second thoughts.

"I'm gonna make that whore pay."

"I don't think you should be saying this to me, Henry."

"Who the fuck are you?"

"Somebody who's going to save you twenty thousand dollars—if you keep your fucking mouth shut." Henry was the type of guy who responded to foul language.

The only way she could make a deal to get Robin Ripley back in Los Angeles was through contacts. She and Ralph had ledgers filled with names and address of people who owed them favors and to whom they owed favors. It was the way of the bounty-hunting business. Without this bartering system things didn't get done, at least not in a hurry.

She spent a half hour searching through her Chicago contacts and landed on half a dozen possibilities. She had to be careful in her choice, weighing the favor and from whom she wanted it. The call she made was to the commander of the Cook County Women's Detention Center, Betsy Flagg. Three years before Ralph had personally flown Betsy Flagg's two-time loser nephew back to Chicago for his aunt to read him the riot act. Betsy had been grateful.

On the phone, Dottie told her about the Robin Ripley situation. "No problem," Betsy promised. "When Robin goes to court in a month or so, I'll get the soliciting charge dropped." No one, not even Betsy, seemed to be in a hurry to uphold Robin's right to a speedy trial. Dottie asked her to try.

Betsy called back in an hour. "We have an option," she said. "Robin Ripley can spend thirty days in the Cook County jail on soliciting charges, or she can plead guilty and pay a fine, in which case I'll take her to O'Hare and put her on a nonstop to Los Angeles. Day after tomorrow."

"We'll take Option Two."

When Dottie explained to Myrna and Brandi that fugitive hooker Robin Ripley would be flying into town the next day, Myrna let out a whoop, pulled a joint from her bra and lit up.

"Not in here, lady," Brandi said.

"Oh, come on, honey," Myrna said, "this is a celebration."

"You're not stinking up the house with that stuff."

"This has been treated with Kama Sutra oil. You'll love it."

"Smoke it outside. I'm not going to say it again."

"On the street?" Myrna turned to Dottie. "Isn't that a plain-clothes cop out there?"

"Don't worry," Brandi said, "he won't bust you."

"The sun hurts my eyes," Myrna said, "and is murder on my skin."

"Mom . . ." Brandi said.

Dottie was torn, but finally had to say to Myrna, "Why don't you hold on to it and I'll drop over to see you later on."

"Dopeheads!" Brandi said and stalked off to her room.

After she was gone, Myrna said, "Tell me I'm wrong, but is she getting more set in her ways? She sounds like Ralph."

"It's the stress."

"I love her, God knows, but the girl needs a Quaalude and a choreographer. I mean, rigor mortis at her age? Come on, we'll light up in the back yard."

Eight

■ ■ ■

OUTSIDE THE HOUSE on Otsego, Q. D. Reese sat across the street on a bus stop bench. As he was transforming himself at the makeup mirror earlier this morning he decided to say farewell to the old-man-walking-his-dog getup and become a gay man who had recently lost his lover to AIDS. In the conservative attire of a local college professor, with glasses and exaggerated feminine gestures, he opened the chemistry book he had brought along.

He relished the quiet, needed to think, to watch, to get comfortable in this new persona. This was good exercise for his part as villain in the movie he was shooting up in Malibu Canyon. The lead villain was a good credit. His performance, he knew, had already raised the picture above its trashy Grade D level.

He watched the house, checking for Ralph's women. The thought of them sent an adrenaline rush through him. He could clearly see the evolution of his intentions here, the moment by moment execution of his desires, the acts he would commit upon these women.

The air was sweet, heavy with moisture. The temperature hovered near ninety. He felt the perspiration squeeze out of his pores and run over the angular contours of his flesh, streaming down his face. In baptism, he reminded himself, impurities exit their host.

He closed his eyes. At times like these he wore his memories like manacles. Of Ralph Thorson, his young wife Dottie and their beautiful daughter on that summer afternoon many years ago. The pain of remembering made him ill. The brutality of those moments had sustained him for the eight years he'd spent in that cell, and now here he was, preparing to collect his reward.

Sweat soaked through his lightweight shirt and T-shirt that read *Make Movies, Not Love* and down into his socks.

Through the overhanging tree branches he could see the white stucco house perched on its tiny knoll, and into the living room where Brandi, strong-featured and nubile, stood by the bar. So beautiful, yet fragile, ripe like a sweet melon. Soon he would dig into her like a human spoon, and devour her.

He saw Dottie, reedlike, the red-haired witch, coming in behind her daughter. He would snap her like a twig in two.

The family, what was left of it, together this morning, how sweet.

"Patience," he whispered to himself.

The front door opened and the one he heard called Myrna waddled out. Q. D. remembered her from the old days. In black Spandex and tall black hair, she bounded girlishly down the steps and across the street—toward his spot on the bench. An idea struck him.

As she drew nearer he lowered his head and began to weep. He could sense her stop and pause, looking down at him.

He lifted his eyes to meet hers. This would be a test of his cosmetic aptitude. He had produced a couple of tears that now rolled down his cheeks. He saw her ridiculously long eyelashes, her melodramatic outpouring of sympathy for him.

"Sir?" she said, clasping her hands. She moved cautiously forward until she stood over him. He let out a whimper, a signal for her to sit down beside him. She reached into her handbag and produced a tissue, handing it to him.

"Thank you," he said, "you're so kind. I have just lost a dear friend and . . . it's so difficult. But you don't want to hear all this."

"There, there. My name is Myrna, and I'm here to help you in any way I can. Please." She slid closer to him and laid a hand on his arm. "You can tell Myrna anything you wish. I'm here for you."

Nine

■ ■ ■

BRANDI SHUT HER right eye and sighted down the barrel. She smelled gunpowder and listened to the pop-pop of weapons fire down the line. Just a little more, she told herself, and squeezed her trigger finger, slowly, slowly, lowering the sight until the target rose into view . . . now. Crack! The recoil rocked her back. Her right heel dug in, counterbalancing. The barrel threw her head into the air. Her right eye opened, refocused and she could see the dark silhouetted shape of a man flat on the ground now flipping forward, back into position. A hole appeared in the figure's chest, just above the heart. Bingo. Dead meat.

In the next booth she watched her mother, straight-backed, two hands gripping the .45, feet apart shoulder width, right foot slightly back. Boom! The shot rang out, the .45 bucked, the kick drove her back. Down range, the target folded. A tiny smile appeared on her mother's face, then vanished. Good shot.

She admired her mother's precision, the way she unflinchingly, one by one, blew holes in the target. She shucked the empty clip, locked and loaded, and fired again.

A firing range was not for the timid. Her father had brought her to ranges from the time she was six. By age ten she was proficient in two dozen weapons, marksman status. She glanced at the men on the firing line, the veterans who couldn't hear you if you stood next to them and shouted but who could I.D. the caliber of weapon chambering at thirty yards. She could tell the veterans by the cigarette filters instead of half-dollar plugs they wore in their ears.

Brandi had convinced her mother that if they were going to chase down fugitives and deal with low-lifes like Robin Ripley's pimp, they had better bone up at the firing range. They had packed their arsenal in the trunk: a .38 police special (her dad's legacy); .22 handgun; Winchester 12-gauge pump shotgun; M1 Garand; AR15; 30-30 Winchester lever action rifle; SKS Soviet carbine; .22 Ruger rifle and an M1 carbine, .30 caliber with a folding stock.

Brandi preferred outdoor ranges where you could bring your own targets: Coke cans, pictures of ex-lovers, anything as long as it wasn't breathing. Her mother used to carry a box of bills with her, draw a picture of Mr. Bill Collector and plug him between the eyes. The downside of outdoor ranges on sticky days like this were swarms of wasps and squirrels stupid enough to race across the field under whizzing bullets.

This range was on Sepulveda, housed in a concrete building located in the city's industrial section on the edge of the projects. Not exactly the safest place to sell and shoot guns, but a prime business location for the yahoo trade.

Brandi had forgotten her glasses and had to tie a bandanna over one eye. She was rusty and there wasn't anything you could get rustier at in a short period of time than firing a weapon. You had to practice, and she decided that at least twice a week she would have to drag Mom down here to spend an hour.

They had been here for about an hour, in soundproof booths, headphones on, plastic safety goggles over their eyes, firing at silhouette and bull's-eye targets. Dottie had switched from an M1 carbine to the .45, Brandi from the Winchester to the .38. The .38 was one of a set of two that her father had told Dottie to trade for his life if he were ever captured and held for ransom in Mexico.

Ralph used to say that Brandi had come out of the womb packing a .38: Look out, world. But there had been times when guns got in the way. On her twelfth birthday her father had been up north of San Francisco, in San Marino County, campaigning for a state senator. He hadn't bothered to phone with a birthday wish and she was mad at him.

She called her mother to her room and announced that she wanted to remove the fifty-odd guns spread out on the extra bed. They had been on the bed for two weeks and enough was enough. "There's no place for you to sleep in here with me," Brandi told her. When her parents fought, her mother moved into her room. "So it's time for them to go."

"What do you suggest we do with them?" said Dottie.

This was a stumper. If they took them out of the bedroom—which was off limits to everybody, visitors, baby bounty hunters, etc.—and stored them in another room, somebody would find them and sooner or later a weapon registered to Ralph and Dottie Thorson would reach the street and be used in a felony.

"Never mind," Brandi said. "I'll hide them myself."

Actually she hid only one, a pearl-handled .38 that she gave to herself as the birthday present her father hadn't sent. The others she gave to him when he returned from San Marino, never telling him (she was never asked) about the missing .38.

A tapping noise on the booth's glass brought Brandi out of her reverie. When she looked up and saw her mother, she nodded once, laid the .38 down and took off the headphones and goggles.

A range employee reeled in the sets of targets, which they took into the ratty lounge area to examine. "Mom," Brandi said, looking them over. "I think you should ditch the forty-five. It's too clumsy."

"I like the forty-five."

"Liking it and being able to use it are two different things."

"Look what I did to this guy." Dottie held up the paper

silhouette of the man. "Twice in the shoulder, his chin, the top of his head, his chest and twice in the . . ."

"Balls. Now *that* was fancy shooting."

"I am quite capable."

"Are you going to have the time in real life you have on the range? No. You have to be fast, accurate, take the thirty-eight."

"I'll use the forty-five, thank you."

"Mom, this is for your own good."

Dottie gave her a tight smile. "Thank you for your concern."

Brandi silently packed the guns away.

"Anything else?" said Dottie.

"It's your funeral."

"What a delicate way of putting it."

"You know what I mean."

Dottie threw her can of Coke into the trash bin. "I'll think about it," she said.

"See," Brandi said, holding out her hand, "we can discuss some things after all . . . partner."

Later when they were finished and met in the parking lot, Dottie leaned against the Cadillac's door, twirling the keys around in her fingers. Brandi was on the hood holding her face up to the sun, feeling the warmth. The only sounds she heard came from muffled reports inside the building and the occasional crunch of truck tires rolling over the parking lot's loose gravel. And of course the irritating jangle of the keys.

"Would you stop that?" Brandi said. Dottie, looking confused, turned to her. "The keys, Mom. Please stop playing with them."

Dottie grabbed the keys and dropped the ring into her purse. "Your father irritated me a lot of the time."

"Dad was good at a lot of things."

After a moment, Brandi, who felt her mother's uneasiness, said, "What's eating you?"

"Nothing much."

"If it's nothing much, why don't you tell me?"

"A promise I made."

Brandi waited.

"That I'm about to break," Dottie said.

Brandi said nothing.

"He made me promise never bring you into the business."

"Ah."

"So I'm having trouble with it."

"It's a good thing you had your fingers crossed when you told him that one, isn't it?"

"I promised him many times."

"Did you mean it?"

"Yes."

"I mean, *really* mean it? Or were you just doing what you had to do to prevent an argument. You know, 'Yes, Ralph. Of course I won't, Ralph'—which as far as I'm concerned is no promise at all. That kind of promise doesn't cut it, Mom. Don't worry about it."

"If anything ever happened to you—"

"You'd blame yourself. C'mere." Brandi took her hand and looked her in the eye. "First of all you can't make a promise like that when the decision's up to somebody else, in this case, me. Second, he was an old-fashioned guy and you know how old-fashioned guys feel about women doing anything that isn't womanly. We'll be fine. We have to do this. It's not a matter of choice anymore."

On the way home Dottie drove slowly, steering the great tub of a car along the narrow neighborhood streets. She was driving so slowly that Brandi glanced over at her a few times wondering what was the matter. What she saw was her mother zoned out in thought, the tight jaw, the forehead wrinkles more pronounced as if she were trying real hard to work through something.

Dottie said, "I'm sorry your father and I were such lousy parents."

Brandi thought about that a moment. "Is this a confession?"

"Probably."

Brandi swung a leg under herself and twisted so that she faced the driver's side. "Cherish and Precious have a drug addict father and a mother who's never home, and when they are together at rare times they don't even talk to each other, and when they do talk they fight. Those are lousy parents. You and dad, as bad as you were, were never that bad. I always knew you loved me. And we did have good times."

"If anything ever happened to you, I'd never forgive myself."

"I told you, I'm going to be all right. We'll protect each other. You think I'm going to let you go after these creeps alone? We're a team, Mom. We stick together."

"You've got your whole life ahead of you."

"Will you please keep your eyes on the road? We tried to come up with a better way to make money but we couldn't. So let's live with it. It'll work out, don't worry."

Dottie pulled over to the side of the road, turned off the engine and handed Brandi the keys. "Maybe you ought to drive," she said.

Brandi took the keys. "I don't know about you sometimes. First you do want to do this, then you don't, then you can't make up your mind. If you start doing this in the middle of a pickup, I'm going to shoot you in the foot."

Dottie looked up fiercely and stuck out her hand.

"What?" Brandi said.

"The keys."

Brandi handed them to Dottie, who straightened up behind the wheel.

"Mom?"

"It just came to me."

"What did?"

"I don't know why I didn't see it."

She started the car and tore off down the street. Kids yanked their bikes out of the way. Brandi saw elderly couples on their afternoon walks stop and turn the way old people do, with their entire bodies all at once, to watch them race by.

"Any chance of letting me in on this?" Brandi said, watching the trees whiz by.

"Tiny Bellows. It all has to do with Tiny Bellows. It was what your father was talking about the morning he . . ."

"Died."

"What?"

"Died, Mom. Dad died. You can say it. It's probably better that you admit it. Not that it's easy, but it's better, believe me. Now, Dad was saying what that morning?"

"Remember, he was talking about things going to change, about buying a new car. And that folder he was waving around, remember that? And did you happen to catch the name on that folder?"

"Tiny Bellows."

"Tiny Bellows. He knew where Tiny was hiding, had to, I'm sure of it. It's in that file; we'll find it."

"I thought you weren't interested in Tiny Bellows, as dangerous as Benito Cruz, who killed his own brother."

"If we're going into the business, we have to be prepared to take risks. You know I've never done anything halfway, why start now?"

Brandi looked at her, searched her face for the joke, seeing none. She threw herself back against the seat and let out a whoop, "That's my Mom!"

Ten

. . .

AT THE HOUSE, Dottie listened to messages on the answering machine. Nothing critical. Brandi had gone off to change her clothes and rid herself of the smell of the firing range. "It's your turn to scrub, spray and polish," Dottie said, meaning the guns.

Dottie found the Tiny Bellows file, carried it to the bar and went to work. The first time through it she found nothing except the standard rap sheet, the priors, the prison terms, parole officers' reports and Ralph's scribbled notes, which she could barely decipher. Just like Ralph to keep the conclusions in his head. She would have to backtrack, try to trace his thought pattern, chart the course he had taken to locate Tiny.

She spread the pages out on the bar and dug deeper. When Brandi joined her she told her to sit down and read along. "Tiny (Walter W.) Bellows," Dottie said. "I'll bet he loves to be called Walter."

"By his mother," Brandi said.

"This time he's wanted for jumping bail on a bank

heist . . ." Dottie counted on her fingers. ". . . almost six months ago."

"We'd better get a move on then," Brandi said.

"We have less than a week."

"Second thoughts?"

When Dottie hesitated, Brandi leaned forward, staring her down. "We need the . . . go ahead, finish the sentence."

"Money. Okay, the six months are up Saturday. So, lookit here." They tallied up Tiny's life of crime as it appeared on a three-page rap sheet. Of his forty-two years, Tiny had spent thirty either in detention (from juvenile to Folsom maximum security) or running from the law.

Two hours passed. They got on the phone looking for telephone numbers to Tiny's thirty-four previous addresses. Most of the numbers belonged to somebody else now, the others no longer existed. Dottie called Lloyd Battaglia, computer whiz, and left a message for him to trace the whereabouts of, or anything having to do with, one Walter W. "Tiny" Bellows.

By four in the afternoon they'd gotten nothing but migraines. The only consistency was a pattern of small pencil dots beside certain addresses: five here, four there, two here. Dottie made a list. After a few minutes she looked at what she had and discovered that the pencil dots—obviously Ralph's—indicated the number of times Tiny had returned to a particular location. Okay, she thought, and?

She cross-referenced the locations with a number of factors, the prisons he had just gotten out of, the time spent in the prisons, the crimes committed.

"Well," Brandi said, "how about that."

"Got something?"

"Check me, but isn't it funny that when Tiny spent the most time in prison he went here. Take a look. Three years at Soledad, four years at Folsom, four at Folsom again, and where did he go after each hitch . . ." She aimed her finger at an address in Barstow, a weigh station in the Mojave desert between Los Angeles and Las Vegas.

"And Tiny's last stretch before pulling that bank heist,"

Dottie said, "was at Vacaville, three years, got out seven months ago. It could work."

"Remember Dad mentioning the desert that morning? So, if you trace this particular address, you'll notice this is where Tiny goes to cool out. In the desert at Barstow. In a trailer, it says here. It's out of the way, a perfect place."

"If Tiny is in fact the right guy," Dottie said.

"Right guy? Of course he's the right guy. What have we been doing for the last five hours?"

"All right, let's see what we've got. The morning he died Ralph said he was going out to the desert and in the next breath said he was buying a new car. Cause-and-effect situation if there ever was one. He was looking for nobody else that I know of. He had Tiny's file out here on the bar the day before. That should do it."

"We're brilliant, Mom."

"What a team."

"So all we have to do is go out there, get Tiny away from his guns . . ."

"And maybe his friends," said Dottie.

"Ahh."

"Who are probably armed to the teeth."

"No doubt."

"In the middle of the desert with sight lines all around them for miles."

"So they can spot somebody coming in. Which is why they chose the spot in the first place."

"There's something else, honey," Dottie said. "A big if. We have to convince the bondsman that we're the ones to bring him in. Without giving too much away, in which case he'd give the job to somebody else."

"Who is the bondsman on this one?" Brandi looked at the signature at the bottom of the bond certificate: "Oh, man," she said. "Paulie Dortmunder."

THEY WOULD HAVE to lie like mad, or rather, Dottie would have to lie like mad because, as Brandi reminded her,

"You're much better at it than I am, Mom, and, anyway, I'm into telling the truth."

Dottie called Paulie Dortmunder and told him she needed to talk to him privately, about a piece of critical information Ralph had shared with her concerning a fugitive that Paulie would love to find, whose identity she would only reveal to Paulie's face. When could she see him?

"How about now?" Which was exactly what Dottie thought the impatient little snake would say.

Paulie's office occupied a wing of his home down near Dodger Stadium on a middle-class residential street. How Paulie ever managed to zone his house commercially in this pleasant middle-class neighborhood was one of the great mysteries on Bailbond Row, and Paulie wasn't talking. Manicured hedges surrounded his trim little German palace. Wooden lawn figurines of fat Bavarians in lederhosen were clustered together in familial tableaux on a perfectly cut lawn. Paulie had painted the shutters and house trim to match the color of the grass, and had bleached the sidewalk in front of the house a pearly white. This was Paulie's own gingerbread kingdom.

As Dottie and Brandi drove up they saw Paulie pacing the sidewalk. She had never liked the little shit. Short, thin, about forty-five, an ex-bantamweight, Paulie acted tough, thought he was God's gift to women, a real man. In reality he was a back-stabbing punk who even screwed the cops if it was to his advantage. Paulie thrived on being abrasive, demanding, head-strong and always right.

"Dottie, Dottie," he said, greeting her as she stepped out of the Caddy. His attention was suddenly caught by a lovely young woman emerging from the passenger door. "And who is this?"

"You remember Brandi?"

"*Liebling*," he said, hurrying around the car, arms outstretched in an attempt to hug her. Brandi managed to avoid his clutches by bending over to adjust her boot.

With his spirits soaring at the prospect of this lovely creature in his midst, he led them to his office.

As bailbond offices went, Paulie's was the tidiest Dottie

had ever been in—small, clean, antiseptic, like Paulie himself. Photos of Paulie—in boxing trunks, flexing his pecs, posing with dignitaries—lined the walls.

"So," he said, "what's this dark secret you couldn't tell me over the phone?"

"Tiny Bellows," Dottie said, waiting for the reaction.

Paulie's cheeks popped and his piggy blue eyes contracted, which told Dottie what she had already suspected: that Paulie knew time was running out on Tiny Bellows's bond.

Ralph had been called in as a last resort when the LAPD Fugitive Detail couldn't find Tiny. Neither could Tiny's own biker gang, which had put up the collateral—cash and a piece of land—to guarantee Tiny's appearance in court. Tiny didn't appear and now $100,000 was at stake. If Tiny wasn't found, the gang would have to pay up and Paulie would be on their shit list. The word would get out to other biker gangs (who were usually reliable when posting bond for their members) and Paulie Dortmunder would lose a nice chunk of his yearly income.

"As you probably know," Dottie said, "Ralph—"

"Is no longer with us. I heard." No condolences, no nothing. That was Paulie, sensitive to a fault. "And?"

"We know where Tiny is."

"Fantastic. Where, and I'll get somebody right on it."

"There is somebody on it."

"What? Who the fuck is it, I'll rip his you know what off."

"Me."

"Us," Brandi said.

"Us," Dottie repeated.

It took a minute, but Paulie was starting to get the picture. "You're just like Ralph, always with the jokes. Come on, now, we only got a coupla days."

"Brandi and I will bring him in. I guarantee it."

Now Paulie got the picture. His jaw muscles made a bundle around his mouth. He clasped his hands behind his back and paced stiffly across his office floor. "This will never do," he muttered, "two broads going after Tiny, and then I'll have your deaths on my conscience."

What conscience? Dottie thought.

"And my reputation, what would happen to that?"

"As a lying sack of trash?" Brandi mumbled.

"What was that?" Paulie said with sudden anger.

"We'd never have to tell anybody about it," Brandi said quickly.

Dottie, picking up on this, said, "We know how important your reputation is, Paulie. We'll get Tiny, bring him back, you slip us our fee. We tell no one, you tell no one. We all make money, shake hands and go home?"

"Fee?"

"The standard, for a felon of Tiny's stature."

Paulie narrowed his eyes, one of his intimidation tactics to reduce their take.

Dottie had decided not to cave in; she had the advantage of time. "Twenty percent of the bond. That would be"—she read down along the brown Defendant Information envelope to Amount of Forfeiture, which read $100,000—"twenty thousand."

"Dottie, Dottie," he appealed. "This Tiny Bellows is a piece of cake. By this late date he thinks he has it made. He won't be looking out. You know where he is, you go pick him up, bring him in. Takes you three, four hours at most. I'll give you a thousand apiece, a nice evening's work, yes?"

"Brandi, you have the rap sheet on Bellows."

"All three pages?" Brandi produced the sheet and began to read. "You mean where it says he's been busted for eight armed robberies, aggravated assault with intent to commit, pistol whippings, two second-degree-murder convictions, that part?"

"Overturned!" Paulie shouted.

"Reduced," Dottie corrected him. "There's a difference. He spent fifteen years in jail for those crimes alone. This is no two to three hours' work, Paulie."

"There's no way I can part with twenty thousand dollars."

"Good," Brandi said, "I didn't want to go anyway. Let's head home, Mom."

Dottie nodded and stuffed the paperwork into her bag.

"I could come up a little," Paulie said, "to two thousand apiece."

"This guy is a killer who in three days will cost his biker gang a lot of money, one hundred grand to be exact, because you were too cheap to pay us, who *know* where Tiny is, the standard fee, which we are due."

"You think the biker gang would be interested in hearing about this, Mom?"

"Gee, I don't know, honey. How would that affect Paulie? I wouldn't want that on my conscience."

"Stop. My heart is bleeding all over my new shirt."

Dottie stared unblinkingly at the worm.

"This makes me sick," said Paulie. "Four thousand apiece, that's my limit. Eight thousand dollars."

"We have no insurance, the bills are mounting."

"Okay, ten, and I never want to see you again. I mean that."

"Twenty. With three days left it should be thirty-five or forty."

He took a long look at her and something—Dottie wasn't sure what—passed through his eyes. He shrugged. "Okay, twenty. You drive a hard bargain."

Uh-oh, Dottie thought, this was suddenly too easy.

"You won't regret this, Mr. Dortmunder," Brandi said sweetly.

"You're just like your father."

"Oh, and Paulie," Dottie said, "we'd like an advance."

"Forget it."

"You gave Ralph one."

"That was Ralph, forty years in the business."

"This is me, twenty years in the business."

"Not the same."

"How are we going to pay road expenses?"

"Use your imagination. You're a bounty hunter now. Good-bye, I have business to do."

"Two thousand."

"You must prove yourself. I know you, but I don't know you can do this. You understand me?"

Paulie turned and marched to the door, holding it open for them. Dottie was about to make another pitch. Paulie put up his hand. "Say one more thing and you go with nothing, no

Tiny Bellows, no work, nothing, plus I call the biker gang and tell them you know where Tiny is and won't go after him for twenty thousand dollars of their money. You understand this, I'm sure."

Dottie looked at Brandi, whose expression said they had pushed Paulie as far as he would go.

Eleven

. . .

Q. D. WATCHED AS Dottie and Brandi left Paulie Dortmunder's office. Q. D. knew the kraut bastard from his baby
bounty hunter days and wondered why the girls had gone to
see him. Whatever had happened in there, they seemed to
like the results, judging from the way they bounced along
the sidewalk to the car.

Dottie started the engine and pulled away from the curb.
Q. D. heard the muffled sound of their conversation through
the bug he had installed in their glove compartment.

He pulled out and followed them to the Hollywood Freeway, keeping them in range. He fiddled with the receiver
beside him on the front seat and listened to their conversation:

DOTTIE: Paulie is such a weasel.
BRANDI: You're talking about a weasel who's going to
    give us twenty thousand dollars.
DOTTIE: We're going to *earn* twenty thousand, and save
    Paulie's butt from the biker gang, and he knows it.

BRANDI: Mom.
DOTTIE: What?
BRANDI: Did you just pass gas?
DOTTIE: What?
BRANDI: Fart. Did you just fart?
DOTTIE: I most certainly did not.
BRANDI: Somebody did. Jesus, isn't it awful! Are we going
    by a paper factory or something?

Up ahead Q. D. watched as the Cadillac turned off the
Freeway onto Figueroa.

DOTTIE: What *is* that smell?
BRANDI: I'm turning on the air. Close your window.
DOTTIE: That is not coming from outside.

Through the Caddy's window Q. D. saw Brandi lean over
the back seat. He heard her scream. The Caddy swerved
across two lanes, cutting off a pickup truck, then spun back
into the center lane.

BRANDI: (*shouting*) Mom! Mom!
DOTTIE: What's the matter?
BRANDI: Oh, my God, oh, my God! Pull over. Anywhere.

The Caddy eased into the breakdown lane and came to a
stop. Q. D. drove on by them a couple hundred yards and
pulled over.

DOTTIE: What is it?
BRANDI: Wait a minute, let me get the wrapping off. . . .
    Oh, my God. It's a . . . Jesus!
DOTTIE: What is it?
BRANDI: A dog, it's a little dog. Jesus. Still warm. What
    kind of sick person would do this?
DOTTIE: Dead?
BRANDI: For a couple hours at least. Look at this. Some-
    body smeared lipstick on it. God Almighty. I'm getting
    it out of here.

Q. D. heard the sound of the car door opening and closing. He glanced back down the highway and saw Brandi carrying the dog through a field and into some trees. She emerged a moment later without the bundle.

DOTTIE: What's this on the seat?
BRANDI: What's what?
DOTTIE: This key chain. Recognize it?
BRANDI: (*pause*) Yeah, it's . . .
DOTTIE: Myrna's. Her lucky charm.
BRANDI: How did it get there?
DOTTIE: How should *I* know?

Q. D. didn't have to listen any longer. He put the Jag in gear and pulled forward into traffic. Ralph's women, he thought, and this was just the beginning.

Twelve

■ ■ ■

"HE WAS THIS gay guy who told me he lost his boyfriend to AIDS," Myrna was saying over the phone. "Right outside your place, on the bench across the street. He was crying and I felt so sorry for him. I don't know, the key chain must have fallen out of my purse. He was wearing makeup, I remember that gay men do that. It was beautifully applied."

"Or he might have taken it out of your purse," Dottie said. "During the intense soul-baring you had with this guy. Myrna, did you tell him anything about us?" Myrna's pause told Dottie that she had. "What did you tell him?"

"Oh, I don't know, Dottie, he was in such bad shape, and you know how I ramble when I get emotional. I kind of told them about, you know, Ralph and what his loss meant to you. Trying to make him feel him better about his own loss. But no, I didn't give him details, if that's what you mean."

Dottie didn't have time to interrogate her further. At eleven she and Brandi were supposed to be at LAX to pick up Robin Ripley, Henry the pimp's hooker, who was flying in from Chicago to stand trial for stealing her john's wallet. She said goodbye to Myrna and warned her about talking to strangers, realizing that nearly all Myrna's friends fit into that category.

On the way to the airport, she said to Brandi, "We have a real dilemma."

"Oh?" Brandi had become sullen and incommunicative since the dog incident.

"If we report the dead dog to Bill Sallie, he'll put more surveillance on us."

"And prevent us from going after Tiny Bellows."

Brandi shifted in her seat. "What would Bill Sallie do if he found out we decided to take over from Dad?"

"We did inherit the business, after all. By right it's ours."

Brandi nodded vigorously. "Like any other business that passes down to the heirs. All right, let's break this down. First, whoever put the dog in the back seat was not some loony. Not with Myrna's key chain right there on the seat. Second, the same guy who put the dog back there was the one who put the bomb in the Banana. Okay, but why the bomb then and now a dead dog? Why not just another bomb? It doesn't figure. Not if it's the same person. Could there be two separate people? Maybe, but in my gut I think it's the same one."

Dottie looked at her. Just like Ralph, she thought; the way she thought, the logic, the point-by-point delineation, talking to herself out loud.

"No doubt about it," Brandi said, "we have one sick bastard here."

And now she was swearing, Dottie thought. Little Ralph unleashed.

DOTTIE HELD THE grainy photo up to the dull airport light and tried to match it with the passengers emerging from Terminal B. Patti Ashbury had sent Robin Ripley's photo and rap sheet. The sheet said that Robin had been picked up for soliciting and other related prostitution activities a dozen times, had used a knife on three occasions. She had drug busts, DUIs, a grand-theft indictment, possession of a deadly weapon. Her own pimp's rap sheet wasn't as extensive. The sheet also said that Robin had just turned nineteen.

Dottie, who carried her usual mystery novel in her purse, sat in one of the fake leather chairs and read. Ralph had always accused her of reading mystery novels as an escape from real life, which was true.

"Mom," Brandi said. "Yoo-hoo."

Dottie looked up from her book. "What?"

"The plane's empty. Aren't those the pilots?"

She saw two gray-haired men wearing blue uniforms and pulling suitcases on wheels emerge from the flight tunnel. "I had better call Chicago to see what happened."

Walking between the two pilots, she spotted a lovely reddish-blonde-haired girl with blue eyes and wearing a white dress, white shoes and a ribbon in her hair. She looked thirteen, very pretty, the girl next door. Yet there was something about the way she walked and turned her head, and in her expression, that told Dottie that this was no innocent young thing.

Dottie approached her. "Robin?" she said.

"Oh, this must be your mom, Robin," one of the pilots said. "Ma'am, your daughter has been telling us all about you."

"Is that so?"

"And I'm Brandi," Brandi said to the pilots, "her sister."

Robin exclaimed, "My word, how you've changed, Brandi. I almost didn't recognize you, it's been so long."

"Uh-huh. You have luggage, sis?"

"Of course." She turned to the pilots, holding out her hand. "Gentlemen, thank you for bringing me safely home to my family. I felt so secure in your care."

The pilots were besotted by her, a regular Little Bo Peep in virginal attire. Dottie had to remind herself that this girl was Henry's number one money-making whore, a thief, bail-jumper and God knew what else.

At the baggage claim, with mascara-blackened tears running down her cheeks, Robin nervously kept looking around. Presumably, Dottie thought, for Henry.

Brandi waited with Robin while Dottie brought the car around. By the time Dottie returned the two girls had become fast friends. They shared a mutual love of AC/DC, Soundgarden, *The Crow*, big exotic knives, .22 rifles (easy shot, no kick), "X-Files," "Tales from the Crypt," fish tanks, Chocomilk for hangovers and all things the color of peach.

On the drive back to the house Robin poured out the tale of woe that led to her flight to Chicago, the jail time and the return. "That old man in the motel room was the most horrible person," she said, her eyes filling with tears. "He was mean and wanted me to do all these disgusting things. When I said no, he called the police with the missing wallet story. I wanted to kick him in the balls!"

"Good for you!" Brandi blurted out and grabbed her hand over the seat. "Don't you worry, we'll take care of you."

"You mean you didn't have his wallet when the police caught you?" Dottie said.

"Oh, I had it all right. I took it when I finally managed to escape from the room. He wanted to tie me down with his necktie and his belt, so I ran. The only thing I took was his wallet and of course my clothes."

At home, Brandi and Robin played video games and talked about fashion and men and other things Dottie couldn't hear over their hushed tones. She didn't like all this chumminess, except that it seemed to calm Robin down.

Dottie heard Robin make a half dozen phone calls, hopefully none of them to Henry. Dottie made a call to Patti Ashbury, who told her that Robin's arraignment was set for next morning at eleven, at Santa Monica Superior Court.

"If you happen to talk with Henry," Dottie told Robin, "under no circumstances do you tell him where you are. He will come over here and hurt you, and probably us. If he does come over here and we manage to live through it, not only will I be mad but I'll make sure you go to jail for many years. No Henry. Is that clear?"

"Yes, ma'am."

Dottie couldn't dislike this kid, no matter what she'd done. Either Robin had been royally mistreated as a child or was the greatest little actress west of Denver. Both, Dottie decided. It took most of the night, but Dottie—even though she knew better—finally came around to believing that Robin had been horribly victimized and needed love.

By the time Dottie climbed out of bed next morning she had decided not to let Henry Fowler get his hands on this poor girl. After calling Patti and explaining her change of heart, Dottie phoned another bondsman and asked him to post Robin's bail, which meant that Robin would be handed over to that bondsman, thus avoiding Henry.

Once Robin left her custody and was presumably safe in the hands of the new bondsman, the plan was for Dottie and Brandi to pack their gear for the trip into the desert and Tiny Bellows. The thought of tracking down Tiny was beginning to make Dottie nauseous, so she did what came naturally when an ugly thought crowded her conscious thoughts: she took measures to ensure that it didn't exist. She smoked some pot and went to bed.

Around eight the next morning Robin appeared in another of her cute-little-girl-in-pigtails outfits, her court clothes. On the drive to Santa Monica, she nervously told them how she had ended up with Henry.

"When I was thirteen and living near Fort Sill, Oklahoma, one night I was baby-sitting for a neighbor's little girl. The girl's mom and dad came home and her dad offered to drive me home. As we came up to my house he sped up and drove right by. I asked him where he was going and he said he had a surprise."

In the rearview mirror Dottie saw Brandi hunker down in the seat, her eyes dropping skeptically into the half-mast position.

"In the woods about a quarter mile from the house," Robin continued, "the man pulled over and grabbed me, ripped my clothes off and took his thing out and made me put it in my mouth. I gagged and threw up all over him. While he cleaned himself off I managed to get the door open and ran.

"Behind me I heard his car engine and saw the headlights sweep in front of me. I was crying and screaming. His car was getting closer, I cut across lawns.

"I finally reached my house and ran inside where I found my mom and dad in the kitchen. I told them what had happened. My dad ran out, screaming about killing the guy, my mother went off to call the police. I was alone in the kitchen, crying and half naked. All I wanted was somebody to hold me."

"They just *left* you?" Brandi said.

Robin nodded solemnly. "Later, the man who did this said I had enticed him, acted like a little whore. He was a church deacon and respected in the community and cried loud about how innocent he was, which made it so hard for my mom and dad to live in the town anymore that we had to move away. We went to Chicago but the pressure got to Mom and Dad and they split up. I came out here to live with my aunt.

"I was in bad shape. Every time I got near a boy who tried to kiss me I'd throw up all over him. Then one day about two years ago I met Henry. He treated me real nice, even though I was still throwing up. He was kind to me, helped me get over my problem. I was so grateful to him that he asked me to do him a favor and be with one of his friends. I said okay and that led to another favor and another and eventually he turned me into his . . . you know."

They arrived at the courthouse where Dottie presented a certified copy of the bailbond to the court bailiff, who seated Robin in the jury box and pulled the case file. An attorney Patti Ashbury used for bail motions such as Robin's had been waiting for them. Dottie spoke briefly with him and then sat down to wait for the case to be called.

The judge, a no-nonsense, severe-looking Asian woman with jet black hair pulled back tightly on her small skull ran her court like a military operation. Crisp, short with defendants and prosecutors who got out of line, she dispatched case after case with astonishing speed. Dottie had faced Judge Ishi before; she was fair and actually had a sense of humor, if you listened hard enough.

Robin sat stiff-backed and alone in the jury box, looking scared. Dottie saw her flinch when a wiry, well-dressed black man strode into the courtroom and sat down. The notorious Henry Fowler, pimp. Dottie could just imagine what this creature would do to Robin if he got his hands on her.

The new bondsman had not arrived and the time for Robin's case was drawing near. Dottie sent Brandi out to make a call. She returned and said, "No answer. He must be on his way."

When the bailiff called the case the bondsman had still not arrived. Robin was called up and stood before Judge Ishi, who glanced at the file and listened to both sides present their arguments. Robin's attorney asked for a release on her own recognizance (O.R.). The D.A. opposed this, pointing out that Robin, a legal resident of Chicago, had skipped on a surety bond, showed no means of support and had no place to stay in Los Angeles.

After a five minute recess the judge returned. "Having looked over the defendant's prior . . ."

Dottie knew what she was going to say—that Robin's bail would be set and whoever could make it could have her, meaning Henry—and so she blurted out, "Your Honor, I have arranged for a bondsman to be present. He must be stuck in traffic."

"And who might you be?" the judge asked.

"Dorothy Thorson, Your Honor. I work for the bondsman who originally posted bail on the defendant."

"If you want to get the bond exonerated, you have to file the proper papers . . ."

"Excuse me, Your Honor, I don't want to get the bond exonerated. I do and I don't . . ." She could feel the blood in her face and a twitch began behind her right ear, a longtime sign of nervousness. "But that's not what I'm asking right now."

"What *do* you want, Ms. Thorson?"

"I want to advise the court that another bondsman has agreed to post the bond, and also that I picked up Ms. Ripley at the airport yesterday after she had voluntarily returned from Chicago to take care of this matter."

"Well, Ms. Thorson," the judge replied, "it seems that you are impressed with this young lady. I'll tell you what. I will exonerate the bond the defendant forfeited when she failed to show up for court, and I am going to O.R. her . . ."

Dottie felt a wave of relief. "Thank you, Your Honor."

"Ms. Thorson, I am not finished with my ruling."

"Sorry, Your Honor."

"I am going to O.R. the defendant to your custody until her next court date, is that agreeable?"

Dottie felt herself panicking: My custody? She looked at the judge, who wore a half-smirk on her face, then at Robin and her angelic smile. She glanced at the D.A., who couldn't believe what he was hearing and finally at Brandi, who whispered, "Go for it, Mom."

Minutes seemed to pass.

"Is this agreeable to you, Ms. Thorson?" Judge Ishi asked.

Dottie stammered, "Yes . . . yes, Your Honor, it is agreeable."

She barely listened as Judge Ishi told the court, "Bond exonerated, no court costs, defendant released forthwith to the custody of Dorothy Thorson until her next court date, which will be . . ."

As she waited for Robin to be processed, Dottie thought, so here I am presented with a nineteen-year-old bouncing baby girl who becomes my legal responsibility until the court date, one month away.

On their way through the parking lot to the Caddy she told Robin, "We could really use an extra hand at home while we're out of town during the next few days."

"You must be joking," Robin said in a very grownup voice.

"I don't do housework."

Thirteen

...

"I'D BETTER CALL Myrna," Dottie said, marching through the front door. The house was dark and cool. Sun slanted through the venetian blinds, laying patches of rectangular light on the beige carpet. The whir of overhead fans and the steady rattle of the refrigerator made a little symphonic interlude.

For Dottie, the ride home from Santa Monica Superior Court had been a nightmare. Once Robin—sweet, innocent Robin—found out she wouldn't be going to jail, at least for the time being, she turned from the warm, vulnerable teenage victim of men's oppression into a haughty first-class bitch. She made a list of the things she would and would not do, the latter far outnumbering the former. She made demands: she wanted silence in the mornings before ten because she needed her sleep; she wanted no visitors to the house after ten in the evening because she needed to regain a semblance of peace after the traumatic jail time she had spent in Chicago. She sounded like an irate hotel guest.

Brandi leaned back against the door, staring at Robin, checking out this new twist.

"This place really needs an overhaul," Robin said.

"This is where you're staying for the next month, honey," Dottie told her. "If you don't like it, I know a cell where the state would be happy to put you up."

"Right."

"One phone call and the sheriff will be here for you in a squad car."

"Oh, sure you will." Robin tossed her jacket over the back of a chair.

"Try me."

Robin must have caught something in Dottie's expression because, like magic, her arrogance evaporated. "Who's Myrna?"

"Your babysitter for the next couple days." Dottie picked up the phone and dialed.

"I'm beyond babysitters."

"It's a babysitter or a matron, your choice."

Robin didn't like the sound of that. "Well, where are *you* going?"

"We're bounty hunters, Robin," Brandi told her. "We've got a busy schedule."

"Well, la-di-fucking-da."

"House Rule Number One," Brandi said. "No swearing on the premises."

"What is this, a convent?"

"It's either that or . . ."

"Yeah, yeah, I know. You guys are repeating yourselves already."

A half hour later the doorbell chimed and Myrna pranced into the living room in a forest green Spandex outfit, a wedding shirt, gold chains around her waist, and gold lamé pumps. She had piled her hair into some kind of a tiara twirl and stuck a gold pin in the center of it. This extravagance was where most of Myrna's monthly allowance check went.

Dottie had grave reservations about leaving Robin with Myrna while they went after Tiny Bellows, but what could they do? "Is this the poor little darling?" Myrna exclaimed

and hurried over to Robin, in shock at the sight of this
woman who was now smothering her in her fleshy arms.

"Get *away* from me!" Robin shrieked. "You smell like a
vanilla factory."

Once Robin stopped pissing and moaning, Myrna, who
took it all in stride, said with great sympathy, "I'd be upset,
too, if I had gone through what you have. Let it out, honey,
it's good for the bio-rhythms."

Dottie warned Robin that she had better be on good behavior while they were away.

"Oh, I'll be good, all right," Robin replied, leaving for
Brandi's room, which she had commandeered as her own.

Dottie led Myrna into the kitchen and sat down with her
at the table. "You parked your car where?" she said to her
friend.

"Where you told me to, next street over, in front of the
Murphys'."

"Tell nobody where we've gone. If anybody asks, we're
visiting relatives up north. The plainclothes cop assigned to
watch the house is still there. The gay guy on the bench. If
you see him, call Bill Sallie, have him picked up. And don't
let anybody in the house." She decided not to tell Myrna
about the dead dog. Dottie was still stumped by that one.
"And thanks for taking care of Robin. She's not going to be
easy."

"She just needs a little sisterly advice."

"And stay away from the dope."

"You know me."

Dottie knew Myrna; that was the problem. When Dottie
returned to the living room she found Brandi on the couch,
wearing a long face. She sat beside her and brushed her hair
away from her face.

"What's the matter, pumpkin?"

"I have my midterm Monday and with everything going
on around here, I haven't got a shot at passing."

"Bring your books with you."

"Oh, right."

"It's a long drive to the desert. We'll need time to stake
out Tiny, then once we get him, you'll have the trip back.

Plenty of opportunity. And don't forget to wear something warm."

One of the duties Ralph had assigned them was to make sure the briefcase he carried on pickups was properly stocked with booze, glasses, playing cards, Maalox, a gun, extra ammunition clips, breath freshener, extra handcuffs, proper surrender papers for each bailbondsman, business cards, toothpicks, writing paper and case files on each fugitive.

For this trip, Dottie added the SKS Soviet carbine, the .22, a .38, and just in case, the 30–30 Winchester. They dressed in oversized black sweaters, shirts and jackets and blue jeans tucked into black calf-high boots.

At seven that evening they said goodbye to Myrna—Robin was pretending to sleep—and slipped out through the kitchen door. Cutting through back yards, they arrived at the Murphys'. Myrna's car, a vintage Mercedes convertible, sat against the curb. They loaded the bags and weapons in the trunk and drove off.

It occurred to Dottie just then, as they hopped on the freeway toward the desert, what exactly she was doing. The implications of the trip, what could happen, how things could get totally fucked up, lives lost. She should have been having second thoughts, but she wasn't. She couldn't wait to get out there and on the job.

Fourteen

...

DOTTIE LOVED THE desert the way she loved snakes, uncooked food and bondsmen like Paulie Dortmunder. To her, the desert was a vast, dangerous place where everything bad could happen to you and usually did. The only thing she liked about the desert was the absence of roads on which she could get lost, or more specifically, the simplicity of directions and a kind of straight-forward way of getting places. Go a hundred miles, turn right at the gas station, go fifty miles, turn left at the Caesar's Palace billboard. Simple.

She used to travel through the Mojave with Ralph on the way to Las Vegas to chase desperadoes. The desert's silence, its eternity of size, its smell of death, intimidated her. She'd always thought of herself as a survivor, but compared to the things that survived in the desert, she was an amateur. The world and the law stopped at the desert's perimeter. A curtain fell between civilization and the great expanse of sand and rock. She imagined a signpost: ONLY THE MAD AND STOUT OF HEART OUGHT PASS BY HERE.

They drove east under a gaping black canopy of night. A

full moon hung above them. Brandi pointed out Jupiter and
Venus standing side by side like bright sentinels. Ralph used
to take Brandi outside after dinner to point out the stars,
telling her stories about them, some made up, some not. At
the kitchen window Dottie would listen, watch them standing
together, heads tilted toward the heavens. She felt a stab of
regret.

"Do you miss Dad?" Brandi said.

"Yes."

"How'd I know you were thinking about him?" Brandi
turned the interior light on and opened her criminal psychology book. She'd been studying psychology since the
eighth grade when her father told her that the only way to
understand people was to understand why they acted like they
did, and there were only two ways to do that: watching and
reading.

"Sorry about your test," Dottie said.

"It's okay."

"I feel terrible about it."

"I'll make it up."

"Really, if there was something I could have done—"

"Mom, I'm trying to read."

A few miles down the road, Dottie said, "I worry about
leaving Myrna with Robin."

Brandi closed the book and sighed.

Dottie said, "I should have been more forceful with the
judge, maybe let the court have Robin."

"Oh, so Henry could have gotten his hands on her."

"Actually, it's not Robin I'm worried about, it's Myrna."

"Myrna can take care of herself."

"Something's wrong."

"Like what?"

"I don't know."

"You don't know? Then why bring it up?"

"Something's wrong with Myrna. You haven't noticed,
huh?"

"No."

There had been something. Lately Myrna seemed frightened, like a small animal. Dottie knew the look; on occasion she had seen it in the mirror.

Up ahead Dottie saw a cluster of lights in the darkness and slowed. She pulled into the small silvery oasis with a fast-food joint/filling station/T-shirt shop.

"You need nourishment," she said.

"Here, at the home of eight billion calories?"

Back on the road, with fries and a greasy hamburger in her lap, Dottie wondered how she could take Brandi's mind off Tiny. Talking about it, not talking about it. She decided on the latter.

Twenty miles deeper into the desert, she saw that Brandi hadn't touched her food. "You have to eat," she said.

"Not right now."

"You know how you get when you haven't eaten."

"I'll get to it later."

"It'll be cold."

"This is exactly what they're saying."

"Who's saying?"

"About how it happens."

"How what happens?"

"This control you try to have over me." She picked up her psych book and flipped to a page. "Right here. It says here that everyone has three personalities: the child, the adult, and the parent. You with me?"

"Yes."

"Like now, when you badger me to eat, you're playing the parent talking to the child. Except that I don't want to be treated like a child. I'm an adult. The adult says, 'No thank you, I'm not hungry.' But you won't let it go, you don't want to hear it. That's where the problems begin."

"Let's see if I've got this right. I should be aware of what you want and adjust to it."

"Exactly," Brandi said.

"Even though I know that eating is good for you, I should step back and let you have your way."

"I'm not having my way. I'm just not hungry."

"With this line of reasoning, I should always let you do what you want, to avoid an argument."

"Not always," said Brandi.

"Where do you draw the line?"

"We work it out. Compromise."

Dottie thought about that. "By recognizing where you're coming from and meeting you in the middle."

"It's logic, Mom."

"Logic."

"Which you've never been good at."

"Stop treating me like a child."

Brandi threw her head back against the seat. "Very funny."

FROM A RIDGE high above the desert floor, Dottie and Brandi were not admiring the beauty of the cacti and suaro in the blue moonlight. Like cavalry scouts, they were flat on their stomachs, binoculars up to their eyes, focused on a cluster of trailer homes in a treeless oasis surrounded by miles of barren rocks and sand. Tiny's place.

"If we assume he's in there," Brandi said, "the question is, is he alone?"

"Whatever," Dottie said, "we can't let him see us coming."

"We don't use headlights."

Dottie reached over and took her hand. "Just because we've come out here to do this," she said, "doesn't mean we can't be smart, turn around and go back."

"Yeah, yeah. First we should figure out the right approach. Circle the wagons in a wide circumference, find the least obvious angle in. Whaddaya say, Mom, before we change our minds."

They removed the weapons from the trunk and loaded them. Dottie steered Myrna's Mercedes, engine purring like the night creature it was, lights out, down into the valley.

After a spin around the area, Brandi suggested an approach from the north as the least risky. Only one of the four trailers showed lights. Dottie took some comfort in this because when bikers partied, they partied as one.

Dottie parked two hundred yards away, behind scrub. On Brandi's advice, she decided on the .22 caliber Stinger, a six-shot automatic with a powerful wallop for its size, and a

Prowler Fouler stun gun. The Prowler Fouler, which shot a
nitrogen-propelled bean bag, shocked the system on impact.
She slipped the .22 Stinger into an ankle holster that Ralph
had convinced her to wear when they'd first gone on pickups
together. Brandi tucked the .38 Special into her belt and carried the Soviet carbine on her hip.

Dottie said, "We're sure about this?"

"Twenty grand is good enough reason for me."

In a low crouch they angled toward the trailers. Closer in,
Dottie saw the flickering blue light of a television. She heard
country music and rough male laughter.

"There's your answer," Dottie said. "Tiny's not alone."

"I'd say two, maybe three."

"Let's check the other trailers. I want no surprises." They
peeked through the windows of the three dark trailers; nothing. From the lighted trailer Dottie heard a woman's voice,
which now put the number at three, possibly four. Lousy
odds. And partying bikers were nasty bikers.

"You remember what Tiny looks like from the photos?"
Dottie said.

"How could I forget?"

Whatever else Dottie could say about Tiny Bellows, he
wasn't the typical biker with scars and dinks, mad pig eyes,
tattoos and mounds of fat. In the photos he looked thin and
dressed conservatively.

In their final approach Dottie's stomach grumbled. She
found an old milk crate and placed it under the window, and
climbed up for a peek. Inside she saw two large men in T-
shirts drinking beer at a table, arguing over the clamor of
country music. Two rifles, a handgun and grenades sat on a
counter beside empty beer cans.

Tiny came out of the back room. Tall, rangy, clean-shaven,
he wore a starched white shirt and a pair of chinos. Under
other circumstances she might have mistaken him for a lawyer. At his side was a tall, slender, black-haired woman, naked except for a thin silver chain hung low from her waist.

"What's going on?" Brandi whispered.

"Tiny plus two and a girl."

Brandi climbed up for a look.

They angled around behind the trailer until they found the rear entrance.

"I'm going through the front door."

Brandi's eyes flashed. "Why?"

"Listen for me, and when you're ready, storm in. We'll make it work."

Brandi didn't look so sure.

"I love you," Dottie said. "Please be careful."

They took their positions. Dottie checked the Stinger in its ankle holster and crept around to the front door. She counted to five, exhaled and knocked. Inside, all conversation ceased.

A curtain parted, the door swung open and Dottie, trying to look lost, which wasn't all that hard to do, stared up into the dark slit-eyed presence of Tiny Bellows himself.

"Whoa!" he exclaimed. "There's an angel at the door, boys. Good Christ, I must be dreaming."

"My car broke down about a mile down the road," Dottie started to explain.

Tiny reached down and lifted her off the ground and into the trailer where he held her up like a trophy before his friends.

The naked woman squealed. "Tiny opens the door and out jumps a fox!" The woman stood in front of Dottie, breathing sour liquor into her face. "These boys done wore me out, honey. I need a rest and you're it."

They all thought that was a riot, slapped their knees and swigged their beer. They seemed to believe that fate had sent her to them as a gift.

Tiny grabbed her purse and rummaged through it.

"My car . . ." Dottie said.

"Your car will be fine," one of the men at the table said, "and so will you."

"And so will we," the other man agreed.

That brought another set of guffaws. Where was Brandi, who should have been through the back door by now?

Satisfied that nothing in her purse looked suspicious, Tiny said, "Tell us something about yourself, little girl." He popped a beer and handed it to her. As Dottie accepted it, Tiny cupped her breast and squeezed.

"A feel for a beer isn't in my bartering system, sir," she said.

"Well, it is in mine, little girl."

She didn't like his condescending to her and remembered Brandi's words. She stared directly at Tiny. "I'm treating you like an adult here," she said, "and you're treating me like a child, a plaything. I want to be treated like an adult. Only then can we can communicate on an equal level. Come to some understanding." As she listened to herself, she imagined Brandi forming the words. Tiny cocked his head, confused. The woman, bony and blotchy-skinned, reeking of sex, sniffed around Dottie as if she were her next meal.

Dottie stared at the back door, worried that someone might have come out of another trailer and surprised Brandi—except that she would have heard about it by now. This still left her with Tiny, his naked girlfriend, now fingering her shirt, and the two fat boys leering at her from the table.

The ankle holster pressed against her shin.

"My sisters are waiting for me back in the car," she said. "Can you help me?"

The room lit up with new interest. "Sisters?" one of the fat boys asked. "How many?"

"My two baby sisters are back there in the dark. I'm worried about them."

"Where'd you break down exactly?" Tiny said.

She tried confusion. "Over in . . ." She pointed over the girl's skinny shoulder. ". . . that direction . . . or maybe in that direction. Jeez, I can't remember."

"Where were you coming from?" Tiny said.

"Las Vegas," she said, "Janey Mae hit the jackpot and we were so excited we must have made some wrong turns."

That did it. It *must* have been fate. Three solo women *and* a pile of money dumped on their doorstep. Almost too much, Dottie thought. Tiny, no stranger to a con, studied her through the dark slits, as if to say, *Okay, little lady, turn that story up another notch and let's see how real it sounds to me then.*

"Look," Dottie said, "I apologize for interrupting your

party. Thank you for your time. I'll try one of the other trailers—"

Tiny blocked her path. "We'd be happy to offer you some assistance, little lady."

"I bet you would," the girl said.

"Load 'em up, boys," Tiny said to his buddies, "we got a little business to tend to. Lorita," he said to the girl, "clean up this pigsty while we're gone."

Dottie waited while the men hitched up their pants, pulled two six-packs from the fridge and grabbed their weapons.

"After you, young lady," Tiny said, holding the door. Dottie stepped down into the darkness. A blanket of crisp air carried the scent of desert flowers on it. Three moonlit Harley-Davidson hogs stood under a tree like eerie pop art gravestones.

"You can ride with me, honey," Tiny said, kick-starting his bike. Except that it wouldn't start, and neither would his pals'. A lot of "What the fucks!" filled the night.

Brandi, she thought. Dottie was grateful for Brandi's exboyfriend, the despicable Darrel, who'd taught her how to "fix" motorcycles—the only thing he'd taught her, except maybe how to whine. As Tiny and the boys tried to figure out what had happened, Dottie eased back into the darkness and pulled up her pant leg for easy access to the Stinger.

After a few more failed attempts at starting their engines, one of the fat boys said to Dottie, "Hey, bitch, whad you do to our bikes?"

Two headlights snapped on, flooding the area. A voice belonging to Brandi said, "Don't even think about going for those guns, fellas."

Tiny and his friends didn't know what to make of this female voice or where it was coming from, so they stayed where they were, waiting. "Very good," Brandi said. "Now, Tiny, I want you to walk in the direction of the headlights, with your hands up. I said, with your hands up."

"Fuck you."

A shot rang out. Dottie jumped, though she couldn't tell right away who had fired it. A moment later she saw Tiny holding his bloody forearm. Flesh wound.

"Mom," Brandi said, "have you got these other two covered?"

"I do" Dottie had the Stinger out and aimed at the two fat boys, hands raised.

"Very good," Brandi said. "Now, Tiny, get your sorry ass in front of the headlights unless you want a matching hole in your head."

Tiny, who now understood this was for real, came forward.

"Mom, about that girl inside . . ."

The trailer door swung open and the naked Lorita, with a rifle in her hands, came out shooting. Dottie spun around, fired twice at her, then dropped to one knee, spun and fired twice more in the direction of the fat boys. Other shots erupted from where Brandi had been standing.

In no time it was over. Dottie listened in the silence. She heard Brandi say, "Mom, would you mind picking up that rifle you knocked out of the woman's hands? Seems she's decided to take a late-night jog in the desert."

When Dottie stole a glance at the men she saw that Tiny hadn't moved. One of the fat boys lay on the ground, holding his gut, moaning. The other fat boy stood beside him, hands above his head.

"Now, Mom, keep the rifle on these two while I put the cuffs on our friend here."

After Dottie had dressed Tiny's wound and loaded him into the Mercedes' back seat, she used the phone in the trailer to call the Barstow police. Brandi asked the biker with the stomach wound if he wanted something for it. He did. She went to the trunk and returned with a powerful pain killer from her father's briefcase.

"That was some very fancy shooting there, Mom," Brandi said when they were able to relax.

"Yes, well," Dottie muttered. They both knew that knocking the gun out of the girl's hand was probably the luckiest shot either of them would see in five lifetimes.

"You didn't do such a bad job yourself," Dottie said. "By the way, why didn't you come in through the back door?"

"The hinge was so rusty and squeaky I would have blown

it," Brandi said. "Instead, I fixed the bikes." She looked radiant, her eyes shone.

The police and an ambulance arrived and Dottie presented to the cops the bond and accompanying papers authorizing her to return Tiny Bellows to the L.A. County lockup. She handed the other men over to the Barstow sheriffs to do with as they wished.

It was nearly three in the morning when they started back across the desert toward Los Angeles, with a disgruntled, handcuffed Tiny Bellows quiet as death in the back seat. Brandi had curled up against her mother's shoulder like a little girl, trying to sleep.

She plugged Ralph's *Rosenkavalier* tape into the car stereo. On cue, majestic predawn colors sprayed the Mojave with early morning light.

At one point, a few miles into the journey, Dottie swore she could see, out there in the semi-darkness, a skinny naked woman who looked remarkably like Lorita streaking through the night.

Fifteen

...

"WHERE ARE WE?" Brandi, bleary-eyed, peeked out of the folds of the blanket Dottie had draped over her during the ride in from the desert. Dottie pointed to the blue neon sign above them. "Inner City Motel," she said. "Says it all."

Brandi sat upright and watched pale sunlight struggling through the smog. "What's here?"

"We are, for the time being. I did some thinking on the way in."

A terrible noise erupted from the back seat. Tiny, hand-cuffed and hung over, and bunched up against the armrest, snored off a bad dream.

"God, he's ugly," Brandi said. "They have coffee here?"

"There was a French writer—something Balzac—who died from drinking too much coffee. Fifty-four cups a day. Tore his stomach lining to shreds."

"Mom, give it a rest." She looked out at the industrial-park atmosphere. "What *are* we doing here?"

"Making sure we don't get screwed."

Dottie asked for and got a room around back that faced a

battalion of dumpsters and a wall of corrugated buildings belonging to an industrial park. They transferred Tiny from the car to the room where they dragged a chair over to an exposed pipe and handcuffed him to it.

Dottie called Paulie Dortmunder.

"You got Tiny?" he said.

"That's what I want to see you about. I'm not far away. Ten minutes."

"What about Tiny?" she heard him shout just before hanging up on him.

"I hate to ask you to stay here with this guy," she said to Brandi, who had brought in the carbine and the .38 Special from the trunk. Brandi, drinking coffee she had found in the lobby, was watching Bryant Gumbel interview another expert on government waste.

"Don't worry about me." Brandi was looking at Tiny as he slid his chair around so that he too could watch "The Today Show." "If he gets out of line, I'll shoot him. Right, Tiny?"

Dottie searched through Tiny's key ring and found the one that unlocked his wallet from his belt loop. Over his protests, she slipped the wallet out of his back pocket and put it into her purse.

"Be back in no time," she said and closed the door behind her.

DOTTIE STOOD BEFORE Paulie Dortmunder, her arms stiff by her sides. "Don't do this to me, Paulie."

She could barely contain her anger, but she wasn't going to give the little shit the satisfaction of knowing how furious she was.

They stood in the tidy bailbond office where Paulie had just informed her that he had no intention of paying her the $20,000 he had promised. In fact, he seemed to be saying that he was not going to pay her at all.

"Ralph owed me one," he said smugly. "And I'm collecting."

"Ralph's debts were his own," Dottie said. "According to

my figures, you owe him about three thousand dollars."

"Ah, but he's not around to corroborate this, is he?"

"So let me get this straight. You're saying that you're not paying me for picking up Tiny?"

"You catch on quick, girlie. Now, if you'll excuse me, I have work to do."

She went to the door, paused for a moment, then turned to face him. "Then what do I do with Tiny?" she said innocently.

"He's out of your hands," Paulie said. "You got nothing more to do. Go home and find a proper job for you and your daughter. Where is that lovely young lady?"

"Guarding Tiny."

"What's that?" Paulie looked puzzled.

"Guarding him. Not far from here, but well hidden."

"What are you saying here?"

"I had a feeling you'd pull something like this, Paulie. I don't know why, you're such a straight shooter. We have him and you owe us. When you pay up, we take him downtown and hand him over."

The expression on Paulie's face was almost worth the $20,000. "If you refuse," she said, "we cut him loose."

Paulie turned the color of raw beef. "*You* threaten *me*, Mrs. Thorson? Who the hell do you think you are?"

"Someone who's not going to get fucked out of my money, Mr. Dortmunder."

"I'll put the word out that you—"

"Did a job that you refused to pay me for? That you contracted for and reneged on? Yes, yes and yes, Paulie. And after I cut Tiny loose, I'm going to the biker gang that put up the collateral and tell them how, in order to save a few thousand dollars to pay your help, you cost them a hundred grand."

As Paulie thought about this, Dottie saw his conniving wheels turning, searching for another way to wriggle out of the debt.

"Today's Tiny's deadline, Paulie, one hundred eighty days on the nose, at midnight, so if you'll hurry up, I have work to do."

"How do I know you have Tiny?"

Dottie reached into her purse and took out the wallet, which she flipped open and let Paulie see but not touch.

"You could've got that anywhere. And how do I know, once I hand over the money, that you'll turn him in?"

"Unlike you, Paulie, we like to think of ourselves as honorable."

"You left Tiny Bellows with that young girl of yours? For all we know"—Dottie could tell Paulie was about to say something unspeakably lewd but at the last minute decided against it—"he broke free and is gone."

"That girl is Ralph's and my daughter. Tiny Bellows has gone nowhere."

"Maybe I don't want him brought in," Paulie said. "Maybe you should cut him loose. Maybe this property the biker gang put up as collateral is valuable, worth a lot more than a hundred grand. I could come out rich."

"Really? Did you check out the property value, Paulie?" She knew he hadn't; he never did. "It could be a bogus trust deed, and where would that leave you? But hey, if you're willing to take the chance . . ."

His expression told her he wasn't. "Okay, look, I can't pay you the whole twenty grand, period. I don't have the . . ."

"Stomach?"

"You could say that."

Dottie made no move to leave.

Paulie said, "I have three grand in cash, take it or leave it."

"One of your regular bounty hunters would have contracted for forty thousand, we settled for half. Now you want to give me three? Goodbye, Paulie."

At the door she heard him say, "Check the cash drawer, it's all I got."

She thought about this. If she took the three, she'd sue him for the rest in small claims court and put a lien on his property. She *had* to think about this. Out of spite, she'd seen Paulie walk away in the past, and she had bills to pay. Her heart ached, it beat so hard. Stomach acid bubbled. She breathed in short, ragged bursts. She wished she had Ralph's cool at times like these.

"All right," she said.

"Two."

"What?"

"Two thousand. I just remembered I only have two."

She opened the door and walked out.

She heard him scuffling down the sidewalk behind her. "All right, three," he said, pulling even with her.

She kept walking, shaking.

"I said three. You can have the three."

"Six," she said.

"What?"

"That little maneuver just cost you. Six now and the other fourteen within the month."

"Forget it."

"Okay." She reached the Mercedes, climbed in and started it up. Paulie stood at the window, knocking. She rolled it down. "What?"

"Four," he said, as if this were the most loathsome word he had ever spoken. "I'll write you a check."

She wouldn't be out of the neighborhood and he'd be on the phone canceling the check.

"Five, and I want cash. I'll write you a receipt."

He stormed off. A minute later he was back with the cash, in two stacks of twenty-five hundred-dollar bills. As she counted the money she could feel the ballast of debt lifting.

She scribbled a receipt and made him sign a note that said he still owed her fifteen thousand, payable in one month. She stuffed the money into her purse.

"I don't like doing business with you, Mrs. Thorson," Paulie said.

"The feeling's mutual."

As she drove away, she looked in the rearview mirror at Paulie's scowling face vanishing into the pale.

Sixteen

. . .

SURRENDERING TINY WAS going to be easy compared with explaining to Brandi why she had $5,000 instead of $20,000.

"Stay here, Mom. I'm going back," Brandi told her, waving the .38. "I'll make sure that creep pays up."

"It was all he had," Dottie said feebly.

"Yeah, and this"—Brandi held up the weapon—"is all I have."

"Which will land us in jail, with *no* money. I know Paulie. You pressure him, he'll turn us in."

"We can't let the Paulie do this to us. We have to fight back." Brandi gave her a sad, pathetic look that made Dottie weak with self-loathing. "I know," Brandi added, "you're too tired to fight back. Well, I'm not."

"We have bills, this is cash money. Even if it means going to small claims, I will get the rest."

"Yeah, sure."

"Will you two put a lid on it?" Tiny said. "My head is fucking killing me."

"Tiny," Brandi said, "shut up."

Tiny said, "You heard of prisoners' rights? Being hand-cuffed to this pipe is cruelty. The cops will hear about this."

"I am this far from shoving your prisoner's rights way up your ass," Brandi said. She turned to her mother. "He's been driving me crazy, Mom, three hours of nonstop yak. I could do him by mistake right here; nobody'd ask questions."

"Oh, is that right?" said Tiny. "I'll call some friends of mine, pay you a visit, see how fucking cool you are."

Brandi walked over to Tiny and stuck the barrel of her .38 up his nostril. "I wouldn't mind explaining to the cops that you committed suicide while sitting in this motel room. They'd be happy to get rid of shit like you."

Tiny thought Brandi's tough-chick act was a riot and laughed in her face.

"Okay, Tiny," Brandi said, "Where do you want it? Nose, eye, mouth, ear, your choice. It's messy, but I'll do it again. Step back, Mom."

Something about the *again* woke Tiny up. He said, "Get the fuck away from me!"

"Come on, Tiny, pick your spot. I'm getting impatient."

Dottie saw something in Brandi's expression that said this was no longer a game. "Brandi," she said.

Brandi pushed Tiny as far back against the pipe as he would go and urged the barrel further up his nose. "Time's up, Tiny," she said. "Where?"

"Fuck you."

"Wrong answer."

Blood appeared on the ridge of his nose and seeped over the end of the barrel.

"Brandi!" Dottie shouted, grabbing her shoulder.

"Fuck you!" Tiny shouted.

"And fuck *you*, Tiny!"

Tiny winced in pain. His eyes popped. Brandi's finger squeezed the trigger.

Dottie, now frantic, lunged for the gun. It exploded, and everything went white. Dottie heard screams, one of them her own. When she opened her eyes Tiny's mouth was in the middle of a scream, covered with blood.

Bits and pieces of something rained down on them. Chunks of plaster. The bullet had struck the ceiling. When the echo faded, Dottie felt Brandi slumped against her. Dottie steered her to the bed and sat her down, rocking her.

In his chair by the pipe, Tiny sat, head between his legs, trembling.

Slivers of pale daylight poured through the slats in the venetian blinds. Outside the motel window Dottie heard distant car horns and trucks rumble by. She took a deep breath. "It's okay, baby," she whispered into her daughter's ear.

AT THE CENTRAL jail downtown, Dottie surrendered Tiny Bellows to the jailer, filled out the paperwork and called the attorney who would file Tiny's bail motion when they went to court.

On the way home, Brandi leaned against the passenger door, saying nothing. Dottie had tried to talk to her but Brandi was stonewalling.

Dottie kept thinking that she'd screwed up, taking Brandi on this stupid desert pickup. She worried about Brandi, if she should take her to the emergency room, have her checked for shock. She thought about the five thousand in her purse and made a list of creditors the money would help get off their backs. She thought about the two of them actually bringing Tiny in. It was like watching a movie starring two women who looked like her and Brandi.

She parked Myrna's car where she had picked it up, two blocks over in front of the Murphys', and nudged Brandi.

"I'm awake."

They removed a bag of guns from the trunk and walked back through the yards to the house. It was almost noon.

They dumped the guns on the kitchen table. Dottie noticed that the place was immaculate. The counters sparkled, appliance stains had been removed, floors waxed. In the living room, somebody had swept, dusted, washed the windows, cleaned the carpet, polished the furniture.

Dottie heard a sound, a human voice strangling, or suffocating. Brandi heard it, too. She picked up the .38 and handed the Ruger to Dottie, and they started down the hall. They peeked into Brandi's bedroom, which was empty, and continued on to the master bedroom, where Brandi, gun leveled, swung into the doorway. Dottie moved in behind her.

On the bed they saw the naked sweaty back of a young girl with short reddish-blonde hair. Below her were two large male feet, a pair of hairy legs and an erect penis on which the girl was pumping up and down.

Dottie looked at Brandi, whose lower lip had fallen open, eyes glazed over.

"Robin," Dottie said. The movement stopped. Robin's little girl's voice squeaked, "Shit!" She turned back and, with an apologetic shrug, climbed off the penis.

"Get dressed," she snapped at the man beneath her, as if this were *his* fault.

Brandi laughed out loud and walked back down the hall toward the kitchen. Dottie recognized the man, her neighbor, Bill Feydeau, from two doors down. "Hello, Bill," she said to him. Bill rolled off the bed and grabbed his clothes, refusing to look at her as he slinked out of the room.

"And you," Dottie said, addressing Robin.

"I've been in jail," Robin said, pulling a one-piece cotton bodysuit over her. "A girl needs her pleasure."

"Not in my bed."

"How did you like the house?"

"What?"

"The house. How *clean* it is. You didn't notice? Maybe you wouldn't."

"What's *that* got to do with *this?*" Dottie said, fuming.

"Bill, sweetie," Robin called out, "don't forget to paint the porch. I'll have a special treat for you when you're done. Go on now." She turned back to Dottie. "As you might have noticed, Bill cleaned a lot more than my clock, Ms. Thorson." With that, she strode defiantly out the door.

"Where's Myrna?" Dottie called after her.

Robin rolled her eyes. Dottie didn't know whether to grab her by the throat or tear the sheets off the bed.

Dottie heard Brandi yelp. She rushed down the hall to the living room, where she found her standing with her hands on her hips, glaring at a woman in leotards, a peasant blouse and gold jewelry, passed out in a chair.

"Myrna," Dottie said.

Myrna's head lolled off to the side, a bloodshot eye flopped open. A shock of recognition filled the eye. "Oh, God, Dottie, it happened. It truly happened."

Dottie turned to Robin, who said, "Let her, she tells it better."

Myrna said, "I met *him* last night."

"Last night you were supposed to be watching her," Dottie said, pointing to Robin.

"She is incorrigible, this . . . this . . ."

"Say it, Myrna. Slut. You said it enough last night."

"I bring this perfectly lovely gentleman over here . . ."

"This creep."

". . . and she prances around with almost nothing on, sticking her thing in his face."

"Still having trouble with words, Myrn? Pussy. I stuck my *pussy* in his face. Which I did *not* do, except in your paranoid imagination. I wouldn't stick a cattle prod in that jerkoff."

"Because he ignored you, because he was a gentleman. Dirk."

"Dirk," Robin said. "As in Dirk-bag."

"Who was this guy, Myrna," Brandi said, "and what was he doing in the house?"

"I can't bring someone by? Besides, we knew each other."

"Oh?" Dottie said. "From where?"

"Downtown somewhere."

"But you don't remember exactly."

"At a party or something. He remembered."

"Hell," said Robin, "it sounds like love to me."

"Shut up, Robin," Brandi said, turning back to Myrna. "We ask you to do a simple thing: watch Robin. You get drugged up, pick up a stranger and we find Robin bopping our neighbor on Mom's bed. Does this sound like responsibility? We don't want you here any more, Myrna. You're excused."

Myrna looked to Dottie for help. Tears sprang to her eyes,

rivers of mascara cascaded down her cheeks. "Is this what you want, Dottie?"

"Why don't I help you—" Dottie extended her hand.

"I'm banished?" She looked at Robin. "What about her?"

"I'm responsible for Robin," Dottie said.

"I thought you were my friend. You said you loved me."

"Somebody get a shovel," Robin said, plugging a cigarette between her lips.

"Robin," Brandi snatched the cigarette out, "one more word and I swear to God we're taking you downtown."

Dottie walked Myrna to the front door and out to the steps by the ivy. The sun was bright and Myrna, who suffered from, among dozens of other allergies, light-sensitivity, threw her hand up to her eyes. "My astigmatism," she cried. "The sun just brutalizes me."

She took a moment to recover. "I screwed up royally, didn't I? I couldn't help it. There he was in the Seven-Eleven, buying flowers. We struck up a conversation. I'm a manless, aging egomaniac with an inferiority complex, what could I do?"

"What you promised. You can't just go off and do what you want when you know how important it is . . . oh, the hell with it."

"That Robin is a vixen, a tramp of the worst kind. Little pop tart, all frilly and *lethal*. Do not trust her."

"I don't."

"By the way, your police captain, Bill Sallie, came by. He's furious."

Dottie searched the street for the unmarked car. She saw kids on bikes, a telephone workman, Mrs. Bill Feydeau out hanging laundry. Parked down the street in its same spot she saw the blue sedan with the dark lump behind the wheel. "What'd you tell Bill?"

"That you two went up north somewhere, the pressure was too much for you. He didn't believe me. But you were right, it's a good thing you didn't tell me because I crack easily." Myrna clutched her arm. "Tell me I'm not banished."

"You know how Brandi is. It'll pass." As she said this,

Dottie involuntarily shuddered, as if something had just crawled up her spine.

"What is it, dear?" Myrna said.

"The desert air," she lied and glanced down the street. As if *it*, whatever *it* was, were waiting there. "I'm going back inside," she said.

From the window she watched Myrna, blowing her nose into a lace hanky, patter off down the street.

Seventeen

• • •

ACROSS THE STREET and halfway up a telephone pole, Q. D. Reese, in a phone company's hardhat and utility belt, placed an alligator clip on the appropriate line. Easy matter, tapping into the Thorson phone.

From the pole he could see the women, including good-hearted Myrna Factor, the pushover. First she'd bought the sad-faggot who'd lost his AIDS-infected lover story, then last night in the 7–11 when Q. D. accidentally on purpose ran into her and gave her the plastic rose. Fell instantly in love with him. A plastic rose, a phony memory about having met before, just like that, and he was in the door. After eight years in prison, he had to admit he still had the touch.

It had been a long time since he'd been inside the Thorson house. Last night he'd sat in the kitchen, where, as one of Ralph's baby bounty hunters, he'd taken meals, and in the living room, where he'd drunk Ralph's booze and where, just before he'd been shipped off to jail, he had blown out Dick Pendergast's kneecaps for fucking around with Bunny, his girlfriend. Property of Q. D. Reese.

Q. D. felt the surge of old resentments. Easy does it, he told himself. You've got time, plenty of it, calm down. Below him, at the foot of the pole, the telephone truck he'd copped that morning sat against the curb.

Inside his mouth he felt the cool cylinder of the bullet roll between his teeth. He ran his tongue over the tip of it and along the smooth surface of the casing.

With the alligator clip in place, he shimmied down the pole and slung his utility belt into the truck's passenger seat. With a last look at the house, he started the engine and drove out of the neighborhood. Ready for Phase Three.

Eighteen

. . .

ONE DAY BLED into the next. They called bondsmen looking for jobs. Brandi went to work at The Biscuit. People who
hadn't been able to make the funeral trickled in to pay their
respects.

It was mid-week, a Wednesday afternoon, and hot. A damp
ribbon of hair fell over Brandi's forehead. She crossed her
eyes and tried to focus on the curl and blew a puff of air at
it. She'd been sitting on the stool staring at a pile of bills.
Her mother sat at the other end of the bar writing checks.
For the first time since her father had died Brandi felt relief,
even hope.

This diminishing pile represented to her a kind of achieve-
ment. By picking up Tiny she and her mother had earned the
right to pay these bills, which, unpaid, had become a growing
reminder of their failure to cope. Paying bills was no ticket
to spiritual salvation or to greater understanding of what it
meant to be without her father, but it cleared a path, supplied
breathing room. She felt a certain pride in being able to watch
her mother inscribing on the checks the names of the debtors

and the amounts she owed. There was money in the bank, *their* money. The hounds had started climbing down off their backs—vultures who, in what seemed like minutes after her father's death, threatened them over the phone and through the mail: pay us now or else.

Her father would have been proud of them, the way they had grabbed Tiny. Of course, Brandi wasn't about to give up her waitressing job. Who knew when the next Tiny Bellows would come along?

Not everything was perfect. She'd done no studying for her psych test. She was dead tired and had to be at work in the morning. And she didn't like sitting here at the bar; it reminded her of her Dad, that she'd never see him again. Like having the plague, the certainty of it. She thought she would explode if the pain got any worse.

"Yes?" Dottie said.

"Yes . . . what?"

"That bubble I see in the corner of your eye, rich girl."

"Yeah, right. Rich," Brandi said. "It's *my* eye and *my* bubble and *my* thought."

"So there."

"Exactly."

"Okay." Dottie went back to the checkbook, which she had the bank decorate with fancy script on ivory paper, as if anybody cared. She did. Brandi did. "This money is not going to last forever," Dottie said. "But it's nice to have it for the moment anyway."

"It's not going to last 'til Monday, the rate you're writing those checks. Don't we get to spend some of this on, you know, rewards?"

Dottie looked up. "Rewards? Why, of course. Like what, for instance?"

"Clothes. I could use some jeans, a pair of boots, something to wear when I go out."

"Out, as in going out on a date?"

"Why not? You remember going out on dates, don't you, Mom? A guy picks you up and you sit with him in the car, you go to a restaurant, have dinner and maybe see a movie later. You remember. You might even hold hands, or worse."

"I'm not into dates. Besides . . ."

"I know, Dad just died. You're in mourning. Come on, you and Dad never went out anyway, except to look for another place to fight."

"Let's drop it then, okay?"

Brandi worried that her mother might become a shut-in, never go out, never see anybody. Not that she should so soon after Dad died, but this could become a habit. Brandi privately decided to take her mother's social life in hand, make sure she didn't become an old maid before her time.

Then again, she thought of the men Myrna dated. The dregs. Ugly, angry, creepy, screwed-up men who preyed on desperate women like Myrna. She wouldn't let her mother fall into that trap either. Myrna's men looked for women to dump on, beat up, take advantage of. Of course Myrna was rich, which made her a natural target.

Brandi decided she'd have to save her mother from Myrna's men *and* from herself. What a task. Of course, Brandi's own lackluster performance in the guy department wasn't any better. She'd been a shut-in all her life. As Ralph's daughter she met bounty hunters, ex-cons, cops—some of them movie-star handsome, fast-talking snake charmers. But it didn't take her long to see that under the slick veneer these guys were miserable, wife-beating low-lifes, thieves, con artists who eventually tried to put the screws to her father, or played up to her to get to him and *then* try to screw him.

She had the reputation for having a first-class bullshit detector, which her father often called upon, or which Brandi herself used to weed out the crème de la crap, as she called it.

With men like these around, she could hardly expect to meet decent types. Could she even put up with a regular guy with a nine-to-five job, a future, babies and a mortgage? Not the ones she met at work or school.

It was depressing thinking about this when she ought to be celebrating their good fortune with her Mom, who was at the moment holding up the stack of envelopes for her to see.

"Here we are," Dottie said, "back where we started. Dead broke."

"Dead broke, but not in debt."

"Dead broke, still in debt."

"Fear not," a voice said from behind them. "Salvation's at your door."

Robin lounged hookerlike in the doorway. She had poured herself into skin-tight jeans and a pink cotton shirt tied at the bottom, revealing a lot of midriff. She looked drunk. Her lipstick cut a dull red swath across her mouth, and her hair, teased to death and sticking out like spikes, wasn't blonde anymore but jet black, blue-black, making her hard and surly-looking and adding five years to her. Robin, street chick; all that was missing was gum and a grungy, tattooed biker by her side.

"I like it," Brandi said.

Robin tossed her butt and slinked across the floor toward them. "I'm in disguise," she said. "In case Henry comes looking for me."

"Very nice," Dottie said. "In a kind of . . ."

"Go ahead, say it. Slutty sort of way. You are what you are. So you're broke again. Maybe I can help."

"This oughta be good," Dottie said.

Robin pulled a pack of Camels out of her shirt pocket. "Not in the house," Brandi said.

"I was thinking in terms of piecework," said Robin, shifting, holding on to the back of a chair for support. Close up Brandi got a look at her thick mascara lines, like gutters, dug in around her eyes. A sad raccoon. Poor Robin, she thought. No family, only a temporary place to live, on her way to court, possibly jail, and her pimp was on the lookout for her. A lost dog.

"You might not like my idea," Robin was saying, "but it has a practical side."

"We're all ears," Dottie said.

"There's a lot of men living in this neighborhood looking for a way out of their misery. A herd of them. I know from watching how frustrated they are with their dumpy old wives."

"You are *not* turning tricks in my home," said Dottie.

"It's not as if you'd have to know. When you're out shopping. It'd be like paying you rent."

Dottie wondered what Robin, who did nothing for free, wanted. "Can't handle it, thanks anyway."

"If you need money, you can't afford to say no."

"Yes, I can."

"You're not a very liberated woman, Ms. Thorson."

"By refusing to turn my home into a whorehouse? You may have something there."

"You don't have to be sarcastic. I was just trying to help."

"I thank you for the spirit in which it was intended."

"What about spirits?" the voice said sweetly.

Brandi swung around on the stool and saw Myrna in the doorway, waving self-consciously.

Brandi, still angry at her for bringing her boyfriend to the house, didn't remember rescinding the banishment. "What can we do for you?" she said coolly.

"Be nice," Dottie said quietly. "We're all she's got."

Myrna held up her hand. In it she held a piece of paper. "I have something for you."

"Lucky us," said Robin, sliding onto a bar stool.

Brandi tried to look pleasant, or at least nonthreatening. "Hello, Myrna," she said.

"You don't mean that."

"Sure I do," she lied. "Hello and come in."

"Bygones be bygones?" Myrna wasn't about to budge until she was given this assurance.

"No problem."

Myrna, holding out the piece of paper like a shield, was shaking more than usual. She wore a frilly summer dress over a forest green leotard and tights, black sandals and orange nail polish. A black satin belt wound around her waist along with a half-dozen gold chains. She had pulled her hair back and secured it with an orange satin scrunchy, whose twin she wore on her wrist.

"I've got something here that can do you some good." She waved the sheet of paper at them. "I won't need it because I won't be around much longer."

"Sounds like a bribe to me," Robin said.

"Don't let the flies in," Brandi said.

Myrna took Brandi's words as encouragement, closed the door behind her and stepped into the room. With a flourish she unfolded the piece of paper. Inside was a check.

Myrna handed it to Dottie, who said, "Well!"

"You need help and I certainly don't require very much to live. The firm"—the firm being the executor of the cosmetic empire—"sends me more than enough each month."

"Why is everyone offering us money all of a sudden?" said Brandi.

"This is really very nice of you, Myrna," Dottie said, "but—"

"It's my desire to help you through these trying times."

"No, thanks," Brandi said. "I mean, thank you, but we'll have to decline."

"Myrna," Dottie said, placing a hand on her arm. "It's not that your generosity isn't appreciated, but Brandi and I are now just starting out, so it's important that we earn everything we get. No charity."

Myrna's eyes turned flame-red. Tears spilled out, irrigating her mascara.

Brandi said, "You don't want to take away our incentive, do you?"

"I just want to help, is all."

Dottie snatched sheets of Kleenex from her purse and passed them over to Myrna, who buried her face in them.

"Now you did it," Robin said.

Myrna's hand shot out from under the bouquet of Kleenex and tore the check away from Dottie. "Fine!" she snapped. She got up off the couch and in a jangle of chains announced indignantly, "This is the final insult, the coup de grace. The door has been slammed in my face for the last time. I came here to make amends and find only rejection. I'm a sick woman, but does anybody care?"

"I didn't mean to . . ." Brandi said.

"I heard everything and understand—"

"Nothing," Robin said. "If they don't want your money, Myrn, pass it over here. I'll blow it, easy."

"Ah, blow. There's *your* operative word, young lady."

"Now, now, Myrn, I'll bet those ruby lips of yours have been wrapped around some strange pipes in their day."

Myrna spun on the heels of her open-toed sandals and made for the door. "I try so hard," she said.

Dottie slipped off her stool and followed, though to Brandi she didn't seem to be buying into Myrna's hysterics this time. "You're always welcome here, Myrna," Dottie told her, "and thank you for your kind gesture."

Myrna paused by the front door. It looked to Brandi as if Myrna might acquiesce, but not today. A lifetime of stubborness stopped her. Like stone, she was unmoved.

Through the window Brandi watched Myrna hurry off down the street. Sunlight dappled off her jewelry and the salon-perfect henna in her teased hair. Part of her wanted to go after her but Myrna wouldn't budge until her wounds, real or imagined, had healed.

"What's all that 'not long to live' stuff?" Brandi asked.

"Crying wolf," said Robin.

"I don't know," Dottie said.

Brandi looked sharply at her. "What do you mean?"

But by that time Dottie was carrying the bills out to the mailbox.

Nineteen

...

FOR Q. D. ACTING was art, the art of losing yourself in another being, and then rediscovering yourself in the expanded world of a separate soul. Big thoughts, major considerations.

As a child his mother had convinced him that he was her masterpiece. She told him he was her only darling, despite the multitude of other darlings—her men—she brought home with her from the lot. She worked as a seamstress at Warner Brothers until her death and always complained that she, and not her more ambitious bosses, should have been up there accepting awards for best costumes in the movies she worked on. He loved her, and he could do no wrong.

She gave him a sense of drama. He would sneak into her room while she was with her men and watch. All that drama. And all that pain. Most of her darlings were not so pleasant when they drank, and rough when they "took their sex," as his mother phrased it.

They took their sex and she gave it to them willingly. And Q. D. could never understand why. Why she preferred them to him, why she went off with them on vacations and left him with Mrs. Mulroy. Leaving him for them. He felt a lot of rage then, against her, against her darlings.

In the bathroom mirror he rehearsed his role in the movie shooting up in Malibu Canyon. "And as far as I'm concerned, Mr. Richards," Q. D. said to his reflection, "I don't care if you like me or not. Our relationship, if you want to call it that, will be over when I pull this trigger . . . in about three seconds."

He tried the speech again, putting more amusement into it. Or maybe he should try *be*musement. Or even irony: ". . . which by my estimation will be in about three seconds."

He had the urge to rewrite the speech but the director loved the writer, who happened to be the director himself. "I don't *care* if you *like* me or not, Mr. Richards. Our re*lationship*, if you want to *call* it that, will last *only* until I pull this *trigger* . . ."

He stood back from the mirror and fixed on his eyes. Those black holes, set deep under a bar of thick brows, leered back at him. These eyes saw everything, understood the motivations behind why men acted as they did, why he, Q. D. Reese, behaved as he did.

Prison had made him illusionless. Like a lot of others, he had fallen into that abysmal well of human depravity and risen to the surface again, stripped of all fear. There was very little he hadn't done or had done to him there. Shredded psyches, plugged orifices. Mutilation, maiming, murder, and mind fuckings until nothing but a pile of ashes remained where once sanity had lived, however precipitously.

In the living room Q. D. checked his watch. He had to be on the set at eleven. Three hours. Take him forty-five minutes to drive to Malibu Canyon. He thought about swinging by the Otsego house, to check on Ralph's women.

Instead, he went out to the deck from which he could view the stretch of L.A. real estate folding down through the Beverly Hills flats to Sunset Boulevard.

He rolled the .22 shell around in his mouth. Old habit from the old days. Loved to feel it between his teeth, Russian roulette of the mouth. He remembered doing it for Brandi, freaked her out, those little eleven-year-old eyes of hers wide with awe.

Before all this was over he would bring Brandi up here and show her what he had to offer. She'd like this view, this place he had secured from his old pal Phillip, the owner, who was in Europe making films. At least that's what he told the neighbors Phillip was not in Europe—in truth, would never see Europe again. Phillip, in fact, was very close by.

His old pal had lent him his home indefinitely. Phillip's mother, upon her death, had left it to him. It was something, this funky treehouse on its own little promontory above the city lights. Furnished, mortgageless. In return for living here, Phillip had asked him to pay the taxes and upkeep.

Phillip, one of those actors who said he could act but seldom did, was the son of rich parents. He hadn't done shit with his life except to squeeze his mother financially dry. And then he had started making outrageous demands on Q. D. Bad move.

Q. D. had been playing Phillip's old-buddy role with the neighbors and occasional callers who wondered why they hadn't heard from him for a while. To these people Q. D. explained that Phillip was in creative solitude in Europe, where he was producing and acting in art films. Truth was that Phillip had found his creative solitude just around the edge of the deck, not ten feet from where Q. D. now stood, in the garden. Creatively contributing to the growth and nurturing of the azaleas, which, according to the next door neighbor, had sprung forth majestically this year.

Q. D. inhaled deeply and went back inside to dress. In a half hour he was out of the house and into the car, driving south on Mulholland.

These old Jaguars were pieces of shit. The rumors about the sleek British-made machines were true. Just like the British. All gloss and veneer on the outside, hiding a cranky, world weary, dysfunctional engine below. Yet he felt rich in this car, he *looked* rich.

By nine o'clock he was on the Ventura Freeway, cutting through North Hollywood toward The Biscuit, a family restaurant of orange and blue motif with a giant biscuit for a sign. He parked out front and went inside.

A hostess led him to his seat, from which he could keep his eye on the Jag. The waitress, whose station he had specifically chosen, approached the table. This would be the moment of truth. He wore no disguise, and though she had not seen him in over eight years, he was worried. He braced himself.

"Can I get you something, sir?" she said.

He looked up into her eyes, searching for a flicker of recognition.

"Sir?" she said.

Nothing. She had no idea who he was. His eyes traveled down to her name tag, which read *Brandi*. Brandi Thorson, after eight years, had no clue. Had he changed that much? Indeed he had.

He plastered a phony smile on his face, and said, "Brandi, what a lovely name."

HE COULD BARELY drive he was shaking so goddamn much. Cold. Quaking. He had closed the windows, turned on the heat full blast, pulled a sweater out of the trunk. Didn't do any good. He felt like ice inside. Outside, sweat bubbled on his skin. He, Quentin Delano Reese, Q. D. Reese, actor, was fucked up.

He tore up Malibu Canyon, climbing among the vertical walls, toward the movie set.

Brandi, Ralph's daughter. The whole nightmare had come back to him. It was all he could do back there at The Biscuit to keep from coming apart. Brandi reminded him so much of the past, of his girl Bunny, whom he had lost when Ralph sent him away. That loss nearly killed him; she'd been his lover, his partner, his friend.

And now here was Brandi, who even *looked* like Bunny, had her smell, like rainwater, her way of walking, speaking. Jesus, he thought, what was happening to him?

"Get a grip!" he shouted into the canyon.

In the restaurant she had brushed against him and at that moment something had happened. They had fused together and she was in him now.

Twenty

...

ONE SUMMER AFTERNOON in Grinnell, Iowa, when Dottie was thirteen years old, she was playing in her back yard when one of her cousins, a boy from the other side of town, said something that so profoundly shocked her that she could neither move nor speak. He told her that the man who brought her up—her father—was not her father at all. Her real father was the man the boy himself lived with, who Dottie thought was her uncle. "I'm not your cousin," the boy said. "I'm your brother."

Something died in her. Her belief system collapsed. She screamed "Liar!" and ran into the house, where she stuffed her schoolbag with books. Back outside she climbed up to her treehouse, where for the next five years she spent hours each day buried in mystery novels and dreaming of escape to Los Angeles and becoming a private eye.

This memory lingered as she drove home from Von's supermarket. She remembered how she'd felt, as if everything had been a lie. That she was alone, stripped of truth. Ralph's death had stripped her, too, but of a different kind of certainty, or stability. Torn from her, just like that.

She wanted to go somewhere, vanish, but how or where, and on whose nickel?

She stopped at a bookstore on Riverton and bought *The Complete Family Home Repair Book, Organize Yourself, Your Erroneous Zones* and *The Anarchist's Cookbook*. Back home she sat behind the wheel and stared at the place they'd lived in for twenty years as if seeing it for the first time.

It was a man's house, rugged and fortified, built by a man for a man, with little concern for what a woman would like. She decided to replace the blinds with draperies or window shades and plant more ivy.

Inside, she put the groceries away and spent the next few hours doing laundry, sanding the dresser and coffee table and listening to Cousin Jack's sermons on tape. Every so often she would catch a scent of something—Ralph himself; his shaving cream, the way he smelled when he woke up—and sure enough, the scent would attach itself to a memory and she'd be lost for a while.

At three P.M. the phone rang. It was Dante Cicollo, the bondsman who had introduced Dottie to Ralph twenty years before. Dante, the lion king of L.A. bailbondsmen, had come west from New Jersey to be a nightclub singer. He found a day job on Bailbond Row and entrenched himself. As Dante's star fell as a singer it rose as a bondsman, and now, two decades later, he was a rich man. He owned, along with real estate and a strong stock portfolio, warehouses in the San Fernando Valley filled with items collected from bond forfeitures: stereo equipment, exercise machines, appliances, the world's largest private motorcycle collection of Harleys, Japanese bikes, even antique Indians. All sat in his warehouses, gathering dust.

"I heard about your success with Tiny Bellows," he said in his smooth Italian accent, a holdover from his Milan childhood. "Congratulations, *cara mia*."

"Thank you," Dottie said, swelling with pride in spite of herself.

"I was also pleased to hear how you stuck it to Paulie

Dortmunder. They'll be talking about that one for years to come."

She laughed. "What a weasel."

"And as a reward, I have something for you."

Dottie had assumed this wasn't purely a social call. With bondsmen, everything ultimately had to do with business.

"Sandor Barsamian. Arsonist."

"I don't know much about arson."

"But you do know about cleaning a house."

"That I do." She wondered what this was all about.

"We have a little undercover work, Dottie. A kind of inside stakeout. As a housekeeper. Short term. A mansion in Van Nuys. Interested?"

"Should I be?"

"Barsamian was picked up for torching a building out near Sherman Oaks. There's not a lot of money on this one, of course."

Come on, Dante, she wanted to say, this is me you're talking to. Dante, like Paulie, was about to use the female thing to keep the price down.

"A few days' work, a little surveillance. You'll keep busy."

"Cleaning a mansion."

"Mansions have a way of never getting that dirty."

"If you have good help."

"I wish I could offer you more money, Dottie, but—"

"I can barely speak through my tears, Dante. How much is the bond?"

"Fifty thousand dollars."

"Who made the bail?"

"A friend who's no longer a friend."

"How much time before this ex-friend loses everything?"

"One week."

"Why'd you wait so long, Dante?"

"It's complicated."

"I'm listening."

"They could grab him on the weapons beef but they want him for the arson."

"Can't anyone be just one thing these days?"

"What can I say, my sweet. It's a violent world."

"Fifty grand on a weapons beef? What was the weapon?"

"Ahh . . ."

"Let me rephrase the question, Dante. What was he carrying?"

"I don't have the, ahh . . ."

"Read the sheet there in front of you." The longer he hesitated the more she started thinking in terms of shotguns, assault rifles, grenades.

"Explosives."

A weapon indeed, Dottie thought.

"But the real issue here is Barsamian's ability to vanish from his home, the mansion where he lives, and torch a place many miles away, then return to his home, seemingly without ever having left."

"He burns down places miles away without leaving his house? Is this a trick question?"

"Sandor Barsamian's signature is all over these fires. The LAPD and I both have surveillance on him. There's no way he could slip by us. But, honest to God, somehow he does."

"Maybe it's another arsonist. Copycat work."

"There are certain details that only he would know. But we can't figure out how he does it. We see him enter his home, and we see him leave. But somehow while he's there, these fires are started."

"Mental telepathy."

"At this point, that's as good an explanation as any. His parents won't say anything, I don't think they have any idea."

"Tell me about them."

"His father owns the oriental rug stores—Barsamian's. They swear their son is innocent."

"Don't tell me Sandor lives with his parents?"

"In their mansion, yes."

"How old is this guy?"

"Twenty-eight. We know he's setting these fires. We need evidence. We need your help. I figure you and Brandi to go in undercover as maids. You check around, keep your eyes open. How about it, *cara mia*?"

"Do you have *any* idea how he's doing this? Things to look for?"

"No."

"Uh-huh. Okay, how much is this worth to you?"

"I can pay you five hundred dollars."

"I can't hear you."

"Each. Hey, this is house-cleaning we're talking about."

"You ought to try it some time." Dottie calculated the price based on danger, the amount of the bond itself and the time remaining before forfeiture, one week. "For a guy out on fifty thousand bail on an explosives rap, we want five thousand total. What's your stake in this?"

"Standard."

Standard was 15 percent of the bail, in this case $7,500. Dottie was certain Dante had built in another $10,000 for himself; he usually did.

He was lying, and he knew that she knew. "I'm already into this for five thousand," he complained. "Plus I owe a favor to the cops." Which meant that Dante had done something highly illegal and the cops were collecting, or extorting. "For old time's sake, Dottie, come on."

"For old time's sake, Dante, why don't you pay me what you would have paid Ralph, who wouldn't clean his own house."

"Does it always have to come down to money?"

"I was going to ask you the same question. For old time's sake, I'll do it for four thousand."

"Two is as high as I can go."

"After the Tiny pickup, Dante, I'm hot, the lines are burning up."

"I can't go higher than three for both of you. I'm strangling myself. Call me if you change your mind."

"Dante?"

"Yes?"

"Call *me* if you change *your* mind."

She sat at the kitchen table, knowing she should take the $3,000. Except that if she agreed to Dante's price, all the favorable word of mouth on Tiny would crumble. Word would get out that the Thorson women were good but could be had cheap.

Plus she wasn't crazy about spending a week cleaning a mansion. She had enough to do in her own home. Although, looking around, she had to admit that Robin was keeping the place ship-shape. But at what cost? An uprising at least, by neighborhood wives when they discovered that their husbands weren't going out for the paper after all but in fact were bopping a nineteen-year-old hooker *and* cleaning the Thorson place.

The doorbell rang. She peeked through the window and saw a short thin man with slicked-back hair, about forty-five, in a suit and scuffed shoes. He wore the beleaguered face of a salesman, but this was no salesman, not with the ferretlike scowl on his face. This guy looked as if he discharged damage into people's lives, and enjoyed it. He carried a well-worn brief-case. One foot tapped impatiently on the concrete. She opened the door.

"Mrs. Thorson?" he said in that low secret voice that almost always identified a bearer of bad news.

"Yes."

"Richard Levine." He handed her his card. "May I come in?"

"Why?"

"Your husband and I had business dealings."

"Tell me about these dealings and then I'll decide whether to invite you in."

This irritated Richard Levine but what could he do? He opened his briefcase and handed her, one by one, documents that explained the situation.

"Bottom line is," he said after the bad news had sunk in, "your husband sold me this house."

"How is that possible?"

Levine showed her the signed deed which said in essence that upon Ralph's death, Richard Levine, North Hollywood real estate broker, in exchange for having paid Ralph Thorson $115,000, now owned the house and property.

"What hundred fifteen thousand dollars?" said Dottie.

"It says it right here."

She rubbed her thumb and index finger together. "But not right here."

"This is his signature, is it not?"

Of course it was his signature, but something smelled.

"You must know how difficult this is for me, Mrs. Thorson . . ."

"Yes, I'm sure, with my husband's body barely in the grave."

"I was very sad to hear of his death."

"You're so kind."

"What all this means"—Levine gathered up his papers like a card shark shuffling his deck—"is that in two weeks I'll be taking possession. You'll notice here . . ." He plucked a paper from the sheath and snapped it in front of her. "It says that unless you pay the sum of fifteen thousand dollars in cash, plus interest, by two weeks from today, I have the right to seize the property and all its belongings."

"What do you mean, belongings?"

"Its contents."

"As in personal property?"

"Not the clothes off your back, but the more worthwhile items. I have a list here somewhere."

She was numb. "Never mind, I'm sure you do."

"If you need a little extra time, of course, I could . . ."

It took everything she had to resist throwing something at Richard Levine, who seemed to be getting a kick out of this, one of the few perks of his despicable occupation.

"This is, after all, business, Mrs. Thorson. But it doesn't have to be. Perhaps we could go to dinner—"

"Get out of here, Mr. Levine. And leave a copy of this with me."

"I'll have my secretary mail it to you."

"And I'll have my lawyer mail you a response."

When Levine drove off in his shiny sports car, Dottie didn't want to stay inside the house. She went out into the back yard where the family had held a thousand cookouts, where she and Ralph and Brandi had set up target practice with the Prowler Fouler, where dozens of friends and baby bounty hunters and stragglers, guys just out of the joint and others on their way in, men estranged from their wives and women hiding from their rabid husbands, stayed in the small apartment with the single window and the slanted roof that always leaked.

Where for twenty years Fang and other noble watchdogs walked their posts and where the Otsego Hill Mob planned their strategies, going to the mat, so to speak, in troubled times: Big Joe Messina, Grandpa Jimmy, the Wild Jew from the Desert, Nervous Frank, Tall Skinny Linda, Little Fat Patty, the Hat, the Neighborhood Watch, Charlie Brown, so many of them.

Dottie sat on a tiny patch of earth in the center of the back yard. As these memories washed over her, she raised her face to the sun and soon felt tears rolling out of the corners of her eyes. Thinking, then not thinking, just sitting with the sun on her face and the tears stinging her cheeks, she smelled flowers and food cooking, and listened to the laughter of children.

Twenty-one

■ ■ ■

"IF MYRNA'S SUCH a good friend, she ought to commit suicide all by herself and not involve us in it," Brandi said, staring out through the car window at the mansions along Sunset.

"Why are we doing this?" Robin said from the back seat.

Dottie said, "Myrna has been a good friend and she is suffering."

"From delusions," Brandi said. "What did she say she was suffering *from?*"

"Her breathing, from those years on drugs," said Dottie. "Cancer."

In the past Myrna had pulled stunts to get attention, but this was not a stunt. Dottie had called Myrna's doctor to find out what was going on. When junkies shoot up, the doctor explained, they use cotton as a filter. Tiny threadlike fibers get into the bloodstream and end up in the lung where they slowly, over time, eat away at the lung's protective lining. With this shield gone, cancer marches in, destroying the lung's ability to function. Once the cancer has feasted on the lung, it moves on to infect other vital organs. The doctor said Myrna had just weeks to live and was in daily excruciating pain.

"I can't go on," Myrna had said on the phone, and she meant it.

It was Friday night, just after nine, and Dottie drove the Caddy down Sunset toward the beach. Robin, now sprawled in the back seat, whistled a tune.

"I'm not going back to jail," she announced.

"Don't worry," Dottie assured her.

"No, you don't understand. I'm not even going to court."

"You are going to court."

"That's what you think."

Robin, simmering with defiance, operated on 90 percent impulse and 10 percent good sense. On the outside she was a young American girl, polite, well-mannered, sultry. Every male's wet dream, and Henry Fowler's number-one whore. On the inside she was like nitro, ready to blow. Dottie had brought her along to keep an eye on her.

Myrna's home, paid for by family money, sat on a finger of land in the Pacific Palisades, a hilly, upscale section of Los Angeles. A gingerbread house, it had a one-car garage, well-kept lawn and a deck out back that looked down through the canyon all the way to the sea.

When they pulled into the driveway the front door opened and Myrna, dressed like a angel in a floor-length white dress and garland in her hair, came down to greet them.

As she drew closer Dottie saw that something was wrong. Her face had fallen. Giant sacks hung under her eyes and her skin, even under the makeup, was the color of paste, as if the embalmer had already gotten to her.

"The cleaning crew just left," Myrna said, "and my interior decorator put the final touches on the room." The room. Sounded ominous.

Myrna led them inside to the living room where she had spread oversized pillows on the floor, harem-style. "You might have noticed," she said. "This is the first day of the new moon. An ideal time for an ascendancy."

Dottie caught a glimpse of Myrna's bedroom, which her

interior designer had transformed into a pink cotton candy universe of pillows, bedclothes, draperies and carpeting.

Once they were seated, Myrna said, "Thank you for coming. It means the world to me that you're here. Dirk was busy."

"Who?" Brandi said.

"Dirk-bag," said Robin. "Her new swain."

"The actor, the man I've been devoted to for—"

"Three days," said Robin, who quickly added, "just to clarify here, Myrna, no offense." Robin stared at her. She looked frightened by what she saw.

"Dirk, as you'll remember, is in the movies. He's on location. He's been so caring."

"If so, he should be here." Brandi immediately regretted the words when she saw the pain on Myrna's face.

"Strangely," Myrna said, "when I told him you would be here, he declined."

"Dirk what?" Dottie said. "Any last name?"

"Oh . . . Dirk is all you need to know." Which said to Dottie that Dirk was all Myrna knew.

"I have been in great pain for some time now," Myrna said, dreamily. "My oncologist told me that I have lung cancer, that it's spread beyond the point of remission and that I don't have long to live."

"Oh, God," Dottie said. She took Myrna's hand and felt the clamminess of death on it.

"Believe me," Myrna said, "it was a relief. The doubt is gone. The doubt was worse than anything."

"What would you like us to do?" Dottie said. "Whatever you'd like."

"I have decided to go out under my own steam, with your help, of course."

Myrna fixed her eyes on each of them. "Your generosity will not go unrewarded. I have provided for you generously in my will, even you, Robin. In the meantime, I have laid out a few things . . ." She indicated an array of expensive trinkets and pieces of jewelry on the coffee table. "I know this is a great sacrifice on your part." Myrna's face took on a holy cast in the room's pale light. "Just know that you are relieving my unbearable pain of living."

She fed them fruit and salad that the housekeeper had made. Dottie asked what part she wanted them to play in this. Myrna rocked back too far on her pillow and nearly fell over. Brandi looked sharply at Dottie, as if to say, she's out of it, let's get this over with.

"The time nears," Myrna said, slurring her words. "The Seconals are taking effect. I need to lie down." She lifted one arm and more or less aimed it at the bedroom. It took the three of them to heft her up and half-carry, half-drag her toward it.

On the table beside the bed Dottie noticed three hypodermic syringes. Brandi and Robin saw them too.

"These three little friends of mine," Myrna said, referring to the syringes. "Each one is filled with heroin. I want each of you to inject me, in whatever order you choose."

"Forget it," Brandi said. "No way."

"Think of it as contributing to my peace of mind," Myrna said. "Cancer races like wildfire through my body. I suffer until I can't bear it anymore. Every hour of every day."

Brandi shook her head. Even Robin, who'd led anything but a sheltered life, looked queasy.

"You promised, Brandi," Myrna reminded her.

"I promised I would do *something*, but not this. I hate needles."

"Overcome it," Myrna said sternly. "This is critical. We are talking about ending my life of torment!" Myrna's fierceness rocked Brandi back. Myrna continued, "Anybody else got the yips? Good. By the time you've finished with this simple act of mercy, I'll have entered an eternal sleep where all the pain and suffering will be done. Remember, the greatest gift is the gift of love. I love you all."

Myrna drifted back into her Seconal stupor, closed her eyes and in seconds was asleep. A moment of awkward silence passed while Dottie prepared her for the injections.

Dottie led them back into the living room, where she said, "All right, I know this is difficult but we're going to have to do it. We'll go in, one at a time, get it over with and go home."

"Jeez, that sounds cold, Mom."

"She's in terrible pain, riddled with cancer. You think this is easy on anybody?"

"Don't leave your fingerprints on the needles," Robin said. "I'm a heartbeat from jail and this won't help."

"I'll wipe the prints and place Myrna's on them," Dottie promised.

"What about these things she left for us?" Robin said.

"Not now, Robin," said Brandi, looking nauseous.

"I've never killed anyone before," Robin said nervously.

"You're not killing her," Brandi said, "you're relieving her misery."

Robin looked at Brandi from under hooded eyes. "Right," she said. "Fine."

They took turns. Dottie first, then Brandi and Robin disappeared into the bedroom, injected Myrna with the heroin, and returned to the living room, looking guilty, color drained from their faces. They rode back to the house on Otsego in silence, street signs, playgrounds filled with children, clouds passing by. The air was thick with tiny specks of white.

Dottie felt as if someone else were driving. Ralph and Myrna, gone. It was all she could do to stay on the road. Was it fair? She didn't know. A thought occurred to her, an old saying really, that death comes in threes.

"MOM," BRANDI SAID. "Wake up."

Through the living room window Dottie saw shafts of morning light. She heard Mrs. Kaharski next door let her cat into the back yard and slam the screen door.

Through the haze of sleep she saw the clock, which read 10:30. Someone had draped a blanket over her.

She thought about Myrna in her pink bedroom. At least, she thought, her suffering was over.

Brandi knelt beside her. "Dante Cicollo's on the phone."

"I'll call him back."

"He says it's urgent. He wants to know if we can start tomorrow. Start what?"

She remembered: the arsonist in the mansion. She also remembered the visit by real-estate viper Richard Levine, which she had chosen not to share with Brandi.

"Can we start what tomorrow?" Brandi said.

Dottie took the phone. "Hello, Dante."

"You ready?"

"Ready?" When you're not sure, repeat the question.

"It's all set. Two thirty-seven Evanston, off Van Nuys Boulevard. I made a deal with the regular housekeepers to call in sick. You and Brandi will take their places for the week, scout around, see what's up with this kid, the arsonist. The LAPD Fugitive Detail has agreed to back off until I give them the word. You with me so far?"

"So far."

Brandi stood over her, hands on her hips, mouthing, *What?*

Dottie held up an index finger. She heard Dante say, "Wear something maidlike tomorrow morning. Nine sharp."

"Maidlike," Dottie said to Brandi. "Do we have anything maidlike?"

"To do what?" Brandi said.

"Maid work," said Robin, at the kitchen door, a half-eaten bagel in her hand. Dottie noticed a cluster of gold bracelets, necklaces and rings on her body. Myrna's.

"Are we getting paid expenses?" Dottie asked Dante, who said, "I'll get back to you on that, but you should. Probably the going rate. In addition to the two grand."

"Three."

"Dottie . . ."

"And if this leads to an indictment . . ."

"Conviction."

"Indictment."

"You are busting my balls, *cara mia*."

"You'll make it an even eight thousand."

"Four."

"Six."

"Five thousand, that's it."

"Done. And with this information you're sending over—

two thousand in cash." She listened to silence. "For old time's sake, Dante."

"Sure."

Dottie hung up.

"Okay, Mom," Brandi said, squatting beside her. "Let's have it."

Dottie told her about Sandor Barsamian, who seemed to be setting fires around town without leaving home, his parents' Van Nuys mansion. Brandi said, "And this maid thing?"

"An inside job. One week."

"You could have said something to me. I have a psych paper and a day job."

"With luck, it'll take a day or two."

"Where have I heard that before?"

"Maybe Lloyd Battaglia can hack his way into getting info on this guy."

"If Lloyd asks," Brandi said, "I'm out of town. I moved to Mexico, if you have to. In Mexico City, working as a maid."

· "Who's Lloyd Battaglia?" said Robin.

"A computer geek who's—how to put it—fallen in love with Brandi."

"Spare me," said Brandi.

"Which makes getting him to work for us not so easy any more."

"Let's drop it," said Brandi.

"Speaking of maids," Robin said, "wasn't Myrna's supposed to call around ten?"

"Robin?" Dottie said.

"What?"

"All that gold you're wearing . . ."

"What about it?" she said.

"It is Myrna's? I mean, it doesn't belong to any of the neighborhood wives, does it?"

The phone rang. Dottie answered it and heard, "You dirty cocksucking, backstabbing bitches! You're all whores and so are your mothers!"

"Myrna?"

The girls crowded closer.

"Who the fuck do you *think?* I wake up this morning with a splitting headache—alive! Alive, you hear me! You can't do a simple thing like an injection, not one of you! And you call yourselves friends! I'm ashamed of you. May you burn in hell." She slammed the phone in Dottie's ear.

Dottie looked up at Brandi and Robin, who stood frozen like statues.

"So," Dottie said, "you didn't inject her. Neither one of you."

"I couldn't," Brandi said. "Just like you, Mom."

"Ditto for me," Robin said, "I mean, I'm going before the judge in two weeks. No way was I taking the chance."

"Well," Dottie said stupidly, falling back into the cushions, "at least she's alive."

Robin frowned. "Which probably means we'll have to give her shit back."

Twenty-two

. . .

To Dottie there was only one thing less enthralling
than cleaning a house and that was cleaning a mansion. This
Van Nuys palace to which Dante had sent her and Brandi sat
far back from the road through security gates, surrounded by
lush landscaping and towering trees, a white manor home
with pillars and verandas, a horse barn, and golden horses
that now, at eight in the morning, were being ridden by
young blonde girls in a ring out back. Closer to the main
house were an Olympic-size pool with a statuary of Greek
goddesses, tennis courts, and leading up the path to the front
door, a black boy statue dressed up in colorful livery.

"I have bad news and good news," Dottie said to Brandi.

"Good, then bad."

"The good news is that you won't have to deal with Lloyd
Battaglia. The bad news is that he's out of town and won't
be able to check on Barsamian."

Brandi looked relieved.

At the rear of the house an elegant older man in a suit—
Forbes the butler—greeted them and gave them a tour. "To-

day you will be confined to the west wing," he told them.

"Confined to the west wing," Brandi muttered.

Forbes explained that it took the regular cleaning staff one week to complete the house, after which they returned to point A and started over again.

"Reminds me of a friend of my father's," Brandi said, "who worked on a Kentucky horse farm. His only job was to paint twenty-three miles of fences. By the time he finished, the paint was chipping back at mile one." Forbes didn't seem to find this amusing and left them to do the dusting.

They started in the library, which held thousands of volumes. After twenty minutes, Brandi, bored and irritable, hunted through the books. She pulled a reference book off a shelf and sifted through the pages, stopping at a particular point. "Here we are. Name three characteristics common to arsonists."

"I give up."

"Sets things on fire as a kid, wets his bed into his teens, is cruel to small animals."

"Really?"

"This could be our Sandor."

"If we run into him, I'll ask."

They loaded the mops and pails on the trolley and wheeled it down the hall to the dining room.

By noon they were exhausted. A middle-aged woman in a crisp white uniform appeared and showed them to a small, cramped room off the kitchen for lunch.

"Why would a guy who lives here want to burn other places down?" Brandi asked, a tuna sandwich and glass of milk before her.

"For the same reason rich kids go on stealing binges. They're given everything, and need to earn something on their own."

"They never heard of a job?"

"Stealing gives you a rush. The risk, the danger. You said so yourself."

"I only hot-wired those cars to visit my friend. She was in the hospital. I didn't do it for the danger."

"Not even a little?"

"We're getting nowhere," Brandi complained.

"Be patient."

"Sometimes you have to make things happen, Mom. I'm going out for a walk."

"Be back in ten minutes."

"Will you relax?"

A half hour later Brandi had not returned and Dottie began to worry. The woman who'd brought them here for lunch had not returned. Dottie walked outside. A stretch of green lawn sloped down to the horse barn, above which one lonely cloud hung silently in the clear blue sky. So quiet. She raised her face to the sun and closed her eyes, feeling the warmth.

After a moment she heard shouts and the sound of horses. She opened her eyes and saw, galloping up from the barn, two horses and their riders. A man and a woman. The man was a good rider, the woman hung for dear life. The woman, Dottie quickly realized, was Brandi, who as far as she knew had never been on a horse before.

They rode up and the young man, in his late twenties with curly black hair and swarthy, movie-star looks, climbed down, dropped his reins and helped Brandi off her horse.

"Meet Sandor Barsamian, Mom," Brandi said. "He lives here."

Twenty-three

...

SUPERFICIALITY SUCKED. Q. D. knew this because Myrna, who sat beside him in the Jag, thrived on it. Underneath her perfume guaranteed to gag a mule, the designer threads, and hair sprayed so stiff even the wind blasting through the Jag's top-down, eighty-mile-an-hour front seat couldn't push a strand out of place, there might once have lived a genuine woman. But no more, not the way she hid under gobs of makeup and glitzy clothing. What was she hiding from, Q. D. wondered. Reality?

Myrna had called him on his cell phone. She was under the weather and wanted him to drive her over to Dottie Thorson's to pick up some things. No problem. He wanted to readjust the phone bugs.

They left Pacific Palisades and took the freeway to Otsego, where Myrna told him to park down the street because she wasn't sure Dottie and Brandi were gone.

"You're ashamed of me, is that it?" he said.

"You? No, my God, you're fantastic."

"Then why do you want me to stay in the car?"

"I have to pick up a few things I had given them which ... they can't accept just yet. Sure, come along. No problem."

Taking his Sony camcorder with him, he followed her down the sun-drenched street to the house, then around back, where she took a key from under a flat rock by the porch, and let herself into the coolness of the house itself.

Q. D. had spent a lot of time here once. He'd sat here in the kitchen with Ralph and Dottie, and with Brandi when she'd been just a pup. A house, whatever else it lost, never lost its smell.

"You go about your business, honey," he said to her, "I'll mosey around. This looks like the kind of place my movie character would live in."

He left her in the living room with a pile of gaudy knick-knacks piled on the bar—the things she was supposed to pick up, she told him—and went back to the bedrooms.

In Ralph and Dottie's bedroom he turned on the camcorder and slo-mo'd around the room. OK, here the great Thorson once slept.

Outside Brandi's bedroom he paused, not knowing why, except for the same unsettling feeling he'd had back at The Biscuit where Brandi had served him breakfast. Pumped. Jittery. Like a kid on a first date. He didn't like it.

It was ghostly in her room. Brandi was sharing it with Robin the whore. He took footage of Brandi's bed, pillows, stuffed animals, photos of Mom and Dad. At the closet he smelled the fragrance on her clothes. He grabbed a handful and held them up to his nose. Sweet, girl things.

The more he shot, the deeper he went. Into her. He was drowning, had to climb out.

He ran his fingers over the glass photo frames on the dresser, across the rough, washed-out texture of her bedspread. "Brandi," he murmured. Good name. Alluring, he thought. "Bunny." The word involuntarily escaped from him. His Bunny. From whom Ralph Thorson had severed him. *An eye for an eye,* he heard himself say, the inner voice, from way down within. *Brandi pays for your sins, Ralph. I lose*

Bunny, you lose Brandi. A life for a life. Until now, he thought. *Until this.*

He heard a noise in the other room—a door opening? Myrna leaving? Dottie back? Brandi? He slipped into the closet, behind the olfactory heaven of Brandi's garments.

He saw a figure in the living room. Not Myrna or Dottie, not even Brandi. It took a moment before he recognized Robin the whore. Looking rode hard, put away wet. Smeared lipstick, stringy hair. Must have had a working night, a good one, by her lazy, satisfied smile and the wad of cash she spread on the bar.

Twenty-four

· · ·

ROBIN WAS THINKING about how much she loved being a whore. Easy money and mostly fun, watching johns pretend they were seducing her, or that she was interested in them, in that way. But she *was* interested in them. She was interested in their money. And though it wasn't romantic—check that, *hardly* ever romantic—she liked to give them pleasure, for which they would pay, liked to see how much she could get out of them. Negotiation. She could have been a great saleswoman; in fact, she *was* a great saleswoman. She got them to believe they were getting a hot young honey who had been saving it only for them, or who'd just been with five black guys, or that they, the johns, had come upon a poor innocent thing whose daddy had fucked her since childhood and now the johns had become daddy figures, protectors. Whatever they wanted; that was the key. She was good at discovering the *thing* they wanted her to be.

Some johns would tell her: "You're twelve and you want to be spanked." Sometimes her pimp Henry told her what they wanted because the johns had told him. "You're a bitch just off the bus, want rent money," Henry would say. "Never did nothing like this before. Got it?"

Perched on a bar stool, with two lines of coke laid out on the wood, she counted her money. A good night. Easy money. What she really wanted was what her friend Erika, a preppy blonde with four regular johns who each gave her $2,000 a month plus trinkets, had. Erika serviced her johns, kept them separate, no drugs, went to school. And no pimp. Very clean.

She was also thinking about being here, at the house, with these two women. Hell, she could have run, lots of times. Just taken off, vanished, gone east or south, anywhere. But she hadn't. She wondered about that. She hated to admit it but she liked it here. These two women had problems, and she could relate to problems.

She was also tired of running. She had a base of operations here, made good money, a place to crash, food in the fridge. This was like heaven, in a way. Plus, what the hell, there was always something going on. And these two were cool, even though Dottie was into playing Mom of the fucking Month. Enough to drive her nuts. But this was good, for the time being. When court time came around she'd have to make some decisions, but for now, hey, it was a lot better than the street.

Robin heard a noise and looked up. She quickly gathered up the money, stuffing it into her purse. Oh shit, she thought, Dottie's back. She picked up the straw and snorted the two lines. The coke whacked her with a force that nearly knocked her off the bar stool. And again! Another whack to the back of her head. Except that it didn't feel like coke this time. "What the fuck!" she said.

"What the fuck is right," the voice said from behind her. Oh shit, she thought, I know this voice.

"Turn *my* tricks, steal *my* money, who the fuck you think you are, bitch, I'll show what happens to shit like you."

"Oh, God," she muttered. "Henry."

"Got that right, bitch."

Whack! He smacked her, the impact sent her flying off the stool and across the room. "Henry!" she shouted. "don't!"

"That's right, bitch, remember my name. It's the last fucking name you *ever* gonna speak."

Whack! Whack! The blows kept coming. They stung her shoulders, her head, they plowed through her hands into her face. His bony knuckles and sharp fingernails pounded, ripped, shredded. She could hear her screams drowning in Henry's grunts.

"You think you can see your old johns and them not tell me? You never did have brains, bitch, nice pussy, *prime* pussy, not brain fucking one."

She started to fade, fuzzed out. Henry's blows didn't hurt anymore. She could barely hear him. She felt numb, which came as a relief. Though she was sick to her stomach and needed to vomit, she didn't really care.

Then everything stopped. The fists, the shouting, the pain. She was on the floor, she knew that. She forced herself to open her eyes, one swollen eyelid after the other. She saw Henry, on his hands and knees, bent over, head down.

Standing behind Henry she saw a man driving something into Henry's back. Blood splashed out of him.

In the guy's other hand she saw a camera. The guy had a movie camera, taking pictures. Of Henry, and of her.

She tried to look away but couldn't. The guy kept beating on Henry with what looked like a wooden hanger. It was the sharp metal hook that he was driving into Henry's back. Taking a movie of it! It occurred to her that she might have died and this was hell.

The man dug the hook into Henry one last time and picked him up like a piece of meat and hurled him against the wall. Then the guy turned to her. Here we go, she thought, I'm next.

She closed her eyes, waiting. The smell of blood sickened her. Moments passed. She felt the guy's hand on her head, on her neck, his fingers across her lips. Smoothing her hair.

Then his touch was gone. She heard the tick of a clock and the Kaharski woman next door yelling at her husband.

She refused to open her eyes, thinking this was a joke, or a test. He had to be waiting to drive the hanger into her. She uncurled herself, straightened one leg, then the other. She allowed a sliver of light to break in through her eyelids.

She saw the window above the bar, the bar itself, the room. Empty. She looked around; no Henry. Only his blood, splattered everywhere.

She heard gurgling sounds, her own, and felt the wracking pains of relief. She brought her hands to her eyes and thanked God that she was alive.

Twenty-five

. . .

"YOU'RE KIDDING ME," Dottie said, driving along Balboa toward home. "That sadist said he wants to take you away somewhere?"

"To Baja," Brandi said, "for the weekend."

"I hope you told him to take a flying leap."

"I told him I'd think about it," Brandi said.

"The guy torches buildings, he wets his bed, he's cruel to small animals. And you said you'd think about it?"

"What was I supposed to say, no, thanks, we're really here on a stakeout and if we tag you, Sandor, you're worth three grand to us?"

"There's a limit to what we're supposed to do for three thousand dollars."

"He wanted you to come along, too."

"Me?" Dottie said.

"That's what he said. 'Bring your sister.'"

"Your *sister?*"

"More interested now, huh?"

"He told you to bring your sister?"

"That's what he said."

"And what did you say?"

"I said, that's not my sister, that's my grandmother."

"You didn't."

Dottie hated it when Brandi laughed the way she was laughing right now: joke's on her. "No, I'm serious," Brandi said. "He really wanted you to come and, no, I didn't say you were my grandmother. As far as Sandor is concerned, we're a sister mansion-cleaning team. What a jerk."

"Baja, huh?" Dottie allowed herself a smile.

"Yeah, Mom, right."

Dottie turned off Riverton onto Otsego. When she thought about four more days of cleaning that monstrosity it made her cranky. And she truly did not like Brandi cozying up to Sandor Barsamian, whose slick Middle Eastern salesmanship she trusted about this much. The guy was a charmer and an arsonist, had his own vanishing act, liked explosives. "Find out anything else about him?"

"I will tomorrow."

"Oh?"

"When he gives me a personal tour of the house, which he also wanted to know if you'd be interested in."

"Oh?"

"I think he has a crush on you, Mom."

"I'm sure."

"You just passed the house."

Grimy, soapy, smelling of Pine Sol and Dutch Boy, all Dottie wanted was to fill the tub and soak.

"Holy shit!" Brandi said at the door.

The first thing Dottie saw was Robin curled up on the couch, head tucked into her chest, whimpering in a torn, blood-spattered dress. Above her, wet smears of blood made ugly red patterns on the wall, like Rorschach inkblot tests.

Brandi kneeled beside Robin, prying her hands away from her face. She looked as if it had been run over by a convoy of fists. Purple bruises blotched her skin. Blood caked her hair. An eyebrow had been all but ripped away.

Dottie grabbed hand towels from the linen closet and hurried into the kitchen for a pan of warm water. It took her and Brandi an hour to clean Robin up and calm her down. No emergency room, she didn't trust doctors, they cut. Not that she hadn't just been cut up real good already.

"At least let us check for broken bones," Brandi said.

"I'm fine," Robin said. "A lot finer than Henry, that bastard. He's not fine at all." She let out a sinister chuckle. In a slurred voice, through swollen lips, she gave them details.

"What did this guy with the hanger look like?" Dottie said. She looked down at her own hands that were shaking all over, and up at Brandi, whose lower lip drooped open, whose gaze had drifted off somewhere away from the scene in front of her.

"Not big but powerful," Robin said. "He kept hacking away with the hook. I don't think Henry's alive, not the way blood was gushing out of him." A silence, then she added, "Plus the guy was taking a movie of the whole thing. With this camcorder he had."

"Oh, man," Brandi said from behind them. "You oughta see my room . . ."

Dottie used an antiseptic that stung, and Robin, actress that she was, made a big production number out of the whole thing. It didn't take a genius to realize bones might be broken. She needed to get to a hospital. But with Robin's pigheadedness, Dottie knew she'd have to rely on her youth to heal the wounds.

"Where's Henry, then?" Dottie asked.

"Dunno. Guy must've dragged him off."

"Jesus Christ!" Brandi shouted from her room. "God damn it!"

"What?" Dottie called back.

Brandi appeared at the door, holding her jewelry box. "Somebody walked off with my stuff."

"Oh, Brandikins, I'm sorry."

"My favorite earrings are gone, the ones Dad gave me." She glared at Robin. "Somebody is responsible and somebody had better find them and get them back."

Robin lowered her eyes and looked at Brandi. "I'll get right on it," she said through bloody, crusted lips.

Twenty-six

. . .

UP ON MULHOLLAND Q. D. Reese, feet propped up on the coffee table, drank a Miller and watched the home movie he'd shot with his Sony camcorder at the Thorson house. Footage of Ralph and Brandi's bedrooms, Brandi's skimpy blouses, silk underwear, the jewelry. He got it all, every delicious frame. He'd even walked off with some of the loot. A pair of Brandi's earrings, for instance, one of them dangling now from his left ear.

On the screen he watched Henry the pimp beating up on Robin the whore. Henry was a pro, must've had practice keeping his girls in line. Q. D. almost didn't want to stop him but he knew that Henry wouldn't quit until his Robin couldn't ever fly again.

Q. D. switched off the projector and went out to the deck. He had saved her life, now he owned her.

He had driven Henry up here in the trunk of the Jag, bloody as shit, and waited till dark to bury him next to his ex-housemate Phillip, in the flower garden.

Brandi would appreciate that he had saved her friend. He

touched the earring, gave it a little tug. His heart gave a tug along with it. Beautiful, pristine Brandi, who used to sit on his knee before her father had sent him to prison and ruined his life.

A tear rolled out of his eye. The irony of it all, he thought, wasn't it cruel.

Twenty-seven

...

"I HAVE NO idea, Horace." Dottie was on the phone to Horace McFeeney, the Thorson family lawyer, telling him about real estate scam artist Richard Levine, from whom she had just received a threatening letter. "According to these papers I have in front of me, Levine paid Ralph a hundred fifteen thousand for the house, and I have two weeks to vacate."

"Drop the papers by and I'll have a look at them."

"Can you do it in a hurry?"

"I've got a full plate, Dottie, but I'll get to them as soon as possible."

"If Ralph and I had had a full plate and got to you as soon as possible when you were up on that morals charge, Horace, right now you'd be bent over a Folsom urinal with ten guys taking turns on you."

This was met by silence on the other end. Then: "I'll get right on it."

"Thank you, Horace."

Lawyers. No wonder Shakespeare suggested having them

all killed. With few exceptions lawyers were unscrupulous, hypocritical shits. Each week, for instance, on an L.A. network affiliate, one of those do-gooders spouted off on legal matters big and small. This "top area attorney," as he was billed, was in reality a bullshit artist whom Ralph got out of legal scrapes a dozen times because the man was incapable of telling the truth and cheated his clients out of big money on a regular basis. It stood to reason that he would go on the air.

"Mom," Brandi said, "we'll be late for our wonderful new job."

Robin appeared at the bedroom door, black and blue, cut up and bandaged. "What about me?"

"You," Dottie said, "should stay in bed."

"Ready, Mom?"

The phone rang and Dottie answered it. It was Myrna, who said cautiously, "Is that you, Dottie?"

"Who else would it be?"

"Is everything okay?"

"Why wouldn't it be?"

"No problems?"

"What kind of problems are we talking about, Myrna?" Dottie remembered Myrna's trinkets that she had left on the bar, gone now. She figured the guy with the hanger had taken them along with Brandi's jewelry, but you never could be sure. She thought she'd take a shot. "You got your stuff?" Dottie said.

"What?"

"The things you bequeathed to us. You came by and got them?"

"Oh, right."

"When?"

"What?"

"When did you come by and get them?"

A long silence followed.

"Myrna?"

"What?"

Dottie could not discount the possibility that she was stoned. "When?"

"Yesterday," Myrna admitted.

"See anything when you were here?"

"No." Not *What, for instance? or Anything in particular?* Just a quick no. Too fast on the uptake, Dottie thought. She decided to try another tack. "Was Robin here when you came by?"

"No."

"She got beat up pretty badly."

"She did?"

"Her pimp followed her, did a real nasty job on her."

"My God."

"Was she around when you got here?"

"I didn't see her."

Dottie was thinking about the second man, who had saved Robin. "How's Dirk?" she said.

"What?" said Myrna.

"Your boyfriend, Dirk."

"Oh, not anymore. He's not my boyfriend anymore."

"Oh?"

"Haven't seen him."

Right.

"Mom . . ." Brandi said. "Cone on."

They were already late and Dottie decided there was nothing more she was going to get from Myrna. It made her angry that Myrna was lying to her—if she was. "Okay, Myrna," she said. "Got to go."

Out in the street, she heard the phone again. Probably Myrna, burning with curiosity, calling back. "Don't answer it," she shouted to Robin.

ON THE WAY to Van Nuys, Brandi drove and Dottie read the L.A. *Times,* the local crime section, to see who among her friends had been arrested, shot or killed. At the breakfast table each morning, she and Ralph had scanned the *Times,* exchanging crime blurbs from the Valley.

The Barsamians' butler, Forbes, led them to the west wing: bedroom/office suite, a child's playroom, gymnasium, indoor lap pool and billiards room with a bar. Brandi hung back, in one of her moods.

It became apparent to Dottie that these quarters belonged to Sandor himself. The child's playroom had gone untouched for years. Some of the toys cost a small fortune. Photos of little Sandor and family members, Middle Easterners all, by the looks of them, sat on oval mahogany tables among blue ribbons won at horse shows and photos of young Sandor in jodhpurs, with bow and arrow, croquet mallet, in bathing suits on private beaches before lavish homes built among sand dunes. This was a life of privilege.

Dottie remembered the information sheet Dante Cicollo had sent over: only child, brought up by governesses, absentee father in the Orient buying rugs. Society mother. Lonely little rich kid, who grew up to torch buildings.

By one they had finished with the game and toy rooms and entered Sandor's private quarters: office, bedroom suite, master bath with gold fixtures, a cavelike bundle of stark, severe rooms.

The single luxury was a giant tank with dozens of fish swimming among rocks and castles and miniature villages. There were no photos in these rooms, no memories, no past. No distractions. This was a utilitarian universe where man and God lived with a single intention: a job to do, a spartan life to live. In the office a simple rigid chair sat before computer hardware worth tens of thousands of dollars.

"Do you know what this stuff is?" Dottie said.

"Yup. Took that course last semester."

Dottie went to the door and looked down the hallway. She said, "Turn it on. Let's see what Sandor has filed away."

"I can't do that. It's private."

"So's this house, and here we are. Let's have a look."

Brandi sat in the chair and turned on the computer. Her slender fingers played the keyboard like a piano, tap-tapping images into being and dashing them with a simple command. "Sandor has everything here," she said with awe. "Makes our school computer look obsolete."

"See what you can find out about . . . arson."

"You mean like through Prodigy? Famous arsonists in history?"

"Private files. The stuff he puts on there himself. A diary, maybe."

"Mom, there are codes. Only he knows what they are."

"Well, then, what about using variations on the word *fire?*"

Brandi tapped away.

"Common sense didn't start with computers," Dottie said. *"Firestarter, flame*—try those."

"Or bed wetting." Brandi zipped through five, ten, twenty variations of *fire* and *arson* and found nothing that would let her into Sandor Barsamian's private files. "He could be using the names of a match company, or even something that has nothing to do with fire."

Standing behind Brandi, looking over her shoulder, Dottie could feel the adrenaline. "The simpler the better," she said. "The easier to remember, the faster to get to."

Brandi cocked her head. "Oh, shit."

"What?"

"Somebody's coming."

She tapped commands, saying, "Come on, come on, come on." One program bled into another, appearing and disappearing, racing for the nearest exit from the machine. "Come on, come on, come on," she chanted.

Now Dottie heard something, from down the hall. She hurried to the door and looked. Nothing. The sound, like a door opening on rusty hinges, was nearby. Somebody grunted, then sneezed. She realized the sound was not in the hall but on the other side of the door, in Sandor's bedroom suite. But they'd already been in there and seen no one. While Brandi stayed with the computer, Dottie pressed her ear against the door. She heard shuffling feet, another sneeze. With a quick look back to Brandi, she grabbed a duster, turned the knob and went through the door.

Dusting as she went, she hummed an old movie song whose title she couldn't remember. Act normal, she told herself. She crouched down, in the event she needed to reach the Stinger nestled in her ankle holster.

"Well, hello there," the voice said from behind her. She jerked up and spun around. It was Sandor himself, dressed in filthy slacks and polo shirt and running shoes without socks. Dust covered his face, arms and hands, and lay in a fine mist on his curly hair.

His eyes were black saucers, wide and startled like those on women with recent face lifts. Red flames burned in their corneas.

"You scared me," Dottie said.

"I didn't exactly expect you either." He approached her as if in a trance. "But I'm so glad you're here," he said.

"Oh?" She realized that she had brought the duster up between them.

"I've got something to tell you," he said.

To confess? she wondered. She tried to steer him away from the door, through which she could see Brandi at the computer.

Sandor's firestick eyes bored into her. He looked manic, probably was, pumped up from his latest job.

"You are very attractive," he said, his breath like charred wood. "I imagine men say that to you all the time."

"Not really," she said.

"You remind me of—"

"Your mother?" she said.

He snapped to attention. "Why'd you say that?"

"I'm old enough to be your mother." *Barely*.

"A woman. Old enough to be a woman."

"Yes, well, that's right, Mr. Barsamian."

"Sandor. If your sister . . . she's really your sister?"

"No."

"Then your partner, young and foolish as she is, if she can call me Sandor, so can you." He forced her back against the sink.

"Watch out," she said, "you're tracking mud and we just cleaned. Mr. Forbes will be unhappy."

She felt the heat from his body. This was getting way out of hand. She didn't want to have to knee him in the groin but that was fast becoming her only option.

"Hey!" she heard. It was Brandi, standing in the doorway, hands on her hips, pissed. "Isn't this nice?"

"I had an overwhelming need to confide in your partner," Sandor confessed.

"My mother," Brandi said.

Sandor, surprised by this, stepped back from Dottie. "You are joking."

"You don't think I'd hang around with her otherwise, do you? Yeah, meet my Mom. If you two want to be left alone, I can always go into the other room and throw up on the rug."

Sandor stepped toward her. Brandi put a hand up. "Thank you, that's far enough."

"I want to explain that something traumatic has just happened and I needed consolation."

"Looked more like rape to me, except that I don't know who was doing the raping." She grabbed Dottie by the wrist and yanked her out of the room.

"Please . . ." Sandor said, following them. "Please, let me explain . . ."

"We're listening," Brandi said. They were in the hall, near the exit.

Sandor, looking small, contrite and petulant, said, "You must forgive me. It's my fault and it won't happen again."

"No kidding," said Brandi.

"Please say nothing and neither will I. Just go about your duties. If you need anything, just ask."

"Well . . ." Brandi said, thinking. "We're leaving for the rest of the day."

"Of course. I will instruct Forbes to pay you time and a half—double time."

"We'll be back tomorrow," Brandi said. "We like to finish what we start."

Outside, they climbed into the Caddy. Brandi drove to the entrance to the Ventura Freeway and pulled into the lot at Von's market. She removed the key from the ignition and turned to face Dottie.

"What was that all about?" she said. "With Sandor."

"Nothing."

"Too fast."

"What?"

"You said that too fast. There was something, wasn't there?"

"Are you serious?"

"Yes."

Dottie took a breath. "I'm sorry it upset you."

"Don't worry, the tears weren't real. I used them all up on Daddy. I want to know what you were doing in a clinch with Sandor."

"He surprised me."

"You could have kicked him in the balls."

"I would have if you hadn't spoken up, thank you."

When Brandi made no reply, Dottie said, "All right, what's on your mind?"

"It's not important."

"Hey, let it out. We're not strangers here."

"It's stupid."

"We've never been stupid before?"

Brandi lowered her head like a young horse, looked away. "Seeing you with Sandor, in that embrace, or whatever you want to call it. It stunk."

"That was no embrace. Sandor Barsamian is crazy. He burns things down."

"I never saw you in an embrace with any man, not even Dad."

Dottie wanted to say that she and Ralph had a lot of affection for each other, but it would have been a lie. She wanted to tell her the truth, that in the last ten years the only time Ralph touched her was when he hit her.

Instead, she said, "Your father didn't like women. He put up with them, he put up with me. He loved you, but you were his daughter. I was a necessary evil. Otherwise, why would he have treated me the way he did?"

"All I do is fight with men."

"You have to compromise."

"And get the shit beat out of me? No, thanks."

"You never have to compromise that much."

"You did."

"I didn't know any better. I tried to fix it. When that failed, I left him."

"A hundred times."

"Better than the alternative."

"Lot of good that did me." Brandi jammed the key into the ignition and started the engine. "Let's go."

"Brandi . . ."

"I have a splitting headache. Besides, we have work to do."

FOR DOTTIE THE north Hollywood branch of the Los Angeles Public Library stood like the last warrior in a long-defeated neighborhood. At a table in the main reading room, she and Brandi sat among stacks of magazines and books. Topic: arson and arsonists.

Outside the dusty windows Dottie saw shadows creeping across mangy lawns and fast-food parking lots. Black and Hispanic kids roamed in packs along dry, sweltering streets.

"All right," Brandi said. "We're here because of that weird stuff I found on Sandor's computer." She opened a book and read: "A profile of the average arsonist."

"I'm listening."

"An average arsonist is," Brandi said, "male, white, sixteen to thirty-five. A loner. Has troubled relationships with women. Sets fires within five miles of where he lives. Lives with an overbearing mother, is sexually inadequate, along with that other stuff about wetting his bed and cruelty to small animals."

"We don't know any of that about Sandor," Dottie pointed out.

"Check this out. Quote: 'Often fixated on mother and older women in general . . . is particularly attracted to women his mother's age'."

"Give me that."

Brandi slid the book toward her and spun it around. Dottie read, and slid the book back. "It says not in all cases."

"Ah," Brandi said, "so it does." She leaned forward so that the others at nearby tables couldn't hear. "In his computer I found that Sandor weighs goldfish in grams and determines how many times you can stick them with a pin before they die."

"What?"

"How many stabs with a pin it takes to kill a goldfish. According to Sandor's statistics, he's killed a lot of fish in those tanks of his. He's also a detail freak. I found data on how many grams of arsenic it takes to kill a cat. He adopts cats from the ASPCA and feeds arsenic to them. Then he cuts off their heads. Nice, huh?"

"We're not going back."

"Not only that."

"Do I want to hear any more of this?"

"He orgasms when he cuts off the heads."

"We're *definitely* not going back."

"Mom, this is a true psycho, you're right. But there's nothing about cruelty to humans."

"They're next. Or rather, we're next. We're off this one." Dottie started to get up until she felt Brandi pull her back to her seat.

"Mom," she said, her eyes round and unblinking, "this isn't Tiny and his bikers. Sandor is *interesting.*"

"No humans, huh? Interesting?" Dottie flipped through the book she was reading. "Let's talk about interesting. Here's an arsonist who poured fire on women and tossed a match on them in churches. Said he was searching for purification. Also to get off. You wonder what it takes to have an orgasm these days. How about this interesting person who set fires with the sole purpose of putting them out and becoming a hero? Or this one who fills a bathroom light bulb with gasoline and waits until his loved one comes home at night and flips the switch. Boom!"

"Dad went after weirdos, lots of them."

"And he's dead. And you're all I've got left."

Brandi lowered her head in thought. "What about the money?" she said.

"You know that old expression, you can't take it with you?"

"Mom, we can get this guy. Think about the damage he'll

do to others if we don't. We have an obligation."

"We pass this on to the cops, who have a lot more expertise in this than we do."

"Where did he get that mud on his boots?"

"You're changing the subject."

"Mom, we're this close."

"Why are you so stubborn?" Dottie said.

"I'm logical. You're stubborn."

The argument spilled out of the library into the parking lot.

At home, Dottie got out and stood by the door. The sun bore down on her. She thought about what Brandi had said. She was right; no one would get as close as they had, and they *did* have an obligation. "Every instinct tells me not to go forward," she said to Brandi.

"All of my instincts say go. Then there was that other thing I found on his computer."

"What other thing?"

"About the tunnel."

Dottie looked at her. "The tunnel?"

"There was something about a tunnel. But that was when I interrupted you and Sandor in your mad embrace."

Twenty-eight

. . .

AT FOUR IN the afternoon Q. D. Reese, driving toward North Hollywood, smelled magnolias floating on the dry air. Last night in his dreams Brandi had been the main character. This upset him. He had always played the lead in his dreams and now he'd been replaced. It was symptomatic. His movie role was not going well. His focus was off. No concentration. To be good, you had to live the part, and he wasn't living it.

He should have been heading for the Malibu Canyon set. Instead, he drove in the opposite direction, toward Brandi's.

At the Riverton intersection he pulled into the 7–11 and made a call to the Thorsons', got the answering machine. Nobody at home? Not necessarily.

He parked the Jag on the next street over from Otsego and scooted through the back yards to the house. He found the key he'd seen Myrna remove from its hiding place and slipped through the kitchen door and down the hall to Brandi's room. He went in and stood on Brandi's bed, took out the kit and removed a tiny Ibex receiver. In the light fixture he planted the electronic bug that could pick up the sound of an ant crawling across the ceiling.

He needed to go but couldn't, immobilized by the scent of her, as if she had her arms around him, suffocating him. He opened a drawer and removed a handful of her underclothes and rubbed his face in them, inhaling. Move, he told himself, take the things with you if you have to. He stuffed the underclothes into his shirt and left the house.

With one hand on the Jag's steering wheel, and the other turning script pages, he drove, trying to memorize his lines. Good luck.

Brandi. Jesus. He hadn't felt this way about anybody since Bunny, and how long ago was that? A fucking lifetime. He could not let this happen again, this giving of himself to someone, handing himself over to love or whatever it was. The same thing would happen, he knew it. It'd be taken away. She'd go off, find some other guy, better guy, guy with more than he had. Sharper, richer, whatever. And he'd be left again, fucked over and alone. Remember what happened with Bunny, remember what happened with the others.

He was having a hard time breathing. "Don't do this," he said aloud, feeling a sickness settle in.

Twenty-nine

■ ■ ■

"MYRNA GOT THE blues, so we're doin' Euthanasia Two . . ," Robin sang.

Brandi told her if she heard it one more time, Robin could prepare herself to be kicked out of a moving vehicle.

When Dottie returned from the Barsamians' she found a message on the answering machine from Myrna, pleading with her to hurry, she needed her in the Pacific Palisades before it was too late. When Dottie called back Myrna did not pick up. Dottie corralled Brandi and Robin into the car and now, two hours later, they pulled into Myrna's driveway.

The door opened and Myrna stepped out into the sunlight, shading her eyes. She looked as if she had hours, if not minutes, to live. She had aged a decade in the past few days. Her face, normally pasty, seemed to melt off her bones.

"Jesus, Mom," Brandi said. "She looks dead."

Myrna, in another of her angel dresses, beckoned to them. At the door she handed Brandi a list of items she needed from the store and told Brandi to take the Mercedes. "Fill it up at the service station," she said. "The grocery is next door."

Inside, nothing had changed from the last time. Myrna had lit candles, prepared a light meal, laid out the same items she wanted each of them to have. After a while Brandi returned from her errands and took her place on the sofa.

Now that they were all seated, Myrna dilated on her gratitude and woe.

Brandi blurted out, "No more shooting up."

"Don't worry, dear, I've made other arrangements."

After prayers and meditation, Myrna led them out through the kitchen to the garage.

"You, too," Myrna said to Robin. "Or you don't get your incentives," she added, indicating the pile of goodies on the table.

"I'm such a whore," Robin said, climbing to her feet.

In the garage Myrna pushed a button and the automatic door closed. She said that a mason had come by and caulked the entire inside of the garage, making it "tight as a tomb."

"I have decided to make this my final resting place." She climbed into the front seat of the Mercedes and turned on the engine.

"I love you all," she said.

"Sure you do," said Robin.

Myrna turned to her and said sadly, "Why are you so bitter, Robin? I'll bet underneath the caustic exterior there's a real sweetheart."

"I wouldn't know," said Robin.

"I'll pray for you."

"You'd better hurry up."

Dottie could tell that the Seconals Myrna had swallowed were taking effect.

"Now, go, my darlings, the housekeeper will find me in the morning. I've left instructions for her to call you. I love you . . . I love you."

Dottie herded Brandi and Robin from the garage. At the door she turned and saw Myrna's frail body draped in its angel dress, her head back against the car seat, off to one side, facing her, a faint smile on her lips. Her eyelids stood at half mast, in a dreamy haze. She tried to lift her hand to wave goodbye but could not.

DOTTIE DROVE IN petrified silence. Back in North Hollywood, she and the girls climbed the steps into the cool, dark house, which smelled of last night's pizza and something else that Dottie could not identify—after-shave lotion? Dottie thought about the bomb, about the stranger who had hacked up Robin's pimp.

She locked the doors, went to bed and tried to sleep, but guilt kept her awake. With a stronger effort, she might have helped Myrna kick her habit. She remembered the dozens of times Myrna had come to the house to dry out, only to use again after a week or so. For heroin junkies the habit was entrenched, like eating. They never quit, they O.D.'d. Or like Myrna, they simply expired

Dottie got up and went into the office where she pored through active case files. She thought about Brandi's tunnel reference on Sandor Barsamian's computer. She was itching to get back to the mansion but they weren't due to clean it until the day after tomorrow.

"What's this?" Brandi called from the other room.

"What?"

"This." Brandi stood in the doorway, waving a letter.

"Oh . . . that." Dottie had decided to tell Brandi about real-estate con man Richard Levine, but not yet. "I was going to tell you."

Brandi looked at her sharply. "When?"

"I didn't want to upset you."

"We're going to lose our home and you didn't want to upset me!"

"I called Horace. He's looking into it."

"You get that guy over here," Robin called out fiercely. "I'll fix his fucking tank."

Brandi stormed around the living room, hands on her hips, jaw clenched, pissed. "This is just great. No money, no home, no nothing!"

"I'll get him all hot and hack his dick off, shove his balls in his . . ."

"Robin, shut up." Brandi glared at Dottie, who saw the old craziness in her eyes. "Mom, this is unacceptable."

"It certainly is."

"I'll shoot him up with AIDS blood, shove pineapples up his ass . . ."

"Robin, shut *up!*" they both shouted at her.

Dottie said, "I suggest we use all this energy to find ways to make money to pay Levine off. For fifteen thousand we can get him off our backs. Temporarily."

"Temporarily," Brandi said, scowling.

The phone rang. Dottie answered it. It was Patti Ashbury calling with the name of a fugitive who had jumped bail, an easy pickup for which Patti would pay Dottie a quick $2,000.

"Is this fate?" Dottie said.

Business as usual, Patti said. "It shouldn't take you more than an hour." The fugitive, Arnold Bell, managed a Burger-Land, a family restaurant on Sunset Boulevard. Mr. Bell, up on his third DUI, had failed to appear in court. His mother, Eunice, had put her house in Reseda up as collateral to guarantee that her alcoholic son would appear in court. Like so many other shitty sons, Arnold didn't give a damn about his mother yet still had the gall to keep his job, live at the same address. Actually, as Dottie knew, it was an understaffed LAPD Fugitive Detail who didn't have the manpower to hunt down a bail jumper who hadn't changed a thing in his daily routine.

When Dottie hung up, Robin said, "I've got it! I have the answer to all your problems."

Dottie looked at her wearily.

"How to make millions!"

"Not now, Robin," Dottie said.

"No, seriously, I have the answer."

"So what is it?" said Brandi.

"Check it out." She snatched up the receiver. "What's that I-Team investigation squad on TV, the ones who do the crime stuff?"

"Channel Seven," Dottie said.

Robin called information and got the number for Channel 7. She cleared her throat and dialed. She told whoever answered that she had a hot story and wouldn't talk to anyone who wasn't in charge. She was put through to a program producer.

"My name is Robin Ripley," she said, "A friend of Dottie and Brandi Thorson, a mother-daughter bounty-hunting team living right here in Los Angeles. You've heard of Ralph Thorson, the bounty hunter who Steve McQueen played in his last movie, *The Hunter?* You have? Great." Robin raised her eyebrows and gave Dottie a reassuring nod. "Well, as you may know, Ralph Thorson recently died and his wife Dottie and daughter Brandi have taken over his business. That's right, they're bounty hunters now, and tomorrow morning, if you're interested in a hell of a story, they're going to capture a major bail jumper at BurgerLand on Sunset Boulevard in Hollywood. On-the-scene capture, and you can have the exclusive if you want it. I think your station is the best, so I thought I'd go to you first before I went to the competition. You are? Okay, you can reach them at five-five-five, two-two-four-six, in North Hollywood. I think they're there now. They have all the details. Robin Ripley. R-I-P-L-E-Y. You bet. 'Bye, now."

"What do you think you're doing?" Dottie said.

"Making you rich, which I should get ten percent for, a finder's fee."

"Robin," Brandi said, getting exactly what Robin had in mind, "you are a genius."

"A genius for getting us into trouble," said Dottie.

Robin twirled around once in a gesture of pride and said to Dottie, "Do you have any idea how many people watch Channel Seven news? Millions. And do you know how many people have people they want found, people who've jumped bail, who owe them money, who they want bad things to happen to, whatever? With you and Brandi on TV, now they know where they can go for help. For a price, of course. I *am* a genius."

Dottie stuck a finger in Robin's chest and pushed her back across the room. "Do you know how many nuts are out there who'd just love to get their hands on two women bounty hunters, or how many jerks out there would love to be bounty hunters who will find us and badger us day and night? This has already happened, Robin Hood, savior of lost souls, to Ralph and me when Ralph went on TV under similar circumstances. We had every nut case in Southern California and twenty states at our door looking for jobs or autographs or who just plain wanted to be Ralph."

"No," Robin said, "I didn't. I was just trying to help."

"She might have something, Mom."

"Yes, a pea for a brain."

"Well than, fuck it," Robin said. "Leave me out of it. Don't go. There's the answer. Say some dumb chick must have called in, pay no attention."

"Well then, see, you *are* capable of a sensible thought every once in a great while."

"I think we should do it, Mom," Brandi said.

"Oh you do, do you?"

"Or lose the house. Two thousand dollars for an hour's work on TV?"

The phone rang and Dottie answered. It was a woman, Bethany something, from Channel 7, who started asking questions. Dottie half listened to her, keeping her eye on Brandi in the center of the room, staring back at her. She looked so much like Ralph it was scary. Face granitelike in its intensity, her piercing, unwavering blue eyes. Not a muscle moved, not a thought betrayed, just the inscrutable, icy stare of a woman who knew she was right on this one. It made Dottie start to question herself, as she had so often with Ralph. But this time she could be wrong. Her decision had to be based on reason, not obstinacy.

"Ms. Thorson?" the woman said. "Are you there?"

"Just a moment, please," Dottie replied, looking deeply into her daughter's eyes.

After a moment: "Ms. Thorson?"

"Okay. We're picking this guy up tomorrow at noon, at BurgerLand, Three-four-five-two Sunset Boulevard in Hollywood. We could meet you at, say, eleven-thirty, if you'd like."

After they exchanged details, Dottie hung up and said to Brandi, "There, are you satisfied?"

"We don't have much choice, Mom. Levine wants fifteen thousand dollars and we don't have it."

Dottie sat on the couch and closed her eyes, inhaling the aroma of Brandi's one extravagance, her perfume.

"Let's think positive about this, Mom," Brandi said.

Dottie took a deep breath and thanked God she had her daughter to give her strength.

Thirty

. . .

AT SIX THE next morning Dottie awoke to Mrs. Kaharski banging around in her kitchen next door, screaming at her lazy husband.

Dottie had spent a restless night, filled with dreams about drowning. According to the psychiatrists Ralph had sent her to, these nightmares defined her need to survive. It seemed to her that she had been fighting for survival from the moment she'd taken her first breath. During her first six months of life her mother, who was mentally ill, kept holding her head under water until she was blue. The psychiatrists explained to her that these attempted drownings prevented her from learning to swim or allowing shower water on her hair and face. Under water of any kind she blacked out. The fear of drowning had always haunted her.

As she lay on her stomach, staring out over the white-sheeted valley where Ralph used to sleep beside her, she could smell him, feel his presence in the room. In the half light she could see the mountain of his body and hear his breathing.

By nine she was up and calling around to bondsmen, looking for work. Dante Cicollo must have put the word out that he'd hired them, because the bondsmen weren't as patronizing as they had been. Dottie also began to think that Robin's phone call to the TV station might have been a good idea after all.

"Do we wait for the call about Myrna?" Brandi said from the kitchen table where she and Robin were eating breakfast.

Myrna, she thought. Jesus. "We have to be out of here at the latest by ten-thirty." She wondered if she should call over to the house.

Robin emerged from the bedroom in a beige dress with matching shoes and bag, gold jewelry, looking like a model. She was a good-looking kid; in this getup she looked gorgeous. She had even managed to cover up the black and blue marks left by Henry.

"What do you think?" she said proudly.

"Where are you going?" said Dottie.

"With you."

"Like that?" Brandi said.

"Whose idea was this in the first place?"

"Robin . . ." Dottie said.

Brandi said, "Look, Robin, we're working. It could be dangerous."

"So you want all the credit. Great."

"I knew this was a bad idea," said Dottie. They could pick up Arnold Bell any time. If he hadn't bolted by now, he never would.

"Yesterday I'm a genius," Robin said, "today I'm a ditz."

Dottie said, "Isn't that what you told them—mother-daughter bounty hunter team. Not mother-daught*ers*." As soon as the words left her mouth, Dottie knew she'd made a mistake.

"Mother-daught*ers*. Perfect," Robin said. "We'll just tell them when we get there. Hey, I know how to do this shit. I've been watching."

"I am not going to tell the world that you, who are under my court-appointed custody, are my daughter. They'll lock us both up, Robin. Forget it."

This seemed to strike a note of plausibility in Robin, who frowned. But the gears were grinding in that scam-infested head of hers.

"All right, then I'll go as a bystander."

Dottie looked at Brandi and they both said in unison, "Fine."

By 10:45 they still hadn't heard from Myrna's housekeeper. Outside on the front steps they made plans to stop by Patti Ashbury's office to pick up the paperwork on Arnold Bell before heading to BurgerLand.

Through the street's hazy sunlight Dottie saw a Yellow Cab careening towards them, kicking up dust. The cab pulled to a screeching halt. The back door swung open and there, framed in the doorway—sickly green and looking nauseous—was Myrna herself, her face blown up out of proportion, her angel dress wrinkled and bile-colored.

Her mouth moved but the words she tried pushing out wouldn't come. For a woman on the verge of extinction she moved with amazing agility. Her tiny red-rimmed eyes were trained on something. She pushed up the steps, knocking Dottie and Robin aside, and went straight for Brandi, whom she grabbed by her shoulders and shoved into the ivy.

"You!" Myrna screamed, standing over her. "I give you a simple thing to do, and you fuck it up!"

Dottie vaguely remembered the list that Myrna had given Brandi yesterday up at her house.

"Fill the car with gas. You remember me saying that!"

Brandi lay in the patch of ivy, speechless.

"I was doing just fine! Had everything figured out, the pain was leaving my body and heaven was minutes away . . . and the fucking car runs out of gas! Out of gas! How could you be so insensitive! My God, what does it take to convince you how serious I am about this?"

Myrna buried her face in her hands. Dottie looked at Brandi and over to Robin and plastered a hand over her mouth to suppress the laugh. Pretty soon Robin was doubled over, holding her stomach. Brandi went into convulsions.

Even Myrna, who was now seeing the ridiculousness of it all, stopped what she was doing and began to laugh.

"Oh, shit!" Dottie said, seeing what time it was. She turned to Robin. "You've got to take Myrna to the emergency room. Here's some money, take the cab."

"What about the show?" Robin whined.

Dottie took her aside. "If you're real good to Myrna, she might let you keep the stuff she gave you."

This registered with Robin, who reluctantly agreed.

On the way to BurgerLand, Dottie said to Brandi, "Did you purposely not fill Myrna's gas tank?"

"Mom, I forgot, honest."

"This is definitely a sign—*two* signs—that it is not Myrna's time to die."

"Or just another example of how she screws up everything she does."

Thirty-one

■ ■ ■

THE DAY WAS cloudy and windy, rain threatened, and Dottie worried that the TV crew would find some excuse for not coming. When she thought about it she realized how uncomplicated things could be without Channel 7. They would pick Arnold Bell up, take him to Central Booking, cash in. No fuss, no muss. Clean and simple, the way she liked it. Then again . . .

Brandi spent the ride to BurgerLand inspecting herself in the visor mirror and offering solutions on how Robin could straighten out her life. "She'll be gone in two weeks," Dottie reminded her.

"Don't bet on it," said Brandi. "I'm gaining a little more respect for Robin. She's no fool."

Dottie gave her a look.

"Just an observation."

"Don't forget what she is."

"Yeah, yeah . . ."

"Whore, thief, drug addict. Assault and battery, weapons possession . . ."

"Like we've never seen that before."

"Just an observation," said Dottie.

BurgerLand, a typical family greasy spoon/fast-food diner, was packed with construction workers and old people who could afford nothing better. Dottie cruised through the parking lot looking for a late-model white Chevrolet Celebrity with California tags—Arnold Bell's car, according to Patti Ashbury's paperwork. She found two white Celebrities but neither bore the tag number on Arnold Bell's sheet. The two cars stood next to one another with a space in between, which Dottie pulled into and cut the engine.

"You checked to make sure he's working today?" Brandi said.

"No, I thought we'd just sit here for a couple of days."

"Mom . . ."

"Arnold's in there somewhere, managing his little ass off."

Brandi led the way into the restaurant, where they took a booth with a clear view of the parking lot and the counter from which, Brandi knew from experience, restaurant managers kept watch on their operations.

"I don't see the guy," Dottie said.

"He may be on break. Or in the back ragging on some migrant dishwasher for leaving crap on the plates."

A few minutes later a man matching Bell's description came through the kitchen door. Five-eight, Caucasian, hundred and eighty pounds, dark hair, mustache, balding, wearing a name tag. Brandi slipped out the booth and walked to the counter. She returned with a handful of napkins.

" 'Arnold Bell, Manager.' And does he have the shakes. No wonder he's got three DUI's, he's probably nipping on the job."

"Good." Dottie glanced out the window, searching for the TV crew.

"Maybe not so good."

"What do you mean?"

Brandi leaned forward. "I saw the shift schedule posted on the wall. Don't *look*, Mom. Jeez. He's due to get off today at twelve-thirty." She glanced at her watch. "We have fifteen minutes."

"Well," Dottie said, "We can't wait. Let's get him now." She peeked in her handbag at the handcuffs. She felt for the ankle holster with the Stinger in it. "It's only a drunk-driving beef but they can be trouble. So be careful. Ready?"

"No."

"No?"

"We have fifteen minutes. Calm down. Where's our wait-ress? I would have been fired if I took this long."

"What if he takes off? I am not going to lose two thousand dollars on the off chance I'll be on TV."

"Mom, will you chill, people are staring. You're going to spook this guy."

Dottie sat back. She dug into her purse and pulled out a ballpoint pen and handed it to Brandi. "Here," she said.

"What's this?"

"Let the air out of the front tires on those two white Chevys."

Brandi looked at her, not moving.

"Go on," Dottie said, "just in case. I don't want Arnold going anywhere and I don't want a high-speed chase down Sunset. Go on now."

"Both of them?"

"Well, sure, how do we know which one is his?"

Brandi slid out of the booth, through the door and across the parking lot. Dottie kept her eye on Arnold Bell to make sure he wasn't watching when Brandi ducked behind the cars. A few minutes later Brandi was back. "Somebody's not go-ing to be too happy."

"Especially Arnold Bell," said Dottie.

They sat and waited. The waitress came and took their orders and returned with a steaming cup of coffee for Brandi and orange juice for Dottie.

Dottie saw Arnold Bell checking the clock and making moves that told her he was getting ready to leave. "That's it," Dottie said, "we can't wait any longer."

Just then Brandi, nodding to the parking lot, said, "There." Pulling into the lot, they saw a large white van with WABC 7 News and a whole lot of self-congratulatory advertising plastered on the side. The van stopped in the middle of the lot. Out of the back two men emerged carrying a camera and sound equipment, followed by a woman Dottie recognized from Action News, Marilyn Somebody, a Hispanic who had anglicized her name.

By now some of the restaurant patrons were staring. At the cash register Arnold Bell removed his brown and yellow BurgerLand jacket.

"Mom," Brandi said, "go out and tell the newswoman to get ready. I'll keep Arnold busy. There's an employee door in the back of the building. He'll be going out through there."

Brandi slid out of the booth and straightened the dress she wore for the occasion and marched toward Bell. Dottie dropped a five-dollar bill on the table and followed.

Brandi approached Arnold Bell, trapping him in the small space between the register and the coat hanger, and said, "Dad?"

Bell turned and looked at her.

"Dad?" Brandi said, "Is that you?"

"I'm afraid you have the wrong—"

"Dad, it *is* you. Oh, Daddy, why haven't you come home? Mom and I are so unhappy. I can't believe it's you after all this time."

Dottie had stopped by the front door listening to this. She saw Brandi motioning to her to get going.

"Young lady," Arnold Bell was saying, "I'm sure you have me mixed up with somebody else."

Employees and patrons seemed captivated by this domestic moment.

"Oh, no, Dad, you're not getting away this time. I've missed you so much."

In the lot Dottie approached the newswoman, who introduced herself as Marilyn Vanderpost, and explained that the fugitive was inside with her daughter and that they'd be coming out through the employee exit.

The crew positioned itself at BurgerLand's back door waiting for Arnold Bell and Brandi Thorson. Marilyn Vanderpost had the cameraman get footage of Dottie taking the Stinger out of her ankle holster and the cuffs ready to slap on Arnold's wrists. "Think he'll resist arrest?" she asked hopefully.

"Let's hope so," Dottie said, "for the sake of your viewers." Marilyn didn't seem to appreciate the sarcasm.

Another minute passed, two, and no Arnold or Brandi. Marilyn tapped her expensive beige shoe against the pavement.

Dottie saw the doorknob turn and signaled to Marilyn, who said, "Let's get it," to the crew.

Dottie stepped forward at the same time Arnold Bell backed through the door, arms spread in supplication, in a gesture of despair. ". . . I am not your father," he insisted. "This is very embarrassing. I'm not even married."

"Since when do you have to be married to have a child?" Brandi said to him.

Dottie was about to move in when Marilyn Vanderpost said something, causing Arnold Bell to turn. Bell caught sight of Marilyn Vanderpost's severe jaw line and razor-sharp black hairdo. "Mr. Bell, do you have anything to say about . . ."

These were Marilyn Vanderpost's last words before Arnold Bell spun around and knocked the microphone out of her hand and pushed her out of the way. It had taken Bell about a tenth of a second to comprehend what was going on here, and he didn't want any of it.

He bolted, but not before Brandi grabbed one arm and Dottie clipped him on the back of the neck with the Stinger. Marilyn Vanderpost had recovered with a fury. With the microphone back in place, Marilyn waved the crew forward and gave chase. If nothing else, Dottie thought fleetingly, this would probably make the six o'clock news.

Brandi, who was very quick when she wanted to be, angled around to the side to cut Bell off before he left the parking lot. Vanderpost sprinted like a champion herself, even in heels, and Dottie now understood that these skin-and-bone reporters were built like this for more than cosmetically pleasing reasons.

Arnold Bell, a short, overweight drunk, had no chance against these women, who cornered him by the two white Chevrolets, lopsided with flat tires. Arnold denied everything and, once he realized he was being recorded, made a personal—and stale—stink about killers on the loose while he, an innocent man who might have had a few drinks one night, was being pursued like a common criminal. Marilyn cut him off by swinging the microphone toward Dottie and Brandi. She fired off a volley of questions on bounty hunting, motherhood, living in a world of male cops and robbers, being a child of bounty-hunting parents.

Dottie had no idea what she was answering, or time to think. She saw the camera eye blinking at her, felt she had to say *something*. It was all a blur.

Marilyn wanted to come back to the house with them for more in-depth footage. With Robin probably back from the E.R. with Myrna, Dottie decided this would not be a good idea and begged off. Besides, they had to get Arnold Bell to downtown booking and get a good night's sleep before returning to maid service at the Barsamians' in the morning.

Brandi pushed the increasingly obnoxious Arnold Bell into the Caddy's back seat, where she had a talk with him. Whatever she said, on the trip downtown Arnold stared at his lap, saying nothing.

FROM THE EAST end of BurgerLand's parking lot, Q. D. watched the scene. He had to admire these two women; they were making a go of the family bounty-hunting business. Through the phone tap he had listened to Patti Ashbury call in the pickup on Arnold Bell, then Robin the whore alerting the TV station, then Dottie with the TV producer. He had to give them credit. Very smooth.

Q. D.'s own life was not going smoothly, however. Yesterday afternoon he had been chastised by the director for a sloppy performance. He hadn't gotten his lines down, muffed a few takes. It was not like him; he needed to regroup, focus, concentrate. First things first. First the movie, then the Thorsons.

He watched as Brandi loaded the manager into the Caddy's back seat. She was something, just like her old dad. Q. D.

turned the Jag's ignition on, listened to the purr of the engine. Beautiful, sleek. Like Brandi.

Q. D. waved a silent goodbye to her, regretting that he'd have to leave her and get to the Malibu set and pay attention to his craft. He'd be back soon, and he had plans.

Thirty-two

...

AFTER DROPPING ARNOLD Bell at County lockup Dottie drove home, where she found a message on the answering machine from Dante Cicollo. A small office building in Van Nuys had been torched earlier in the day. Had the earmarks of Sandor Barsamian's work. The LAPD was no longer willing to wait around for Dottie and Brandi to find out how Sandor did it.

Robin came banging in at six and turned on the TV. Her black eyes had all but disappeared, her skin in fact glowed. "Your friend Myrna is very sick," she said, clicking through the channels.

"What did the doctors say?"

"They don't know how she's still alive."

"Constitution," Dottie said.

Robin kept clicking away, growing frustrated. "Are you on TV or not?"

"Channel Seven," Brandi told her.

Robin turned to 7 and sat back to watch. "Myrna will be

fine," she said, "but the emergency room doctors . . . they never want to see her again."

"Where is she now?" Dottie said.

"Still at the hospital, resting. Getting out tomorrow. By the way, I had to borrow ten bucks' cab fare from one of the doctors. Real cute guy, asked me for my phone number."

Dottie took a ten out of her purse and handed it to her.

"Don't worry, I won't bring the guy here. I might not even charge him."

"Good for you."

"Why do you hate me so much?"

"Yeah, how about that, Mom?" said Brandi.

"I don't hate you, Robin, it's just that I . . ."

"Spit it out," Robin said. "I'm not a virgin."

Dottie didn't want to go into it.

Robin worked the clicker. "All this bullshit and I actually missed you." She snatched up the phone and punched in numbers. "Hello, yes, this is Dottie Thorson, female bounty hunter. You had a camera crew at BurgerLand today."

"Hey." Dottie was up and moving as Robin said, "Okay, I'll hold."

Dottie grabbed for the receiver. "Give me that thing."

"Chill out," said Robin. Robin rolled her eyes at Brandi. Back into the phone, she said in a saccharine voice, "Yes, I'm Dottie Thorson's niece and I heard that my aunt and her daughter, my cousin . . . they're female bounty hunters who picked up a . . . Oh, is that right? . . . Ah, isn't that interesting . . . Well, I'm so glad to hear that . . . you've been most helpful . . . and your name? I would like to write a letter to your superior stating how thorough you are . . . well, thank you, Helen. Bye-bye, now." She hung up and crossed her legs. "Stupid bitch."

"So?" Brandi said. "What's up?"

"Tomorrow. Big story. Noon, six and probably eleven. They're doing something they call pickups. On the bounty-hunting biz in general. You're suddenly a big fucking deal, thanks to me."

"You're a miracle, Robin," Dottie said.

Robin jumped to her feet and strode across the room to

the bar, where she took out a bottle of vodka and poured herself a drink. She held the bottle up. "Anybody?"

"I'll have one," Brandi said.

After downing a couple of quick pops Robin announced, "You need me."

"We need you?" Dottie said.

"You do. You're too nice, you need somebody who can see the black side of things, like I can."

"Which black side?" Brandi said, pouring them another. Dottie didn't like Brandi drinking like this, and could definitely see the black side of Robin's booze habit spilling over onto Brandi.

"You never would have thought about the TV show without me, which is going to lead to big bucks. You need me to do things you don't have time for, like taking Myrna to the emergency room, like taking care of the phones while you're on a case. Like keeping this place clean when you don't have time. I could go on. What you really need is a partner."

"First we have to take care of this little matter of your court appearance, Robin," Dottie explained. "And then we can see about this other thing."

"If you tell the judge I'm working with you, don't you think she'll go a little easier on me?"

"What about it, Mom?" Brandi said. "With all the calls coming in, we could use somebody."

"What calls?"

"The ones we'll be getting off the TV show."

"How do you know we'll get any?"

"See, you're being negative again."

Robin said, "You're the one who was worried about all the calls in the first place, wasn't she, Brandi?"

"Don't deny it, Mom. I was right here, we both were."

That was Dottie's cue to excuse herself and go to bed. Just what she needed, to argue with two drunks all night.

In her room with the door closed, listening to bursts of laughter coming from the girls, Dottie lay back on the big bed where she and Ralph had slept together for twenty years, and lit a joint. She drifted back to those first magical days when they had met in the fire of youth, in the small flat behind Grauman's Chinese Theater on Hollywood Boulevard. The little village of people back there was like a Broadway stage with its parade of characters sitting on the porches cooking up chili and rice, drinking wine, telling stories.

She remembered those times as if they had happened in another life to somebody else.

Thirty-three

⸱ ⸱ ⸱

AT NINE THE next morning they drove through the gates of the Barsamian estate. Brandi, who hadn't gotten to sleep until after two, was still drunk and hung over. Dottie worried about her drinking; it reminded her of Ralph's. She had never put it together when Ralph bragged about drinking a fifth of Jack Daniels a day that it was the booze that made him angry and eventually—as surely as the bomb did—killed him. Maybe she did understand but didn't make the connection until it was too late. What could she have done about it? Probably nothing. What worried Dottie was that Ralph had passed the gene down to his daughter.

They had been cleaning for an hour when Dottie, who had been doing all the work while Brandi sleepwalked, said, "I'm sorry you don't feel well but you've got to help."

"Not so loud, Mom, I can barely see."

At eleven, while they were working in the library, they heard a loud bang and something heavy slide across stone, and then a door slam. A moment later the library door swung open and Sandor, in filthy overalls, face smudged with dirt and a wild look in his eyes, came into the room.

"Where were you?" he said accusingly.

"When?" said Dottie.

"Yesterday. You never came I missed you."

"We were off," she said. "Forbes knew."

"Forbes said nothing to me about it."

"Forbes isn't a big talker," Brandi snapped. "I wouldn't let it bother you, Sandor. Where've *you* been?"

"Where have *I* been?"

"Yeah, *been*, as in been with all that dirt on you. You've been crawling through something, right? Let me guess."

"What's bugging you?"

"I had a rough night, Sandor," said Brandi, "and so did you, by the look of things."

Sandor said to Dottie, "Could I speak to you alone?"

"We're a team," Brandi blurted out. "We have no secrets. What she hears, I hear."

"Just for a moment," he implored. "Please."

Dottie looked over at Brandi and said, "Why don't you start on the office?"

Sandor led Dottie through the door and into a sitting room. He was very edgy. "Please don't do this again," he said.

"Do what?"

"Not show up without telling me. I thought you had quit or were unhappy here. Call me directly if you have any complaints, or if you are ill. I will secure for you the very best medical attention."

"Thank you." What was *with* this guy?

He took her hands. "Please forgive me for saying so but I am very attracted to you. I don't know what has come over me, but I feel the need to warn you."

"Warn me?"

"About my feelings, so that you won't think I am acting without reason."

Here was a young, virile, good-looking man with mesmerizing eyes making a pass at her. That was all very well, but he was also an arsonist who liked explosives. "Sandor," she said, "I'm in mourning."

"Ah, my poor woman. I am here if you need anything. In

fact, what you might need is a vacation. My parents have a small ocean cottage near Bahia de Los Angeles on the Sea of Cortez, in the Mexican Baja. You are welcome to use it at any time. I go there often to find peace."

She tried again. "My husband—Brandi's father—recently passed away, so . . . what I mean to say is that you're very kind to offer but we would prefer to just clean your—"

"I was so unhappy that you weren't here yesterday that I did something."

She heard a small bell go off. "Oh?"

"For you. Very stupid, perhaps, but I'll let you be the judge of that."

"Of course. What did you do?"

He released her hands and sat back, eyeing her suspiciously. "Why do you want to know?"

"You brought it up."

"You're trying to get me to say something I shouldn't, is that it?"

Oh boy, she thought, this guy was in the lunatic stage this morning. Did he want to confess? To what, another fire? She stood. "I should get back to work."

"I have been to work, Dottie," he said, his eyes soft and pleading. "I need to talk with you about something."

A rap on the door interrupted them.

"What!" Sandor shouted.

The door opened and Forbes took one delicate step into the room. "Excuse me, sir," he said, "there is an emergency call for the lady. A. D. Dante, about her mother."

"She'll call him back."

"Oh, my God, my mother," she said, "she's very sick." This mother thing was a prearranged code she and Ralph had worked out with Dante Cicollo many years before.

"Oh, all right." Sandor fell back into the cushions. "Hurry back."

Dottie followed Forbes down the hall and into the library, where he handed her the phone. "Hello, Dr. Dante," she said into the receiver. "What's her condition?"

"Not good," Dante Cicollo said. "Your mother was burn-

ing up this morning at the Van Nuys hospital. Very dangerous. Maybe it's time to pull the plug."

"What if we hang in a little longer? It's crazy, I know, but
we've come this far."

"It's going to be emotionally rough if we disconnect, but
there's a life-threatening situation to consider."

"I'll have to think about it. We've got so much to do here."

Brandi stood at the door, motioning to her.

"I have to go, Dr. Dante," Dottie said. "Check in with you
later."

Brandi, her finger to her lips, led her down the hall to the
computer room. "Check this out." She handed over three
sheets of paper she had just printed out.

Dottie read what at first appeared to be random thoughts
about life in general but then realized they were parts of
letters to women, from Sandor. How he would snip off pieces
of his skin and send them to the women, how he wanted
them to carve their initials in his back, how he wanted his
penis in them to feel the razor-sharp instruments buried in
their vaginas.

"That's enough for me," Dottie said. "This guy needs help.
And we're not here for that."

"We're not leaving?"

"Yes, we are, and now."

"Mom, we're on the verge of getting this guy."

"That was Dante on the phone, who told me that Sandor
had just torched a building somewhere in Van Nuys. That
look in Sandor's eyes? The building in flames. We are out
of here."

"I have other news," Brandi said.

"Oh?"

"I know how he does it."

Dottie looked at her, wondering if this was a ploy to stay
longer. "Okay, I'm listening."

"Come on, I'll show you."

They slipped down the hall past the sitting room where
Dottie had left Sandor and into his bedroom suite. Along the
way Dottie grabbed the pail and a mob off the trolley. In the
bedroom the television was on. Brandi locked the door and

led her mother into the bathroom, where on the floor they found a pair of filthy, rumpled overalls, mud-caked boots and gloves. The place smelled like a sewer.

"He had to get in here somehow," Brandi said. "The question is, how?"

Dottie searched for a trap or sliding door behind the tiles. Then it struck her. Brandi's discovery. The tunnel. Why hadn't she thought about this before? It was right in front of them, but where? They checked under the sink and toilet, in the shower. Nothing.

Just then they heard the bedroom door rattle. "Oh, Jesus," Brandi said.

Dottie said, "We're here to clean. Do as I do."

Dottie grabbed the mop and filled the pail with tub water. "All right, get the door."

As Brandi headed into the other room, Dottie heard a familiar voice: "A mother-daughter bounty-hunting team in Los Angeles. Meet Dottie and Brandi Thorson, who chase fugitives from justice and bring them back dead or alive . . ."

Dottie rushed to the door in time to see herself and Brandi on TV. "Brandi," she said.

Brandi, who was about to turn the knob, looked back over her shoulder.

"Don't," Dottie said, fixed on the TV, "do anything yet."

They watched as the Channel 7 reporter detailed their exploits. "Let me in there," Sandor said, knocking on the door. Dottie felt the hair stand up on her neck. The spot seemed to go on forever. Finally Marilyn Vanderpost said, "More at six from your I-Team on Seven Action News."

Dottie gave Brandi a look and motioned for her to open the door, after which she returned to the bathroom. She heard Sandor complaining about the locked door, and Brandi saying, "Hey, we're busy, Sandor. You probably don't know what that's like."

"What is this?" Sandor said from the bathroom doorway, hands planted on his slender hips.

"That's what I want to know," Dottie replied. "I don't mind cleaning up after people, but tracking in mud like this, after we already did the bathroom once, is very irritating.

'Light housework' is the job description. This is the second time this has happened. If it happens again, I'm afraid you'll have to find someone else. Plus it smells like a barn."

As Dottie had hoped, Sandor seemed relieved by her outburst. He apologized for his carelessness, adding that he'd been out with the horses. He even offered to clean up his own mess, which Dottie said was not necessary. The job had to be done and she and Brandi would do it.

But he insisted and shooed them out. Unfortunately, Dottie had wanted to keep searching for Sandor's secret passage and also to take the overalls and boots, whose traces of dust and dirt were evidence placing him at the scene of the crime.

It was nearly one and time for lunch. They waited in the hall for Forbes to fetch them. One o'clock came and went, then one-fifteen. Dottie was hungry and decided that they should go ahead without him. Like a pair of weary soldiers they left the library, crossed over a small patch of lawn to the pantry, down one flight and into the kitchen, where they found Forbes glued to a small black-and-white television set.

"Forbes," Dottie said. He turned too quickly, nearly losing his balance, and rose to his feet with as much dignity as he could muster. He mumbled something about having to leave and that they would have to get their own lunch this afternoon. It didn't take a genius to know why Forbes was upset.

"I don't think we'll be going anywhere just yet, Forbes," Dottie said, blocking his exit.

Forbes stood his ground. With his pasty white face and thinning hair, hands clasped together in prayer, he looked like a frightened old monk.

"Sit down, Forbes," Brandi said, pulling over a chair for him.

"We've been watching television, haven't we, Forbes?" Dottie said.

He averted his eyes. A trickle of sweat found its way out of his hairline.

"We didn't look too brutal, did we?" Dottie said. "I can't hear you, Mr. Forbes."

"You were both quite . . . formidable."

"Do you know why we're here?"

The absence of an answer told them that he must have had an inkling about Master Sandor's obsession with fire.

Dottie said, "You've been with the Barsamians for a long time."

"Forbes?" Brandi said, tapping him on the shoulder. "That calls for an answer."

"Twenty-seven years," he muttered, looking sick at having betrayed even this slightest of confidences.

"Which means you've known Sandor and his nasty little habits since childhood. Bed wetting, cruelty to small animals, starting fires . . ." By the spark of recognition in Forbes's eyes, Dottie could tell that she had gotten it right.

"We're here because young Master Sandor has been setting fires around town."

"Big fires," Brandi added, "fires that cost people untold hardships and insurance companies millions of dollars."

"Pretty soon these fires will be killing people, and you will be indicted for murder along with Sandor. Accessory before *and* after the fact. Are you familiar with these terms?"

Forbes lowered his head. His fingers gripped the arms of his chair.

"In fact," Brandi said, "the police have already tagged you for at least five counts of arson—good for life in prison."

"Unless you cooperate," said Dottie. "Forbes?"

"Yes?"

"Where's the trap door?"

He looked up, his face a mask.

"The trap door Sandor uses to get out of the house, the one in his bathroom."

"I . . . I don't know about that . . ."

Brandi leaned forward, face to face with him. "We know there is one. We know he uses it. He comes in, dragging mud and soot from the arson sites. If you don't help us, we'll make sure you *do* spend the rest of your life in prison."

"I believe I should talk to an attorney."

"Fine," Dottie said, "and in the meantime, while Sandor is torching more buildings with your intimate knowledge, the noose tightens around your neck."

"He burned one this morning," said Brandi, "but of course

you know that. And then the one he plans for tonight."

"Good lord," Forbes said, looking genuinely ill at the thought. He took a deep breath and brought his small hands up to his lips. "I have known the boy since childhood."

Dottie knelt before him. "I know how hard this must be for you, but Sandor needs help. A father or father-figure needs to save his only son, Mr. Forbes. Isn't it about time?"

Forbes looked so grief-stricken that Dottie could only imagine the years of torture he must have endured, hiding this terrible secret.

"We can keep this as quiet as possible," she said to him, "if you can show us the how and the where."

"You can't imagine the horror of it," Forbes said.

"Oh, I think I can. Here," Dottie said, standing, "let me give you a hand."

With Brandi on one side and Dottie on the other, they led Forbes up the stairs and back across the lawn toward Sandor's bedroom. As they approached the door, it flew open and Sandor stepped out. "What do we have here, Forbes?" he said.

"I've come to help you, Sandor," the old man said.

"Help me?" he said suspiciously. By his expression Dottie could see that Sandor had just realized something that frightened him. He turned and ran back inside. Dottie said to Brandi, "Call the police and keep an eye on Forbes."

"Mom . . ."

"I'll be all right." She reached down and took the Stinger out of her ankle holster.

"What are you doing?" Forbes said, glaring at the weapon.

"What do you think?"

"I can't allow you . . ." He lurched at her. Brandi stuck her foot out. Forbes's legs got tangled up and he went down.

Brandi said to her mother, "Don't do anything dumb."

Dottie hurried after Sandor. Precious seconds had been lost, and considering how fleet of foot Sandor was, he had probably disappeared, like Alice, down his hole. She rushed through the bedroom to the bathroom where, as expected, the muddy, sooty clothing and boots were gone, along with Sandor. The trap door was somewhere in the bathroom, had to be. She ran her fingers along the walls, pushed at places, and pulled handles. Nothing. It was infuriating. She sat on the toilet to think.

The kid was clever, but *this* clever?

Walls, fixtures, ceiling, floor tiles. She checked under the bath mat. The space had to be large enough for Sandor to shimmy through. She checked for loose particles, dry wall chips, paint scrapings.

And then she saw it, the ever-so-slight curvature that swung out from the bathtub. If she hadn't been sitting on the toilet, under light from the overhead window, she would have missed it.

She went to the spot where the tub met the wall and placed both hands on the porcelain, though it wasn't porcelain but lightweight plastic.

She gripped the inside of the tub with both hands and pulled. Nothing. She tried the other end and this time she felt movement. The tub, and the molding around it, inched away from the wall, as if it were on a track, revealing a hole in the floor wide enough for Sandor to drop through.

It was dark down there and she had no flashlight. Back in the bedroom she rummaged through Sandor's dresser until she found a box of kitchen matches. No coincidence here, she thought.

She carried the matches back to the hole in the bathroom floor and dropped down into it feet first. Her toes found a metal rung, which she tested and put her weight on. Below the first rung she discovered another and another, until she reached the floor. Matchlight illuminated dirt walls and the beginning of a tunnel that led off into more darkness.

The place smelled overwhelmingly of sewer. Holding the Stinger, she followed the tunnel, lighting matches along the way. Each time she struck one she was afraid Sandor was going to jump out at her. It was nerve-wracking, and she was sure she was making enough noise for him to hear everything.

The further she went, the more labored her breathing became in the dusty air. After about fifteen minutes of inching forward, she came to a patch of light some twenty feet above her head. She saw no sky but she did see ceiling, and ladder rungs dug into the wall.

She climbed the rungs, keeping the Stinger above her, barrel pointed towards the light. Her stomach rumbled, her scalp itched, sweat broke out on her neck. Her bra suddenly felt tight. She took deep breaths, listened for sounds.

She paused at the top rung, figuring if Sandor hadn't taken time to close the lid, he was either in a hurry or waiting for her.

Peeking over the edge, she swung her eyes around. She was in someone's home. She saw white sheets draped over furniture, draperies drawn over high windows, thick, dust-moted air.

She climbed up into the room, where she caught the pungent odor of smoke.

"You had to meddle," a voice behind her said.

She turned and saw Sandor standing before the fireplace. He walked casually to the hole from which she had just emerged and closed a metal hatch over it; locking it down.

He said, "Why don't you tell me exactly who you are, not that it matters now, but I'd like to know. You have broken my heart with this behavior. I had plans for us."

She held the Stinger on him. "Take another step and I'll have to shoot you."

"This is meant to scare me?"

"If I shoot you, I'll have to drag you out of here. The imposition's on me."

"This is the kind of wit I appreciate in a woman. My mother has it, of course."

"She gave none of it to you."

A sour look passed over his face.

"This house," he said, "is owned by my parents. They have kept it vacant out of memory for my Uncle Vin, who died here. We are just two streets away from the main house. And the tunnel underneath? I discovered it as a child. It's part of an old underground river that runs in bits and pieces through Van Nuys and other Valley communities. Dates back to the last century. I used to play down there as a child. I would leave the other house, escape through the tunnel and visit my

Uncle Vin. We played many games together."

Something, Dottie thought, was wrong with this scene. She had the gun, but he acted as if he were in charge.

"But all good things must end," he said. "Can you smell that, the smoke?"

She nodded. She could.

"It's fire." He sat in a chair and crossed his legs. "A fire I prepared for long ago, for just such an occasion."

"Oh?"

"On the occasion of my near-capture. Notice I said *near*-capture. How can this be, you might ask? Here you are with a gun, I am defenseless. A fire burns in the other room; in fact, in a number of other rooms. It is a fire that burns from the outside in, all around us and moving towards the center. In a few minutes you will be consumed by it."

"Then I think it's time to go, Sandor."

"Do you, now?"

She noticed smoke seeping from under two doors leading into the room.

"Suit yourself," he said. She went to the front door and turned the knob. Locked. Using the Stinger, she shot the handle twice but the door wouldn't give.

"You will discover that there is no exit, neither by door nor window. All steel reinforced. Perhaps a howitzer might put a hole in it, no guarantee." He casually aimed a finger at the floor. "And my trap door. Reinforced steel. Too late."

"If I don't get out, neither do you."

He laughed.

The smoke was beginning to gag her. "So," she said, "my options are limited. I kill you . . ."

"And we both die."

"I shoot you in the leg."

"I live. You die."

"How do you figure?"

"I have a way out."

"On your hands and knees?"

"Why not?"

She was trying not to panic but this was getting out of hand. She coughed, her eyes burned, a lump grew in her throat. She noticed that he wasn't particularly affected by the smoke. Like deep-sea divers who hold their breath under water for long periods of time, Sandor might have prepared for this. He would wait for her to expire, and walk out.

She said, "I'll give you one last chance to tell me how to get out of here and then, as promised, I'll shoot you. Since we're running out of time, I'll count to three. One . . . two. Last chance . . . three."

She pulled the trigger. The Stinger exploded and the bullet ripped into his right thigh. He yelped and grabbed the leg with both hands. Blood squirted out of the puncture. "What the hell!" he shouted.

"So . . . let's talk," she said. The wound was superficial but Sandor probably didn't know that.

"You are crazy!" he shouted.

She was hoping for this reaction, and said, "Okay, now the other leg, or maybe your arm, I haven't decided. One . . ."

"In the fireplace."

The fireplace stood against the wall, a simple pillar of brickwork. "What about it?"

"Help me, I'll show you."

"You've got one good leg." No way was she going to get within two feet of him. "Drag yourself over there."

She heard his wheels turning. He had plans all right, and they didn't include her, or maybe they did, but not in any way that would make her happy. He struggled out from behind the chair and, using pieces of furniture along the way, hobbled to the fireplace. She heard fire crackling in the other rooms. Her breath came in short bursts. She wondered about Brandi, if she was all right. Her mind drifted dangerously away.

Reaching the fireplace, he said, "This is it."

"That is what?"

"My precaution."

"Show me."

He pressed against one of the bricks and a section of the fireplace swung out, revealing a knob. He pulled on it and a section of the fireplace moved out. Dottie looked more closely. Through the accumulating smoke she saw that the section was a glass-enclosed box about the size of an outhouse, built into the fireplace itself. Big enough for one person, maybe two. A small round seat was fitted against the wall.

"What is this?" she said.

"Air-conditioned through a tube connected to an underground tank. It's air-tight and heat-resistant," he said. "We can get in there and the fire can burn around us for hours. Impenetrable glass. And we walk out. Alive."

"Very clever."

He swung the glass door open and started inside. "Hurry, can't let too much smoke in."

"Sandor?"

He stopped. "What?"

"This won't work."

"I have to turn on the air conditioner. We don't have much time."

"I'll do it." She moved toward the booth. "Out of the way."

Sandor shoved past her into the booth and was in the process of closing the glass door on her when instinct told her to reach in, grab him by the jacket and yank him out. Which she did. He tumbled by her and landed on the floor, letting out a terrible yelp.

She had a choice. Critical. She could take him inside the booth with her. She wondered about the oxygen supply for two and what he would try once they were crammed in there together. Or leave him out here and be burdened with eternal guilt. A series of scenes flashed before her of Sandor setting fires, killing fish, chopping off cats' heads. She closed the door behind her and latched it. On the wall she found a switch and flipped it. In seconds cool air began pumping in.

The horrible part was having to watch Sandor outside the booth, struggling, gasping, smoke filling his lungs. She turned away but could still feel him there, his fingers scraping against the glass. Then she could barely see him through the thickening smoke, and he disappeared. She flipped a second switch and the booth retreated back into the fireplace wall.

Sandor, who had lived by fire, would die by it. And she,

who had chronic claustrophobia, had to look forward to hours of being locked in a box.

That is, if this contraption of Sandor's worked. Until now that had not occurred to her. She sat on the small ledge of a seat and began to pray.

Thirty-four

...

BACK AT THE house on Otsego, Brandi had had it with people patting her on the head like a two-year-old, stroking her hair, giving her a friendly rub on the back, with well-meaning, repetitious words of consolation. As if to say, "Oh, you poor thing, first your Dad, and now your Mom, how are you ever going to survive?"

It'd been hours, more than she cared to count, since she'd gotten word about the fire. She'd driven over to the Barsamians', and then to the second house, where they'd found Sandor's charred remains. Brandi led the cops to the underground tunnel that linked the two houses. They scoured the tunnel for Dottie, finding nothing.

How was it possible, Brandi wanted to know, for somebody to disappear like that? She tried to drive out thoughts of Sandor hiding her mother's body in one of the tunnel's thousand places.

At home she paced and drank bourbon. Bill Sallie called to tell her that he'd put his best men on the case.

She answered the phone and sent away people who

showed up at the door, including Myrna, who sat outside in her Mercedes listening to the radio.

Friends from school had come by, wanting to talk about the good old days. What good old days? They had all seen the Channel 7 piece at BurgerLand and told her how proud they were, how brave she was, how courageous. She thanked them and promised to call them later.

Brandi wanted her mother. Wanted to find out what had happened to her and wanted her here with her. She fought back the idea that she was dead, though the harder she tried to bury the thought, the more it loomed up. But she was not going to be a crybaby when she still had hope.

The only person she allowed to stay was Robin, who wasn't one to stand around wringing her hands. The girl was no bullshit. She looked out for number one and didn't care who knew it, and Brandi needed that right now.

"What's going to happen to me?" Robin said. "When they hear your Mom's gone, guess who the court'll come after?"

"Don't worry, Robin, the last person the L.A. court system wants clogging up its works is you."

"Will you plead my case with the same whatever your mother would have used?"

"Sure, why not?"

"We could make money. I'll take Dottie's place in this bounty-hunting thing. I can take these assholes down. If you knew some of the slimeball johns I've dealt with, you'd know how good I am."

Brandi tried to imagine what having Robin as a partner would mean. One thing was for certain, there wouldn't be anybody better at getting money out of bondsmen. Or anyone less reliable when things heated up.

She told Robin not to let anyone in and went into her bedroom to lie down. She lay in bed reading poems she'd written to her old friend, Brandy with a *y*. She sometimes did this when she was manic. Poems where she and Brandy (friends called them Double Shot of Brandi/y) had dreamed about being P.I.'s, "Where people were cool and all the men were romantic, loving, sexy and tight-butted." After a time she fell asleep.

She couldn't tell where the racket came from but it woke her with a start. She grabbed the .22 caliber off the dresser and went to the door. The house was quiet. She eased the door open and peeked through the crack.

It was dark. She looked back toward the bed and on the table read the luminous dial: 10:00 P.M. She had been asleep for six hours.

She heard another noise, from the kitchen. Robin? She could either snap on the lights or sneak up on whoever was out there. She tiptoed through the door and down the hall.

Groggy with sleep, she pressed close to the wall, trying to peek around the corner. She felt the .22's cool metal against her index finger.

The kitchen light showered down on the table filled with leftovers and crusted pans well-wishers had left for her to clean. She saw empty liquor bottles, food cartons and ripped-open bags of cookies.

Seated at the table was a woman with her back to her, head covered by a rumpled yellow rainhat.

She aimed the .22 at the figure and said, "Keep your hands on the table."

The woman obeyed.

"Who are you?" Brandi said.

The woman mumbled something.

"I can't hear you."

"Yurrr mmuuudder . . ."

"Who?"

"Your mother. Who else do you think it is?"

"Mom?" Brandi said. "Mom!" She ran into the kitchen and threw her arms around her. Her mother looked half frozen and nearly as green as Myrna had after her suicide attempt. "Are you okay? What happened to you? Where've you been?"

"Could you please get me something to eat? I'm not feeling so hot."

After Brandi called Dr. Williams at home, Dottie told her about Sandor and the fireplace she'd been caged in for eighteen hours, barely able to breathe. She told her how she'd finally pried the glass door open and stumbled around until a motorist picked her up and brought her home. "Did they find my bullet in Sandor's leg?" she said, to which Brandi had no answer.

Brandi drove her to Dr. Williams's over on Riverton, where he told Dottie she suffered from smoke inhalation, nervous exhaustion, dehydration, cramps, a migraine, and skin disorders caused by extreme heat. Dr. Williams called in three prescriptions and sent her home, saying he'd be by tomorrow to check on her.

Brandi stayed with her while she slept. Robin, who'd been out running errands, returned. Brandi sent her to the store for food, asked her to answer the phone. Robin cleaned the house on her own.

Next morning Dottie felt strong enough to make a call to Dante Cicollo, who had already heard about Sandor.

"Great job," he said. "We were worried. They found a slug in Barsamian's body."

"So it wasn't a dream after all. Dante, would you mind getting the money to us? We need it."

"Right away," he promised.

Which meant that one of them would have to go to his office to plead, threaten and generally humiliate herself to get paid.

Around two-thirty, the phone rang. Brandi answered it. After listening for a moment, she said, "Hang on a minute, my mother is here. Would you repeat that to her?"

Brandi handed her the phone. "This is Dottie," she said.

"I saw you on TV" the woman said. "I heard the news-woman talk about how your husband's car blew up, how he died?" The woman had a sing-songy voice that ended every sentence with a question mark. She sounded about fifteen. "I'm very sorry?"

"Thank you."

"This is real hard for me," she said, "so . . ."

"Take your time. I'm not going anywhere." After a moment, Dottie said, "What's your name, honey?"

"I'd rather not say if it's all the same to you?" She cleared her throat. "I think I might know who did it, the bombing, I mean?" Dottie pointed to the Caller I.D. number on the phone's rectangular window. Brandi copied it down and went to the office phone to run it.

"I knew him . . ." the woman said.

"Really?" Dottie said.

"It was a long time ago but . . ."

"How long ago?"

"This guy I used to date, he used to tell me about Ralph Thorson, how he used to be his best friend until Mr. Thorson . . ." She hesitated.

Dottie waited. "Until Mr. Thorson what?"

"I don't know how much I should say."

Dottie had the phone pressed so hard against her ear it hurt. "You don't have to say anything, except one woman to another. You know what this guy is capable of, and so do I. *I* know what he did. He killed my husband. Except that the bomb was meant for my daughter."

"Oh, my God, that's it!"

"What?" Dottie said.

"That's what he said he'd do."

"That he'd set the bomb for Brandi?"

"Yes. Exactly."

"When did he tell you this?"

"A long time ago. Years."

"This guy told you he was going to plant a bomb for Brandi, years ago? How many years ago?"

"Oh, I don't know. Eight?"

"I think we should meet," Dottie said.

"No, no," said the woman, "you don't know what he would do to me if he ever found out. I know this man, he's capable of worse than putting a bomb in a car." She lowered her voice. "Much, much worse."

"If we don't get him now, he'll keep at it," Dottie said. "Do you want that on your conscience?"

"Oh, God."

"So please, for Brandi's sake, and mine as her mother, let's meet. Somewhere out of the way. You'll never have to go to court or face the man. I can guarantee that."

Dottie listened to the silence on the other end and knew if she didn't keep talking, she could lose this single threadlike lead. "We—Brandi and I—have the means to get him. You saw the TV show. We have resources that others don't have. We have ways of getting to him so that none of us will ever have to worry about him again."

"I don't know . . ."

Dottie tried again. "What if out of the clear blue he spots you on the street one day? What do you think would happen?"

"I don't want to think about that possibility."

"If you meet with us, you won't have to. Don't we both have an obligation to get him off the streets?"

A pause, then: "Yes."

"With your help we can." *Come on*, Dottie thought, *answer me, stay on the line.* "As a woman who knows what this guy is capable of, don't you want to help?"

"Yes, but . . ."

"You'll be totally protected. No one but the three of us will have to know anything. We'll get him, the three of us, before he gets us. Yes?"

"Yes."

"Pick a place you know and we'll meet you there, the sooner the better."

"A place?"

"Where we can meet. A place you're comfortable in."

"I don't want to do this, Ms. Thorson."

"Well, it's kind of gone beyond that now, hasn't it? There's a sicko out there, a murderer and God knows what else, who you can identify before he goes on another rampage. If you didn't believe you had to do something about him, you wouldn't have called."

Brandi returned, holding up a piece of paper that read: *Chatsworth. 2345 Devereau. 7 Star Motel. Public Phone Booth.*

"You can guarantee that I wouldn't be implicated?" the woman said.

"Yes," Dottie said, knowing that if he were brought in, the police would have to ask her some questions. Dottie was willing to say anything to keep this lead alive. Besides, she wasn't exactly lying. The woman would never be safe without him in prison.

"There's a mall at the corner of Devereau and Simenon in Chatsworth," the woman said, "The Blue Hills Mall?"

Dottie picked up a pen and wrote it down. "I'll find it."

"In the mall there's a Gap? Tomorrow after I get off work, say five-thirty, in the Gap?"

"And I'll know you by . . . ?"

"I'll know you, Ms. Thorson. Remember, I saw you on TV."

Dottie hung up and gave Brandi a look. She gazed into the room's half light, trying to keep calm, to digest the information, to think clearly. For eight years this guy had been planning to kill Brandi? And then he blew it?

What, she wondered in horror, was he planning now?

Thirty-five

■ ■ ■

Q. D. REESE WAS on a roll. He'd just spent a solid day
before the cameras, killed a couple of good guys in treach-
erous cinematic ways. Brought evil to the silver screen. He
had that kind of face, they said, wore that kind of scowl,
made people in the audience—hell, on the set, in the supermarket, wherever he went—squirm, wince and turn away
from his baneful sneer. The perfect movie villain's face; he
had it.

Somebody once said he had the look of a man on the cusp
of sanity. The actors playing the good guys were never sure
how far Q. D. the actor, or the character he was playing,
would go. They always showed real fear whenever he came
after them.

He had made no friends on the set of this movie, didn't
try. They left him alone. Of course there were always a couple of women on the crew for whom evil was a draw, babes
who would drop by his trailer for a quick fuck, why not?
They were already so lathered up he didn't really have to be
there, except in dick only.

At six he left the set and drove home, where he pulled the Jaguar into the garage and waited for the electric door to cloak him in darkness.

As he did most every night, he cooked up beans and rice and carried them into the living room, where he played the clear, voice-activated tape of the day's phone conversations at the Thorsons'. He listened for fifteen minutes until he heard something that made him sit up and take notice.

He set the bowl of food down and backed up the tape. Something. He heard a woman's voice, not Brandi's or Dottie's, but one that drove a spike through him.

"*. . . I saw you on TV? I heard the newswoman talk about how your husband's car blew up, how he died? . . . I'd rather not say if it's all the same to you?*" Her throat clearing. "*I think I might know who could have done it, the bombing, I mean?*"

He picked up the bullet from the coffee table and put it in his mouth, rolled it around. He knew this voice *real* well, his mind tumbleweeding back through time.

Bunny. *Not possible.* He rewound the tape. Now he was on his feet. He turned the volume up so he could hear it out on the deck.

Memories broke over him. Bunny. Bunny, his child bride, from whom Ralph Thorson had separated him. Bunny, who then threw him over, stopped writing to him in prison. Couldn't take the loneliness, she'd said. Cut him off. He'd known what she wanted: guiltless fucks with old boyfriends. She'd eliminate the guilt by saying goodbye to old Q. D. Bye-bye, baby, rot in jail, I gotta get laid.

Bitch.

And now? Now he had a real problem. Bunny was about to tell Dottie Thorson who had pulled the trigger on Ralph. Bunny knew. And soon Dottie would know. Then the cops, then it was back to prison. And all because Bunny saw Ralph's women on the tube and made a call. The fucking irony.

"*You don't have to say anything, except one woman to another. You know what this guy is capable of, and so do I.*"

I know what he did. He killed my husband. Except that the bomb was meant for my daughter."

Q. D. closed his eyes, clogged up with tension.

"There's a sicko out there, a murderer and God knows what else, who you can identify before he goes on another rampage. If you didn't believe you had to do something about him, you wouldn't have called."

Q. D. began to prepare himself.

"There's a mall at the corner of Devereau and Simenon in Chatsworth. The Blue Hills Mall?"?

Blue Hills Mall. He committed the name to memory.

"I'll find it."

"I'll find it," Q. D. repeated.

"And inside the mall there's a Gap? Tomorrow after I get off work, say five-thirty, in the Gap?"

"And I'll know you by . . . ?"

"I'll know you, Ms. Thorson. Remember, I saw you on TV."

"And I'll know *you*," Q. D. said.

Thirty-six

■ ■ ■

ALL THE NEXT day Brandi wrote poetry and ate fried shrimp and hickory-sweet barbecued ribs until she was sick. The more coffee she drank, the more hyper she got, until by two in the afternoon she changed to cheap red wine that she knew would give her a headache. She had her Chocomilk handy to take care of the hangover. She listened to Anthrax, Soundgarden, Candlebox and Joe Cocker until Dottie told her to knock it off. She took her pearl handled .22, the .38 police special and a few other weapons into the back yard and with AC/DC plugged into her ears she cleaned them.

Later she burned some cookies. She fed the fish (remembering what Sandor Barsamian had done to *his* fish). She changed the oil in the Caddy. "Mom!" she shouted when she saw how black the oil was. "We're not going to have a car left."

She had a bad feeling about meeting this woman who knew who might have killed her father. Maybe it wasn't the meeting but the memories she was having trouble with. About the fights between her mother and father, the split-ups.

When her mother left home her father started taking it out on her. Finally she couldn't take it any longer and got him to join Tough Love, for drug-and alcohol-addicted children with hopeless parents. Except in this case, Brandi was the hopeless child with an alcoholic father. But when Tough Love suggested that Ralph Thorson might have been wrong about a few things, he stopped going.

Then she ran away. Next thing she knew, there was a run away report on her. Her father lied to the cops, telling them she had broken all the windows in the house with a baseball bat. After Tough Love intervened and Brandi told the police what was really going on, they gave her three choices: live with her father, live with her mother, or go into foster care. A foster home was out. Her father had threatened to kill her mother if Brandi moved in with her. So given no real choice, she moved back home with him.

To more bitterness and anger, and his constant pain. He was on codeine for his foot and nitro for his heart, insulin for his diabetes, pills for high blood pressure and circulation medication, all of which he capped off with mixed drinks and cigarettes. Then he had the nerve to take vitamins!

He was a sad, sick man and Brandi knew she was the only one who could take care of him. Anybody else would have ripped off his money and his pills and left him to die. Despite the hell, she gradually came to understand what made him do the terrible things he did, why he'd been undone by his cravings. He'd fed a beast—alcoholism—who had taken control of him. The bottom line, she knew, was that she loved him and he was murdered, and she wanted whoever had killed him brought to justice. Period.

By four in the afternoon she and her mother were in the Caddy and on their way to Chatsworth, a town out near the San Bernadino foothills. A half hour into the trip, Dottie, who drove, said, "I think we're being followed."

Brandi shot her a glance. "Don't be paranoid."

"No, really, three cars back, a foreign job. It's been bouncing in and out of our lane, take a look."

"Mom, we've been on major roads. People follow other people for hundreds of miles. You're just nervous."

Dottie looked into the rearview mirror. "You're right about that."

They drove for another few minutes and Brandi said, "Is he still there?"

"Nope."

"See?"

"Yup."

"Okay."

"I mean, yup, he's back. A green Jag. Without being obvious, can you make out the license number?"

Brandi pretended to reach for something in the back seat and took a look. "Two something, L, R . . . or maybe it's a P. Too far away."

"Okay," Dottie said, "Let's make sure." She turned onto Balboa and hugged the right side. Sure enough, the Jag turned into her lane, hanging back.

"One more time." Dottie turned up a narrow residential street with boxlike homes on nicely manicured lawns decorated with bleached white religious statuary. She kept looking behind her until she was sure no green Jag was there. "Gone," she said.

They reached the Blue Hills Mall at five and strolled around, checking the place out. They went into the Gap, where Brandi saw her mother eyeing a few things.

"You like that skirt, Mom?"

"Oh, no!" she said too quickly. "I'm just, you know, biding time."

Brandi decided that when the money from the Barsamian case came in they would go on a shopping spree. Her mother hadn't bought anything new in years.

Brandi led the way to the food court, where she ordered an extra large coffee and fired up a Camel, exhaling a cloud of smoke that turned dark blue. "Blue Hills Mall," she said, "now I get it."

"How about something to eat?" Dottie said.

"I'm not hungry."

"Coffee and cigarettes will not get you through the day."

"They've been doing okay so far."

"You don't have any money, is that it? Here." She hauled

her purse up on the table and rummaged through it, coming up with a twenty-dollar bill. "Take this, get something to eat. What would you like?"

"Mom, I'm not hungry."

"You know, I read that if you don't eat, your skin loses elasticity. You have such beautiful skin."

"Lose my skin?"

"Its elasticity, because you don't eat."

"I eat. I even have this." She grabbed a tiny roll of fat around her middle. "This is not from starving myself."

"It's from *what* you eat. If you were eating a large muffin, it'd be eight hundred calories and thirty grams of fat."

"I'm drinking coffee."

"A Big Mac, super fries and a large Coke. Fourteen hundred calories, twenty-five grams of fat."

"Mom . . ."

"Nachos. Seventeen hundred calories, a hundred and ten grams of fat. Here, take this twenty and get something decent to eat."

"Mom, I'm, fine!"

"We don't need to pay the phone bill this month. It can wait!" People at other tables began staring at them.

"Mom, you're overtired. Maybe if we—"

"I wanted to buy you something at the Gap but you have to eat. Eating is more important."

"We're not done yet!" Brandi snapped at a woman who had come up and hovered waitresslike over them. "I'll call you when we're done! You can pick up the trash then."

"Bunny Mulcahe," the woman said.

Brandi looked up and saw a sexy Valley blonde of about twenty-eight or thirty, five-four, slightly plump in a cutesy-pie short summer dress that showed off her curves, white shoes and ankle socks and red lipstick that matched the barrette pinning her hair back behind one ear. She had a bunny-rabbit nose that sort of wrinkled when she smiled, thus the name. Bunny. She was very tanned and stood with the hip-thrust-forward look of girls who were brought up brassy.

"Ms. Thorson?" she said, extending her hand to Dottie, who shook it. "And Miss Thorson," she said in a sing-songy way to Brandi. "I'm Bunny Mulcahe? The one who called about—"

"Sure," Brandi said, dragging a chair over from the next table. "Please. Sit down."

"Would you like something to drink?" Dottie said.

"That would be very nice. Diet Coke?"

The twenty-dollar bill sat like a giant conversation piece on the table before them. Dottie said, "Brandi, why don't you get something for Bunny. And maybe something for both of you to eat."

"What about it, Bunny?" said Brandi.

"Well, sure, large nachos, that'd be great."

"Mother dear, anything for you?"

"No, thank you."

"Be right back. Don't start without me."

By the time she returned to the table carrying a platter of greasy nachos, Bunny had a pile of letters in front of her in thick blue envelopes.

"He was a handsome man," she was saying, "but he had no morals or principles when it came to what he wanted. I didn't realize when I started going out with him that he would try to take over my life. He was always calling me, following me, and finally it came down to where he was threatening me. I didn't consider him a boyfriend, but then he started stalking me and scaring off any guy I would even talk to.

"I was a party girl in those days and not a one-man type. I've sort of sworn off men, at least for now." She lowered her voice. "My choices haven't been that good."

Brandi resisted the urge to ask her what she thought had been her undoing. "How did you happen to meet him in the first place?"

"He was older, about thirty-five and I was nineteen and he had developed a profession as a quick-draw artist. He also had bit parts in movies. That was his big thing, he wanted to be a famous actor. Meanwhile he worked fairs and gun clubs. He was good, maybe one of the best, but he was sick in the head. Had strange ideas about women. Hated them but coveted their friendship and love, you know what I mean? I figured this out later. So possessive. When I said no to him he got so mad. I found out from a friend of his that he'd been locked up for mental observation after run-ins with the cops over the way he treated women.

"He told me he had fallen in love with me the first time he saw me at a friend's house and he sent me two tickets to one of his quick draw exhibitions at the state fair in Pomona.

"I was fascinated by the show he put on. Then when he asked for a volunteer from the audience he picked me. I was his model in the exhibition and I loved every minute of it. So when he asked me if he could use me again, I said yes. That's how the relationship started."

Bunny paused to eat. Brandi watched as she delicately picked at her nachos, protesting that she hardly ever ate this kind of food. In a short while, though, the bites got bigger and the protests smaller until Bunny was attacking the food with the ferocity of a real binge artist. Once she had reached the point of no return, she gobbled the rest, washed it down with Diet Coke and when she came up for air she had a wild look in her eye.

"Can we get you anything else, Bunny?" Dottie asked.

"Jumbo fries?" Brandi suggested.

"If it wouldn't be too much trouble?"

"And a Big Mac?"

"Oh, my goodness, I don't know if I could—"

"I'll bring one just in case. I'll help you eat it."

Brandi could tell by her sour expression that the idea of sharing food didn't sit too well with Bunny, who probably considered this high-fat dinner payment for her willingness to unburden her past to celebrity strangers she'd seen on TV.

"Well," Bunny said, after politely leaving two fries in the paper tub. She patted her mouth and readjusted her body in the chair. "I got tired of him and said I couldn't work as his model at the exhibitions anymore. He told me he understood, he was calm about it, gave me a peck on the cheek and left my apartment. His lips were smiling but I could see anger deep in his eyes.

"That's when he started to stalk me. Wherever I went, he wasn't far behind. I could never see him, but I had the sense he was there. Then he started sending me letters. These."

She plucked one from the pile and read. " 'My darling, you are in my thoughts often and I cannot forget you, though I try hard. I am adrift at sea without your comfort and your love.' He was always quoting things from books." Bunny replaced the letter on the pile and said, "The sex we had, it was . . ." She lowered her eyes and ripped a piece of napkin.

Though Brandi wanted to coach Bunny through this difficulty, she decided by waiting that she'd get the stronger truth.

"Very fast," said Bunny, "very brutal. He never looked at me and afterwards . . . he just got up and left. It was the loneliest sex I ever had. Very creepy, really brutal, cold. He could be so warm with his words of comfort, but he treated sex like it was something he was *supposed* to do, a duty or something. You know what I mean?"

"I do," Dottie said. Brandi gave her a look, knowing what she was talking about, and who.

Bunny said, "I think he hated sex. Plus he had this lightning bolt tattooed on his thing."

"You're kidding me," Brandi said. "Tattooed?"

"It makes me cringe to think about it. Plus it was so weird with that noise he made."

"Noise?"

"From the bullet."

"What bullet?" said Brandi.

"The one he carried around in his mouth. He was always chewing on it with the exploding end aimed at the back of his throat." Bunny shuddered. "It made me so . . ."

"What was this guy's name?"

"Quentin," said Bunny.

Brandi didn't hear the rest of the sentence. She was clocking back through time. Memories jabbed at her. She saw herself at ten years old, out in the kitchen. With *him*. Sitting on his lap, listening to his words, chewing on that bullet, eyes like pinpricks, dilated, crazed. She remembered him swaggering through the front door with that porkpie hat he wore, all in black. And his sudden angry outbursts, his surliness. That vein in his forehead popping out whenever he got pissed at something. She remembered everybody backing away from him when that vein popped. Except her father, the only one who would stand up to him, back him down.

The bullet rolling around in his teeth. "Russian roulette of the mouth," he called it. His hatred of not being the center of attention, the temper tantrums. She remembered climbing up on his lap like young children do and looking into his eye to find out if she could catch sight of whatever it was back there that made him the way he was.

"Short, handsome, mid-thirties, actor," Dottie said, reiterating what Bunny had said about the man. "First name Quentin. Good with guns. Jesus. We know this guy."

"Did you ever see him eat worms out of tequila bottles?" said Brandi.

"Yikes!" Bunny said. "That's him!"

Brandi remembered Quentin Ickes telling her he'd gone into the back yard and dug the worm up before stuffing it in the bottle. When he had eaten it he chewed it real good, opened his mouth and showed her his tongue. Horrified, she'd nearly thrown up. He also used to eat the roach on every joint he smoked, without putting it out first. And snuffed cigarettes on his tongue, even though he didn't smoke.

Brandi found herself staring at her mother, whose eyes were darker than Brandi had ever seen them.

"I can believe it," Brandi said, feeling ill, as if hearing his name had finally made it real. "Quentin Ickes killed Dad."

Bunny said, "He sent me dead animals in the mail, bunny rabbits with their paws, and then their heads, cut off. After a while I couldn't go to the mailbox. I finally had to move away. I got this later"—she produced a letter from the pile and opened it—"when they forwarded my mail to me. Seeing you on TV got me thinking about it." She cleared her throat and read. " 'I'll be going to prison for a long time, my sweet, but I swear to God that the man who sent me up will pay for it. You know how an eye-for-an-eye works. In return for taking me away from you, I will take something from him in kind.' "

Bunny lowered the letter and stared out at nothing, lights

out, lost in thought. "I can't believe I stayed with him so long," she muttered.

"I know the feeling," Dottie said.

"Mom," Brandi said, "wasn't Quentin sent up for what he did to Dick Pendergast?"

Bunny looked up at the name.

Brandi said, "I remember that. Quentin Ickes shot Dick Pendergast over a squabble with a girl, put Dick in a wheelchair."

Dottie said, "Assault with a deadly weapon, with intent to commit. And what about those high-school girls he nearly beat to death in the L.A. Basin?"

Bunny's expression soured, she turned pale. Brandi went off to get her a glass of water. When she returned Bunny was on her feet, stuffing the letters into her purse, suddenly very nervous.

"Is there anything we can do for you, Bunny?" Dottie said.

"No, no, really," Bunny said, backing away, tugging on her dress. "I have things to get here in the mall. Thanks for dinner. 'Bye."

With that she spun around on her heels and strutted off, swallowed up in the crowd of shoppers.

"What was that all about?" Brandi said.

"Too much fat in the nachos?"

Brandi, feeling as if she had missed something here, looked at her mother and said, "Are we just going to let her go?"

"Don't worry," Dottie said, dumping the remnants of Bunny's meal into the receptacle. "I got her address off a bill she had in her purse."

Thirty-seven

■ ■ ■

Q. D. ALWAYS HAD it in his head to play Iago, whose devious whisperings in Othello's ear about Desdemona's infidelity destroyed a man, a woman and a nation.

Cunning and conniving, Iago took a white lie and watched it grow like a cancer in Othello's mind, turning the general mad with rage. What a little dirt can do. Q. D. was thinking these things as he sat in a very uncomfortable green plastic chair in the stink of the Blue Hills Mall food court, watching *them*.

Watching Bunny whispering little complaints in their ears. Bunny loved to bitch. She loved to fuck and she loved to bitch. And she knew what the demon jealousy could do. She knew how to make him, Q. D., crazy with jealousy. Fucking woman, showed it off and when she got you where she wanted you, she slammed the door, cut off your manhood—whack!

And there she was, Bunny, in her summer frock and come-fuck-me pumps, all innocent and lamblike. "I had to run from

Q. D.," he could imagine·her bleating. "You can't *imagine* what he did to me."

He had to look away because any minute he knew he was capable of mowing through the green plastic chairs and grabbing hold of that pretty white throat of hers and snapping it in two.

For an hour he watched Bunny go through a performance he studied carefully for its nuances, its range of emotions, its array of gestures, its pathos, ethos, and Thanatos. She was good. Why not? He had taught her everything. When the bitch had first come up on that stage in his gun act she'd been raw and young and needing to be molded. And he, Q. D. Reese, formally Quentin Ickes, had given her the gift. He'd never had a better assistant. He had loved her malleability. Human clay.

Now look at her, he thought. A junk-food gorging, washed-up has-been from Chatsworth, doing squat with her life. He could almost cry.

If he thought about it, as a gesture of profound goodheartedness, he'd be doing her a favor by putting her out of her misery, poor lamb.

Ah, Jesus. All of a sudden, there were her eyes, fixed on him. Christ. He scratched the side of his face, turning away. Had she seen him? She'd seen *something* because she tore out of her seat, said a hasty bye-bye and it was all that he could do to angle through the tables and chairs to keep her in sight.

But he was a tracker. He'd find her, little lamb, and do what he must to set her free.

In Sears she slowed down, something on the rack caught her eye. A negligee. Never could pass by something for latenight fucking, not Bunny.

He was close enough to catch a whiff of her. Man, did it bring back all that hot and sloppy loving. And then up popped the eternal question: fuck her or kill her?

She started up again and he kept pace. She'd maybe lost a step or two over the past eight years but she still had the old hustle.

My Bunny, he thought, love ya, sweetheart, little lamb.

Thirty-eight

■ ■ ■

ON THE DRIVE back to the house the Caddy's air conditioner conked out. Brandi, irritable from lack of sleep, kept telling Dottie how to drive. Speed up. Slow down. Turn here. This was Brandi playing the hard case she'd been in her teens. Dottie tried to ignore her, which wasn't easy against her in-your-face criticism.

Dottie remembered when Ralph had met Quentin Ickes up in Madeira County ten or twelve years earlier when Quentin was hired by the local sheriff running for office to perform his gun act at an election rally. Ralph had been campaigning for the sheriff, an old friend. Ralph and Ickes had been thrown together and Ralph later told Dottie that he'd never met a man who hated blacks, children, women and Jews more than Quentin Ickes did. Quentin showed up at the house one day wanting to be a baby bounty hunter. Ralph, who was short-handed, believed he could keep Ickes under control, and until the end he did.

"Something's not right about this," Dottie said to Brandi as they crossed over Sepulveda.

"Your driving?"

"What do Quentin Ickes and somebody else we know of have in common?"

"Somebody else, as in who?"

"I'm not sure. I need help here. Somebody we met, or were told about . . ."

Brandi tucked one leg underneath her and twisted herself around to face her mother. "Quentin Ickes and somebody we know? Somebody we've seen recently?"

"Yeah."

"I need more than that, Mom."

"What did Bunny tell us about him?"

"Let's see," Brandi said, sticking her arm out the window for some air. "Quentin Ickes was a gun guy, possessive of women . . ."

"Short, wiry, always wore black."

"Has a lightning bolt tattooed on his thing."

"An actor. Wears black, right, she said that. Likes sex in the dark."

Brandi readjusted herself and looked out the window. "Sex in the dark, wears black, an actor, chewing . . ."

"What?" said Dottie.

"Chewing. Didn't she say he was always chewing?"

"Who?"

"She said his chewing bothered the hell out of her. I even asked her what he was chewing all the time, and she clammed up tight, didn't want to say. That was funny."

"Who are you talking about?" Dottie said.

"Myrna. Aren't we talking about Myrna?"

Their eyes met. "I thought we were talking about Bunny."

"Well . . ." Brandi gave a start. "Jesus. Myrna and her friend whatshisname?"

"Dirk."

"Dirk-bag." Silence. "Mom," Brandi finally said, "this is a stretch, isn't it?"

"Think about it. Sex in the dark . . ."

"I've had guys who liked sex in the dark."

"You have?" No matter how liberal she thought she was

about sex, Dottie didn't like to hear these things from her daughter.

"*I* like it in the dark."

"Well," said Dottie, "who doesn't? We're getting off track here. Dirk always wears black clothes, even in the heat; another of Myrna's complaints, right? She bought clothes for him, he never wore them. *And* he's acting in some movie."

"That's what she said."

"Too short. He was too short for her. And the chewing."

"What about the lightning bolt on his thing?" said Brandi.

"I think it's time we asked."

"Indeed it is."

Thirty-nine

. . .

AT HOME, MYRNA was feeling as joyous as she had the
day she married Sammy Fiedler, the most powerful bookie
in the San Fernando Valley, at Temple Beth-El. She'd spent
five glorious years with him until he was gunned down in
Harry Practicus's motel on Ventura Boulevard. Which was
the worst day of her life. A friend took pity on her and gave
her heroin to relieve the pain, which began Myrna's twenty-
two year love/hate affair with the drug.

Myrna was joyous today because she had just received a
call from her oncologist saying that her cancer had miracu-
lously gone into remission. But, the doctor warned, if she so
much as skin-popped one more time, she could kiss her life
goodbye.

She immediately called Dottie, no answer, and left a message to call her back. She couldn't bear not telling somebody.
Except that her only friends, not counting Dottie, were junkies. If she called them, they'd talk her into shooting up to
celebrate the good news. She couldn't tell Dirk, he wouldn't

understand. She was not willing to ruin what she had with him, whatever that was.

A noise outside interrupted her thoughts. When she peeked through the blinds light scalded her eyes. Out of the brightness she saw two people emerging from a large automobile and coming toward the house.

The doorbell chimed, and she heard a woman's voice shouting her name. Had she ordered something? From whom? A delivery person who knew her by her first name?

"Who is it?" she called.

"Myrna, it's me, Dottie. Open the door."

"Oh, sweet Jesus," she muttered. "What now?" It had to be something horrid. Dottie never showed up without calling.

"All right," she said, "just a minute." She inspected herself in the mirror. She looked like shit. In fact, shit would be an improvement. She tucked her blouse into her pants suit and tried to fluff up her hair. Good thing it wasn't Dirk. One look at this Medusa and he'd be history.

Ready now, she opened the door. "Come in, dear," she said. "It's so nice to see you."

"Me, too?" a second voice said.

"Brandi?"

"It's like night in here, Myrna, how do you see?"

"Quite well, thank you. Come in, come in. Can I get you something to drink?"

"We can't stay long," Dottie sat at the kitchen table. "We thought we'd stop by to see how you were."

"Actually . . ."

"And to ask a few questions," Brandi said. "You're not on the junk, are you?"

"No, no. Drying out, all by myself this time. Proud of me?"

Brandi was prowling around like a cat. "Seen Dirk lately?"

Where had that come from? Myrna said, "Who?"

"Your boyfriend."

"I haven't really been *seeing* him . . . he's very busy acting, you know. He has a huge part in a movie—"

"Which one?" Brandi said.

"Pardon me?"

"Which one? What's the movie?"

"Ah . . . well, truth be told, I don't know."

"What *do* you know about him, Myrna?" Dottie said.

"What's he done?"

"We don't know," said Brandi. "Maybe nothing."

"Then why are you asking me these questions?"

"What does he look like?" said Dottie. "Do you have a photo?"

"Just a minute here, my dear friends." Myrna said. "I don't appreciate you barging in here like this. I'm in recovery and do not encourage this kind of—"

"Just a description. How tall?"

"He's . . ." Myrna thought about this. "He's short, actually, which I kind of like. Haven't I told you this?"

"Short and wiry?" said Dottie.

"Wears black?" Brandi said.

"He likes black."

"And the chewing?" said Dottie.

"The chewing?"

"You said you didn't like his chewing all the time."

"I never said that."

"I heard you, too," said Brandi.

"Well . . ."

"What does he chew on, Myrna?"

"I don't know."

"Does he have a lightning bolt tattooed on his thing?" said Brandi.

"Huh?"

"On his thing, his dick, has he got a tattoo on it? Of a lightning bolt?"

"How on earth would I know?" They both looked at her quizzically. "What I mean is—"

"What do you mean, Myrna?" Brandi said. "You haven't seen his penis?"

"Well, actually, I haven't. I mean, I've felt it, played with it . . . what am I saying here? I'm not saying another word until you tell me what's going on."

"Your friend Dirk might have killed some people, beat women up . . ."

"This is a joke, right? He's the gentlest man I have ever known. The most polite—"

"And he chews on a bullet?" said Brandi.

Myrna pushed her hands under her shawl to keep them from shaking.

"Where can we find him, Myrna?" Dottie said, touching her lightly on the arm.

"I don't know."

Brandi said, "This is not the time to hem and haw. He's the guy who killed Dad. The bomb was meant for me."

Myrna gasped. "I . . . I don't know how to reach him. I call a cellular phone, he gets back to me."

"What's the number?"

Myrna went to her desk and took out her address book, thumbing to the number. She felt confused, as if she were betraying Dirk. She could not believe that Dottie was talking about the same man. If they could only meet him, they'd know. Yet . . .

"Does he have a last name?" Dottie said.

Another mild shock raced through her; he'd never told her. She'd never asked. She felt suddenly as if some other being inside herself were having the affair with him, if that's what she could call it. Not knowing such a basic piece of information as his last name upset her, made her feel like a dupe. "We're on a first-name basis," she explained. "It's better that way. Haven't you ever . . ."

Their silence was all the reply she needed.

Dottie copied down the phone number. "Don't talk to Dirk, and don't see him. He's very dangerous, spent time in prison for assault and attempted murder."

Dottie's arms went around her and she felt safe for a time. She followed them out to their car, shading her eyes against the awful sun.

"Lock your door, let nobody in," Dottie said.

"Nobody," Myrna promised.

She watched them drive off and returned inside. My God, she thought, she hadn't even told them the good news about the cancer remission.

Waves of depression seized her. She opened a bottle of

wine and gulped down two glasses. She picked up the telephone and dialed a number.

A machine picked up and the throaty voice said, "Hi, this is Dirk. Leave a message. I'll call you right back."

She said she had something critical to tell him; that'd get his attention. Sure enough, five minutes later the phone rang. She reached for the receiver and whispered, "Hello?"

"Hello, you beautiful thing."

"Dirk!" *See*, she thought, just the sound of his voice made her feel better. "How are you?"

"Busy. I'm due back on the set. What's up?"

"I was just wondering," she said. "What movie are you shooting?"

"This is the crucial message you have?"

"I won't tell a soul," she promised, though she could tell by his tone shift that he was irked. "Dirk . . . ?" she cooed.

"What?"

"Don't get upset, but some friends of mine have . . ."

". . . have what?"

"Confused you with somebody. A case of mistaken identity." It felt as if ice had frozen the telephone lines. She reached for a shawl and dragged it around her shoulders. "Dirk?"

"Who?"

"You wouldn't know them."

"Who?"

"It's not important."

"*Who?*"

"Dottie said I shouldn't . . ."

"Your friend Dottie and her daughter Brandi? I know them."

"You do?"

"You took me to their home, Myrna."

"Oh, yes, well, I've recently been under a lot of pressure. Which is something I also want to talk to you about, this problem I've had. I've got it under control now, but for some time it's been—"

"Your heroin habit."

She felt as if she'd been slapped in the face. "You . . . knew?"

"An actor knows the world's foibles. I once played a junkie in a film and spent time with junkies. Even shot up with them."

A tingle like an electric wire ran up her spine. "Did you . . . like it?"

"Are you kidding? I *loved* it. I was on fire, I could do anything. You know what I mean, Myrna? Down between your legs, on fire."

"Oh, I do, I do." A warning bell sounded inside of her. "But I'm in remission, Dirk."

"Don't you mean recovery?"

"Both. I could tell you about it."

"What did you tell Dottie about me?"

"Nothing. I said nothing to her."

"What about this mistaken identity?"

"Silly things."

"For instance?"

"Oh, Dirk." Her headache was in the right front corner of her forehead, throbbing like a ball.

"I'm coming to see you, Myrna. And I'll bring something special with me."

"Oh?"

"Something you like."

"I bet I know what it is," she said, fear pouring into her.

"We'll get that sensation between our legs together."

"Oh, Dirk." A laugh suddenly burst out of her. "You have to tell me something."

"What's that, dearest?"

"Promise you won't laugh."

"I can only promise that I'll be there with my surprise."

"Okay. It's a question. Ready?"

"Yes."

"Here goes. Do you have a tattoo of a lightning bolt on your penis?" She waited. "Dirk?"

"I'm listening, my sweet." His voice was so deeply quiet that it seemed to come from out of a cave.

"Are you mad at me?"

"No, no. In fact, I want to see you all the more."

"I'll be waiting."

"I won't be long, my sweet."

He hadn't answered the question about the lightning bolt. No matter. She would find out, even if she had to suddenly flip the light on. She was dying to know.

Forty

...

BRANDI, PRESSED AGAINST the passenger door, said next to nothing on the drive back from Myrna's. She did say that the way things were going, Myrna'd probably be on lithium in a week, or dead.

"There's a pleasant thought," said Dottie, pulling in front of the house.

Brandi said, "Please let's not go to Myrna's any more. I can't stand to see her like that."

She said this with such little-girl hopelessness that Dottie leaned over and kissed her on top of the head. "I love you."

Dottie walked up the steps and into the house. The rooms were dark and musty and felt heavy with memory. Through the dense air she looked down the hall to the bedrooms, where she could hear long-ago voices chattering away.

"We need to spruce this place up," she said.

"I'll check the messages."

Dottie fell onto the couch. She felt tired, beat, old, angry, all of it. She wondered when, or if, this weight would be lifted.

"Myrna called," Brandi said. "You want to lie down?"

"I'll be all right."

"What are you thinking about?" Brandi sat next to her.

"Oh, I don't know. Weary old me."

"Cheer up, things can't get any worse."

"Just wait."

"Come on, we can't let down now."

"Who's letting down? I'm taking a break." Dottie picked up her purse, fished out Dirk's cellular phone number and dialed. An operator told her that the number was no longer in service. She tried again; same reply. She figured she must have copied it down wrong and tried Myrna. No answer. She wondered if Myrna had given her the wrong number on purpose. Possible. In the junkie mentality, paranoia rated high.

"What have we got on Quentin Ickes?" Dottie said.

Brandi had opened her psychology text and was leafing through the pages.

"I'm going to fail this course."

"I know, honey, but unless we get Ickes, psychology tests aren't going to matter any more."

They went to the office files and searched through the I's, arriving at Ickes, Quentin. They found Ralph's hand-scribbled notes on him, revealing suspicions about him from the beginning. Dottie found a list of priors for aggravated assault (four for brutally assaulting women), breaking and entering, various weapons violations—for which he'd spent a total of three years in local lockups and at Lompoc, Chino and Vacaville.

A psychological report from the Metropolitan State mental hospital said Ickes suffered from paranoid schizophrenia with homicidal tendencies (two distinct personalities merging with a third); had a severe love/hate relationship with his mother until her death; was in love with guns, treated them as people, talked to them, worshipped and fondled them; was a Jekyll-and-Hyde perfectionist.

"Why did Dad let him stay around for so long?"

"Why did your father let half the people he knew stay here? According to the dates, your father had compiled this data not long before Ickes was sent up."

They found photographs of Ickes and Ralph, and a dozen or so other baby bounty hunters, some with Brandi, at around age eleven, sitting on Ickes's knee.

"Look at my expression," Brandi said. "I want to get away from the creep." Looking closer, Dottie saw real anxiety on her face. Her expression was not, as it first seemed, that of a child in glee but in terror.

They found photos of Quentin Ickes with Dick Pendergast, whom Ickes shot in the kneecaps over a stripper Ickes had been dating. And though Dick Pendergast wanted nothing to do with her, when Ickes caught them in a clinch he shot him.

"This is good," Brandi said, "but we're going to need more."

"I'll call Lloyd Battaglia."

"If he's back from whatever garbage can he's been rooting in."

"Is that nice?"

"Bake a pie, eat a pie."

"What does that mean?"

"Make your own bed, lie in it. That's Lloyd."

Dottie dialed Lloyd Battaglia's number. His voice mail answered, "If you have a message for me, please leave it after the bell." After a soft tinkle, Dottie said, "Lloyd, this is Dottie."

"Hi, Dottie, what's up?"

"Lloyd? Is this the real you?"

"It is."

"You're back," Dottie said.

"You can't ever know if I was gone, can you?"

Lloyd was so weird, but there was no better hacker. "I have somebody," she said. "A real twisted one who we think killed Ralph, and is now after us. We have some details, like a beeper number that's been disconnected. We need help." She read the number to him.

Lloyd said, "Okay, fax me what else you have on this guy. In the meantime, write down whatever comes to mind. If I can expect Brandi to be with you, I'll fit you in sooner."

"Brandi, coming with me?" Dottie repeated aloud so that

Brandi, who was never enthusiastic about seeing Lloyd, shook her head vigorously.

"If she can recover," Dottie said into the phone.

"Recover?" said Lloyd, genuinely concerned.

"From . . ." She looked to Brandi, who pinched her nose and crossed her eyes and made a throw-up face.

"Stomach cramps."

"Let's put it this way," said Lloyd. "I need you both here if you want the job done right. I'm very busy."

The message was clear. Dottie said, "She'll be with me."

"An hour and a half," said Lloyd.

Brandi jammed her hands into her pockets and marched off to her room. When Dottie hung up she heard Brandi shout from the bedroom, "Mom, he gives me the *creeps!*"

Dottie stood in her bedroom doorway. "Please, or we get nothing from him." Brandi was by the bed, facing a photo of her father in his favorite chair, smiling, happy, a drink in his hand, listening to music.

"Please."

"Every time I come back from his place I have to take a bath."

"Just this one last time?"

"You said that the last four times."

"Okay." Dottie turned and walked away. "I've made my thoughts clear." She got all the way to the kitchen before she heard, "Jesus! All *right!*"

FOR DOTTIE, LLOYD Battaglia's North Hollywood neighborhood, half of which still lay in shambles from the earthquake, was an odd mix of tiny but comfortable two-bedroom homes with tightly clipped lawns, plaster divinity tableaux and ramshackle dumps with old car parts and metal odds and ends and heaps of garbage lying in piles out front.

Lloyd had lived with his mother until she passed away two years ago and was now alone. Lloyd would pick up a stray woman every so often who needed a place to stay and these women would end up ripping Lloyd off for a few thousand dollars of equipment before running off. This was, as Lloyd explained, another of life's compromises in the universal bartering system under which Lloyd and his hacking-world compatriots lived. Lloyd's one true love, as he was fond of repeating, was Brandi.

When Dottie pulled up in front of the house, Brandi took a quick breath and shut her eyes.

"I appreciate your doing this," Dottie said to her daughter. Poor thing, she'd had to endure Lloyd's devotion. He had written love letters, sent candy and flowers, promised her anything, no strings attached. No strings attached to Lloyd meant a spider web of obligations as intricate as any of the systems he hacked into: IRS, FBI, ITT.

"Anything?" Brandi once said to him. "How about doing twenty years without parole?" Ralph, who relied on Lloyd's genius, made Brandi write a letter of apology (reiterating her wish for no relationship, other than professional, with him).

And here they were again, walking up the dreaded trash-strewn pathway to Lloyd's front door. Brandi, hands jammed into her pockets, head down, eyes lowered, walked behind. Dottie knew that Lloyd's motion detectors had picked them up while Lloyd, at his monitors, was probably ogling Brandi through the fisheye of a surveillance camera.

Before Dottie had a chance to knock the door swung open and there was Lloyd, a tall glass of water in his hand, with straight brown hair falling over unflinching eyes. His narrow face and reddish lips made him look clownlike, demented. He wore a T-shirt that read LIFE: THE BOX WE LIVE IN, black jeans, faded pink clogs and a flowered shirt that Ralph had given him at least ten years before, and looked it. Lloyd had the palest blue eyes Dottie had ever seen, suggesting a kind of otherworldliness. It was like looking into a future where wisps of things rather than objects lived, of images and numbers, conceptual and ephemeral. Like Lloyd himself.

"It's great to see you," he said in his goofy, unmodulated voice. "Come on in, can I offer you some food for thought? Harbar."

"Your sense of humor hasn't changed," Brandi said.

"You think I should reconfigure it?" he said earnestly. "I

will. Do you have any suggestions? Really, just say the word."

His place was its usual shithole, with stacks of newsletters and manuals piled so high they created paths to adjoining rooms. Crusted dinner dishes from past millennia sat on the coffee table.

Lloyd led them to the main office, where he unlocked the deadbolt and other alarm devices. Inside was typical of rooms where rogue hackers like Lloyd spent their days: a window-less shell of a room, choked with stagnant air, piled high with data relay systems, computer parts, mother boards, electronic chips, several different modems, computers wired to each other, open pizza boxes, soda cans, plastic utensils.

This room was where Lloyd raided the world through his computers. He once boasted that in five minutes he could retrieve enough unsavory or damaging information on just about anyone on the planet to lay to ruin an entire lifetime.

"Here, sit here." He dragged chairs over for them. Brandi chose to stand, arms crossed, feet apart, dead-eyed.

"Boy," said Lloyd, "have I got a big nothing for you on this guy Quentin Ickes."

"Nothing?" Dottie said.

"Oh, lots of *stuff.*" He fell into his high-tech chair and spun it into position, long fingers dancing over the keys like a pianist's. "That beeper number went out of service today."

"Myrna," they both said simultaneously.

Lloyd said, "I've got gobs of data on him, but nothing you can use to locate him in the next ten minutes, which is about all the time you seem to have, am I right?"

"Or less," said Dottie.

"Okay," he said, bringing up on the screen boxes that appeared and vanished with astonishing speed. Watching the screen, Dottie felt like a modern-day Alice, traveling into a wonderland of encoded data. "I have scuffled around the IRS," Lloyd said as he continued to tap away, "ransacked the Justice Department, FBI and LAPD, prison records at Vacaville and Lompoc, found names of Mr. Ickes's parole officers, dates of release, visitors to prison and people he wrote letters to, with names, addresses, phones numbers, credit cards, bank accounts going back twenty years, residences, bad checks, arrests, detentions, everything you ever wanted to know about this fellow, a bad boy to be sure.

"I avoided the Feds' security watchdogs with their ears perked, cryptically decoded their security passwords. I have bounced their traces from city to city, off satellite relays and even, on several occasions, in order to get their security hounds off my trail, through European and Asian countries, by running a program that led those hounds up some tall phony trees, down some dark dead-end trails. Har!"

All of this braggadocio was for Brandi's benefit, and by the looks of her, she was impressed enough to move closer behind Lloyd, her eyes locked on the screen.

"In each case, in and out in under a minute," Lloyd said, "I snatched the data and split. Har! Fast enough but they weren't far behind. But me and Mr. Sloan outfoxed them."

Mr. Sloan, Dottie knew, was Lloyd's handle for his main computer, named after his hacker mentor, Harold K. Stone, a legend in the trade. Lloyd's eyes seemed to glaze over at the mention of his name.

"So," Dottie said, breaking into his self-congratulatory overkill, "where can we find him now?"

"Can't."

"Can't?"

"Your man has taken a detour off the info highway, or is cloaked by new I.D. and Social Security number, assuming that he's being paid a wage, and except for his name or variations on it, I'm afraid I can't find the fellow. I need more than you've given me."

Lloyd spun around to Brandi, who leaped back. His pink lips curled up into a smile, revealing a row of even gray teeth. "It could be days."

"We don't have days, Lloyd," Dottie said.

"You're safe here, you know, with me. No one can get in here. I am hurricane-, fire- and earthquake-proof. If the neighborhood went under, we would feel a light tremor, no more. I have provisions enough to last for months, clean air through pumps lodged between ten-inch-thick steel reinforced walls. I call this my family survival room. After all, for years, we three, along with Ralph . . ." He grew misty-eyed. "My condolences . . ."

"Thank you," said Dottie.

". . . for years I have considered you my family."

Brandi shot Dottie a worried look, not a look saying that she was worried about Lloyd but what she might do to him if he kept this up.

"Movies," Dottie blurted out in a kind of self-defensive reflex.

"Movies?" Lloyd said.

"Yes," Brandi said, "movies. Try the movies. Myrna said this guy Dirk she's been seeing—the guy we're looking for—is acting in a movie."

Back at the screen, Lloyd worked his magic fingers while Dottie watched, astonished by how these two computer lovers, the hacker and the layman, could track a man who had nothing but the letter Q and a possible job in a movie.

"I'm breaking into the Screen Actors Guild," Lloyd said, "which has virtually no security against the likes of me. Actors by the name of Dirk. Twelve. Actors with the letter Q . . . their first names. Twenty-eight. Printing them out. Accessing Social Security numbers, local addresses, six Dirks, five Q's." To Brandi he said, "This Dirk or Q is working locally?"

"Try it."

In minutes Lloyd had narrowed the field of Dirks to two and Q's to three. "Assuming it's his name," Lloyd said, "that he's working as an actor, that he belongs to SAG, so many ifs . . ."

Dottie reached into her purse for her checkbook and said, "Lloyd, you've been wonderful. How much do I owe you?"

"Well, let's see," he said, with his eyes glued on Brandi. "This hasn't been easy. A high priority job, computer time, getting into the Feds, IRS, prison and SAG computers . . ."

"Just give me a figure."

"Had to raise my prices . . . two thousand five hundred and thirty dollars. Forget the thirty."

"Very funny," Dottie said.

"Hey, no, that's the price."

"Twenty-five hundred dollars!"

"Bake a pie, eat a pie."

"What is that," Dottie said, "the new catchphrase?"

Brandi gave Lloyd a look. "Stop being a jerk and give me a realistic figure."

"One date," he said.

"What?"

"With you. I'll pay."

"Forget it."

"She's going with somebody," Dottie said.

"I'm going with somebody," said Brandi.

"Who?" said Lloyd, disappointed.

"Henry," said Dottie, "a new guy."

"He was over the house the other day," Brandi said. "A friend of a friend. It just happened, and you know how loyal I am. Jesus, Lloyd, I'm sorry."

"Oh, man."

"But I promise, the minute Henry and I break up . . ."

"If you ever do," Dottie said.

"If we ever do, I'll call you and . . ."

"You'll take Lloyd out," said Dottie.

"I'll take you out, I promise."

This seemed to make him happy. "You mean that?"

"Yes."

"Okay then."

"So," Dottie said.

"So . . ." said Brandi.

They stood around awkwardly for a moment. Dottie opened the checkbook and clicked her pen.

"So," Lloyd said, noticing. "That'll be . . . I don't know . . ."

"Your going rate," said Dottie. "Let's be honorable about this."

"Three-fifty."

She wrote out a check for three hundred and fifty dollars, which should have been two hundred, but which was, in reality, a nice drop from twenty-five hundred. What was she going to do, complain?

"Thank you, Lloyd, you're the best, once again." She handed him the check.

His eyes were glued to Brandi, pleading, soft, hurt. Dottie felt sorry for him, pathetic guy.

"Don't forget, Brandi," he said, "not that I wish you and Henry ill, but the minute anything happens . . ."

"I have your number, Lloyd," she said, laying a hand on his forearm and quickly pulling it away as if realizing what she had done.

They left Lloyd's pigsty. At the car they both raised their hands and gave him a little wave. Lloyd stood in the door, in his sagging jeans and pink clogs, hair draped over his forehead, besotted with love.

"Never again, Mom," Brandi said as they drove away.

"I promise."

"Yeah, right."

"Plus, Henry would never allow it."

Brandi snorted and looked out the window as the wind beat softly against her face.

Forty-one

...

AT HOME, THE answering machine held messages from a whole slew of people Dottie decided not to call back right away, including Dante, Patti Ashbury with a case, and sleazo real-estate scam artist Richard Levine advising her that it was against the law to yank out the For Sale sign he had stuck in her lawn. He was going to give her the benefit of the doubt this time, but that was the last. She was thinking it was a good thing for Mr. Richard Fucking Levine that he hadn't delivered the message in person.

Dottie called Myrna to find out why Dirk had canceled his cellular phone number so soon after their conversation. What was she hiding? The phone rang and rang. Either she had passed out or didn't want to talk; in either case, why had she turned off her answering machine? That was troublesome.

Brandi came in from the kitchen with a cup of coffee and a glass of juice for Dottie, who said, "Is Robin still sleeping?"

"Out like a light."

"Let's get to work." She took the pieces of paper on which she had written the names and respective information on

Lloyd Battaglia's list of suspects and divided them between the Dirks and the Q's.

Dottie checked Quentin Ickes's date of release from Vacaville prison—three months prior. Using Lloyd's printout, she located his parole officer, Wilson Best, on Waterfront Boulevard, up the coast in Loma Linda. Dottie called his number and a man's husky voice came on the line. Dottie explained the situation. Parole officers had to be careful about who they gave out information to; it might be somebody wanting to gun down the parolee. P.O.'s had heard all the bullshit lines at least a hundred times, and they, better than anybody, could cut the truth out of a herd of lies.

"The first thing I'd do is stay as far away from him as you can," Winston Best said after he'd determined Dottie was legit, "but since you're already locked in, watch out."

"Do you know where he is?"

"No, and I don't want to. I've had some sick ones, but Ickes, he's an actor. Bright, witty on the outside, but, oh, the snakes inside."

Dottie thanked Winston Best and went back to the SAG list. Brandi got on the phone with a production company employing an actor named Dirk Warden. "Hello, this is Beatrix Potter from SAG. I'm checking on the status of . . . Dirk Warden. He wouldn't be available, would he? Ah, well, maybe you could help me. We had a problem down here at SAG with the computer; you probably heard about the fire. His agent is out of town and I need a list of Dirk's recent work—films, TV, and dates, if you have it. . . . Okay, I'll hold."

Brandi covered the mouthpiece and whispered, "How'm I doing?"

Dottie nodded. Brandi, back into the phone, said, "Yes, still here. Oh, good, go ahead." When Brandi heard that Dirk Warden had acted in a TV movie at the same time Ickes had still been in Vacaville, she thanked the woman and hung up.

Dottie was able to strike from the list three other actors who had been at work during the time Quentin Ickes had still been in prison. Three remained.

An hour later they still had not been able to confirm the

remaining three—Dirk Bitteford, Quentin Marsh and Q. D. Reese, all currently working on low-budget features.

At eight the phone rang and Commander Bill Sallie said, "Dottie, I just got a call from the Sheriff's Department. They found a female, late twenties, murdered in Chatsworth. A real horror show."

"Any I.D.?"

Brandi looked up sharply, mouthing, *What?*

"She had a piece of paper with your phone number on it."

Dottie felt sick to her stomach and had to sit down.

"What is it?" Brandi insisted.

"What's her name, Bill?"

"Sylvia Mulcahe."

"Sylvia Mulcahe. Nickname Bunny?"

"You know her?"

Brandi started tearing through files. Back to Bill, Dottie said, "You have a description on her?" She hoped to God it wasn't Bunny but who else could it be? In Chatsworth, same last name?

"Five-five. Blonde, had some priors."

"Oh?"

"Drugs. Solicitation."

"Anything else?"

"Nothing for the last six years. Not been picked up, anyway. So," Bill said, "are you going to tell me about it?"

"Yes," she said, and she did, a blow-by-blow account of how she came to know Sylvia, a.k.a. Bunny Mulcahe.

"You know who might have done this?"

This was a tricky one. "I have an idea, Bill, it's something we're working on. Can you let it go for another day or two while we run down some leads and then I'll tell you everything."

"Does it have anything to do with Ralph's death?"

"No," she lied.

"A couple of days. If I don't hear from you, I'll be over in person."

"Thanks, Bill."

When she hung up, she heard Brandi shout, "It's her! the same one. Holy shit. This is amazing."

"What are you talking about?"

"Sylvia Mulcahe, look, there's even a photo of her with Dad and Quentin Ickes." Dottie moved over to the table, where she saw, in the photo, Bunny Mulcahe from Chatsworth—younger, blonder, thinner.

"The woman Quentin Ickes shot Dick Pendergast in the kneecaps over, the titty dancer. Sylvia Mulcahe, our Bunny."

Dottie said, "I didn't even recognize her." She felt the long arm of guilt taking hold of her.

"She was here like once and I don't even think you were around. It was one of the times you ran away from home."

"I did not run away from home. I was taking a breather from your father. Anyway, that's not important. But my God, what happened? How did Quentin Ickes ever . . ." She stopped and thought. How *did* Quentin Ickes manage to find Bunny in Chatsworth—if in fact Ickes had been the one who had murdered her—unless he had followed them there?

"That green car, the foreign job we tried to lose on the way to the mall."

"We lost it."

"*It* lost *us.*"

"And found us again."

Dottie pressed her fingers hard against her temples. "Let's think about this. There's no way Ickes could have been following us around day after day. I would have spotted him. So why Chatsworth? How would he know to follow us there?"

"Who knew we were going out there?" Brandi said.

"Nobody." After a moment, Dottie said, "The only time we talked to Bunny was over the phone."

Dottie snatched up the phone and with a screwdriver she got from the kitchen drawer unscrewed the bottom and pulled off the plate. She went through the same procedure with the kitchen and bedroom phones. Nothing. Back in the living room she dialed a number. Then she quickly hung up. She whispered to Brandi that she was going next door to call Lloyd Battaglia from Mrs. Kaharski's phone.

"If you have a message for me," Lloyd's recording said, "please leave it after the beep."

"Lloyd, it's Dottie. You there?"

"I am."

"Lloyd, how do you tap a phone line?"

"Uh-oh."

"I think Ickes has tapped into our line. But I checked the phones, nothing."

"Seen any phone trucks in the neighborhood lately?"

"No . . . actually, wait a minute. A week or so ago, there was a truck . . ."

"If you want me to get into the phone company files," Lloyd said, "I can check on service calls to your neighborhood."

"Would you?"

"Meanwhile, if you can climb a pole or if you've got a pair of good binoculars, scan the wires above where you saw the truck and look for alligator clips. You know what they are . . . they look like little jaws."

"I know what you mean."

"And don't use your phone unless you have to. Get a new line installed, or use the neighbor's, which I assume you're doing now."

"I am."

"I'll leave a message on your answer phone. 'Hacker says yes' Or 'Hacker says no.' Something like that. Got it?"

"Thanks, Lloyd."

"Give Brandi my love."

Dottie hung up and sat for a moment. Something nagged at her. Remembering what Bunny Mulcahe had said about Ickes threatening to kill Brandi, Dottie once again wondered why, after the initial bomb, he had not tried again. This was puzzling. Myrna's boyfriend had to be the key, and Dottie decided to wring the truth out of her friend, no matter how painful it was.

She dialed Myrna's number and waited, and waited. If there was one thing Myrna could not do without, it was access to the outside world, though the phone.

Brandi was in the kitchen eating.

"It's not like Myrna," Dottie said.

"What *is* like Myrna?"

"I'm going over there," Dottie said, not wanting to leave Brandi alone, "and you're coming with me."

"Is that right?"

"It most certainly is."

"You're getting mighty assertive in your old age."

"Come on, be a sport."

Brandi stuffed the remains of the pie into her mouth.

"Hey!" the voice said. A sleepy, bedraggled Robin, half undressed, leaned against the doorway. "What's with all the racket? A girl needs her sleep."

Dottie looked at her closely. "Robin?"

"Huh?"

"What are you on?"

"Percocet. What about it? I'm in pain."

"Where'd you get them?"

"Dr. Nudina, your neighborhood pediatrician."

"Dr. Nudina gave you drugs?" Brandi said. "He wouldn't give me an aspirin if I was dying."

"You don't do what I do for the good doctor."

"Oh, gross. That guy weighs three hundred pounds and he sweats like a pig. Robin, you're lowering your standards."

"And you're so lily white."

Dottie said, "When you two are done arguing, Brandi and I are taking a ride."

"I'm not staying here alone," said Robin.

"You've stayed alone for the last twenty-four hours," said Brandi. "Sleeping."

"Are you serious! Jeez." She looked out the window and up at the wall clock. "Okay, so go ahead, come back and find me mangled by that creep you're looking for. I'm expendable."

"Get dressed," Dottie said. "You have one minute."

Forty-two

■ ■ ■

"ONE FOUL WORD," Brandi heard her mother say to Robin as they drove down Sunset Boulevard to Myrna's, "or if Myrna finds one thing missing, believe me, when I take you to court, it's the first thing I tell the judge."

"Yes, mother," Robin said sweetly. "Whatever your heart desires."

Brandi was getting sick of Robin and her antics; at the same time she liked her spunk. There wasn't any either/or with people like Robin. She learned at Tough Love meetings that it's not that you're bad, getting good; it's that you're sick, getting well. These days, that's how she saw afouled people: sick, hopefully getting well. With that attitude she could be more tolerant of those who in the past she dismissed as lost causes. Like Robin.

And then, just like that, she found herself in the middle of a memory she'd been finding herself in a lot lately. It was that morning when she'd run out the front door and down the steps past her mother. She remembered the strange, worried look on her mother's face. The Banana was down on the street and in the front seat her Dad was ready to drive her to work. When all of a sudden—Boom!—the explosion filled the sky, and then *thud*. Right into her brain. Then another *thud*. That one took the air out of her, and the next thing she knew, she was flying backwards when all she wanted was to reach out through the bursts of light, to slow the world down enough so that she could pull him free.

She heard her own voice shouting, "Daddy! Daddy!" Until the roar of her voice drowned the world in silence.

Back now in the car on the way to Myrna's all she wanted was to slay the memory with sleep.

"Mom," she said.

"Yes, honey?"

"What do you think about maybe moving?"

"I'm going as fast as I can around these curves."

"No. *Moving*, as in moving to another house."

"If Richard Levine, real estate shyster, has his way, we'll be doing just that."

"What are we going to do about him?"

Robin piped in from the back seat, "I told you I'd go over there and *convince* him to go away. Hell, let's set it up. I'll do him, you take pictures and we'll blackmail the bastard."

"Done that before, Robin, have you?"

Robin pushed herself back against the seat, crossed her arms and stared out the window. "All I do is try to help and you give me a rash of shit."

"We appreciate it," Dottie said, "but right now we have to figure out how to get fifteen thousand dollars to Levine."

"Doesn't Paulie Dortmunder still owe us that much?" Brandi said.

"Good luck getting money out of that thief," Dottie said. "So. Moving, huh? What brought that up?"

Brandi thought for a moment. "We should give some real thought to it because, you know, every time I walk into the house, it reminds me of Dad, and it's not getting better."

"Ah."

"But I guess we have enough to worry about."

"Maybe we should think about it."

Brandi knew she shouldn't have brought it up, especially

with her mother gazing at her with those oh-you-poor-child eyes of hers. She heard herself say, "You mean, we'll actually . . . *think* about it?"

"We will."

It was true. Every time Brandi walked into the house a pain like a clenched fist erupted in the pit of her stomach, followed by such deep sorrow that all she could think to do was cry.

As they drove Brandi wondered if this wasn't a natural thing for a girl who'd just lost her father, and in time she would get over it. Maybe she shouldn't be worrying so much, which in itself was probably cause for a lot of her anxiety, about what she was going to do without him. Except get on with it.

For Brandi the homes in Myrna's Pacific Palisades neighborhood betrayed nothing of the emotional life of their inhabitants. The homes all projected an unruffled elegance, at peace with the world, safe and secure in a Prozac-like calm. Myrna's was no different, but Myrna was another story. And so, probably, were her neighbors.

They pulled into the drive and walked up the bleached-white sidewalk to the door. Dottie knocked and knocked until Brandi said, "Why don't you use your key, Mom?"

Inside, where it was dark and cemetery-silent, Brandi immediately sensed that something was wrong. Dottie caught it too and took the Stinger out of her ankle holster.

"What's going on?" Robin said, standing just behind Dottie, her eyes on the gun.

"Why don't you say it a little louder?" Brandi said to Robin.

"Wait in the car."

"I could do that." Robin turned on the heels of her hundred-dollar pumps and clicked-clacked back down the driveway.

Brandi reached into her bag and took out the pearl-handled .38, which felt heavy this morning, like her mood.

Myrna's bedroom door was ajar, a crack of dull light peeked through from inside. With her gun barrel, Dottie pushed the door open and stepped back. Brandi moved to one side, pressing her back against the wall, and kept looking at her mother for a signal.

Dottie craned her neck, looked in, and entered. Brandi, right behind her, smelled something metallic. "Mom," she whispered.

"Isn't it funny?" said Dottie.

"What?"

"I have never wanted a cigarette more than I do right now."

Brandi saw that the bathroom door was ajar, through which she saw only blackness.

"Unbelievable!" the voice said from behind them. Brandi jumped. "What a couple of pussies," Robin said. "I could have been out there all day waiting for you two." She marched by them, spiked heels mushing through the deep pile carpet, and into the bathroom. The light snapped on.

Brandi had never heard a scream like the one that came out of Robin. Followed by gagging, coughing and retching.

By this time Brandi was through the door, her mother behind her, hurrying across the gleaming white tile toward the tub, where Robin was bent over like an old woman in prayer, head in her hands.

Beyond Robin, Brandi saw Myrna's naked white body floating in the bath water, still as death. When she drew closer she saw what had freaked Robin out: in the center of Myrna's forehead, a hypodermic needle was sticking out of a thick blue vein.

"My God," Dottie said, removing the needle.

Brandi lifted Myrna's limp arm and felt for a pulse. "Still ticking."

As Brandi dialed 911 she studied the puncture mark on Myrna's forehead, and the trickle of dried blood curling out of the puncture. She gave the information to the dispatcher and then helped her mother lift Myrna out of the bath water, carrying her through the house to the foyer.

An EMT squad arrived, hooked Myrna up to an I.V. and loaded her onto a gurney. Dottie drove like a madwoman following the truck down Sunset to the Santa Monica Hospital E.R.

*   *   *

THEY SAT IN the waiting room amidst broken-boned skateboarders and people who'd slammed their hands in car doors and arthritis-crippled old people, drunks with lacerated faces.

Dottie had a copy of the Los Angeles *Times* in her lap, reading the obituaries. "Myrna wasn't one to shoot junk into her forehead," she said.

"Which leaves Dirk, a.k.a. Quentin or whatever."

"Exactly."

Brandi felt her anger rise. Controlling her voice, she said, "We're going after this guy, Mom, and we're going to get him."

"Before we do that we're going to calm down because without calm we have no chance."

"We'll cut off his hands," said Brandi. "They seem to be doing the most damage."

"Or his head," said Robin, who was trying to light a cigarette.

"Not in here, Robin," Dottie said.

The doctor came out and told them that Myrna had been transferred to intensive care. It was a miracle that she was still alive, considering the amount of heroin injected into her body—a body, the doctor added, that had virtually no immune system after years of ingesting the drug. Her chances, he said, were not good.

"She's got a hell of a constitution," Dottie told him.

"Which may be the extent of her defenses at this point," the doctor replied.

"We never count Myrna out," Dottie said.

Forty-three

■ ■ ■

Q. D. SAT ON his deck above the city, pissed. He drank the rest of his grapefruit juice and threw the glass bottle over the railing and into the scrub, listening to it chink against rocks as it tumbled down the embankment.

Tumble. He'd given Bunny and Myrna one last tumble-fuck apiece before he'd sent them over the border between the living and the dead.

They had betrayed him. But he held no grudges; he'd been creative about packing them off. He gave Myrna, the head-case junkie, a dose of her own medicine, right in her brain's pleasure center.

He admitted he'd not been so delicate with Bunny. He just did her.

He opened another bottle of grapefruit juice, took a swig. He kept *thinking* about Bunny in the old days. They'd been a *team* . . . until he caught her with that fucker, Pendergast. Didn't she know how it would fuck him up?

He had replayed the scene how many thousands of times? Coming into Ralph's house, into that office of his. Dark, late afternoon. He'd heard the sound of something, two people, man and a woman. Didn't think much about it, except . . . he knew that voice, the woman's.

In Ralph's office, on the black swivel chair, Pendergast, his pants down over his ankles, with Bunny, naked, in front of him, bent over, sucking his cock.

Something just shorted; Q. D. felt it. Like wires crossing. He pulled out the .38 and shouted something. Bunny screamed and fell away and he shot out Pendergast's knee-caps. Four slugs, two to each knee. Tore them to shreds.

It was her *fault*, the dumb bitch. Didn't she know what it would do to him? Damn right, she did. She was not stupid, she knew exactly what was coming down. And hey, she finally got her due, deserved it.

"Get off this shit!" he shouted and returned to the problem at hand. With Bunny and Myrna gone, what was he going to do about Brandi and Dottie? It was only a matter of time before they found him. He could run; he could always do that. And he would, but not before he finished what he had started out to do.

Forty-four

. . .

DOTTIE DROVE THE girls home and, leaving them in the living room, stumbled into the bedroom, where she slept for seven straight hours, a record. Next morning she again woke up to Mrs. Kaharski screaming at her husband. The usual. On a cellular phone Dottie borrowed from the neighbors she called the hospital and was put through to Simon Hales, M.D., who told her that Myrna's condition had not improved.

Dottie and Brandi spent the day tracking down leads. With Lloyd Battaglia's help, they made calls to production companies, cross-referenced prison records, badgered theatrical agents, inquired about locations of local films.

Mid-afternoon Lloyd called with news that no phone company truck had been in the neighborhood making repairs on the afternoon in question.

By sundown they had narrowed their list of suspects to two, and even then they couldn't be sure that a Dirk or Quentin or variations on the letter Q was their boy. For all they knew, it could have been Harry, Sidney or Butch.

"We have to go with the odds," Dottie said. "Statistics say

that men and women with strong or unusual first names tend to keep them, changing only their last."

Dirk Bitteford, who lived in Studio City, had an answer phone with a country music tune in the background. The production he was on, *The Punk*, was shooting out near Bakers-field, but had closed down temporarily, probably looking for completion funds. The production company's Culver City's answer phone said to leave a message, they'd get back. Dirk Bitteford, according to SAG records, was forty-seven years old and fit the description of Quentin Ickes. He had recently arrived from Lincoln, Nebraska, no previous address or phone number.

The second possibility was Q. D. Reese, with a Beverly Hills post office box, no phone, also arrived on the scene during the past two months, no previous address. Shooting a picture in Malibu Canyon, *Borrowed Time*. The location supervisor gave Dottie a hard time when she tried to wheedle information out of her. Dottie decided to back off; she didn't want word to get back and spook him. Dottie called Lloyd Battaglia to see if he could break into the post office computers for an address on Q. D. Reese's P.O. box.

Lloyd said he couldn't do it on his computer but told her how she could do it in person.

At around nine Robin, who had stayed in bed all day, blundered out to the kitchen in a wrinkled wisp of a dress she probably used on her tricks. When Dottie saw what a mess she was she decided to make an extra special dinner for them and spend the evening together. Play some cards, watch a little TV, regroup.

But Robin couldn't eat the Hungarian goulash or even string a few words together into a coherent sentence. Dottie didn't know if it was the effects of the beating or the Percocets, probably a little of both. Brandi went into the bedroom and returned with clean shorts and a blouse and tennis shoes. She and Robin disappeared into the bathroom and half an hour later came out looking like the WASP twins, Binky and Buffy, in their smart tennis outfits.

Dottie had kept the goulash warm and now they were ready to sit down and eat. They played cards and talked. For the first time since Robin's arrival, Dottie felt a semblance of family. She regretted having to take her back to court in less than a week.

They lost track of time. At three A.M. Brandi suggested a movie. She put *Heathers* on the VCR and they sat down to watch.

In the middle of the second murder scene the doorbell rang. Before Dottie could say anything, Robin, now full of energy, jumped up to answer it.

Dottie wondered who could be coming by at this time of night. She leaned back over her chair and parted the curtains. On the front steps she saw a man. The overhead light showered down on the uniform he was wearing—that of a security guard, the cap pulled down over his eyes. A quick glance told her he was wearing the proper gear of a security guard except that something was wrong. Too bright, too clever-looking to be a security guard, miscast.

". . . why is it that you want to see them?" she heard Robin say defiantly, and then the man mumble something.

"Yeah, you and who else?" Robin said. More mumbling, and then Dottie saw him reach for something in his pocket. Dottie threw the curtains back and started out of her chair.

She heard Robin yelling something. Brandi got up, a scowl on her face, and turned toward the door. Everything went into a slow-motion crawl. Brandi was now just a step or two from the hall. Some instinct told Dottie to reach out and take her by the shoulder.

She heard Robin shriek . . . and an explosion. A shot, a gun going off.

Dottie lunged for Brandi, who had already made the turn and was heading for the front door. The first thing Dottie saw when she turned the corner was Robin bent over, blood pouring out of her stomach, trying to speak.

Brandi stopped, frozen. Beyond Brandi on the top step Dottie saw the man in the security guard uniform with a gun in his hand, a .45, aimed at Brandi's mid-section. The coldness of him, the look in his deranged eyes, paralyzed her. There was nothing she could do. She wanted to freeze time, to throw herself between them. The man raised the gun. Dottie saw his index finger squeeze the trigger and she let out a scream.

Nothing happened. She saw confusion on the man's face, and sudden anger as he glared at his weapon as if it had betrayed him, as he struggled to eject the jammed cartridge. Dottie pulled Brandi back and threw her into the couch, out of his line of fire.

Dottie raced back into the living room for her Stinger. She snatched it off the table and started back. She heard the slide on the .45 working and the man's furious grunts. She prayed to God she could return before the .45 got healthy again.

In a crouch, she rounded the corner, holding the gun waist high. The doorway was empty. Out on the street she heard the scuffling of feet. She hurried out and down the steps to the street, where she saw him race like a deer down Otsego, out of range.

She caught a glimpse of the unmarked surveillance car, driverless, and could just imagine what Quentin Ickes had done to him.

Back in the house Brandi had covered Robin's wound with towels and was calling 911. Within moments, sirens wailed in the distance.

"We've got a decision to make," Dottie said. "We have the Studio City address on Dirk Bitteford. The other guy, Q. D. Reese, has a P.O. box whose address we can get when the post office opens." She checked her watch. It was nearly four-thirty. Two hours. "I don't want to have to explain everything to the cops."

"Right. Okay." Brandi slid over beside Robin and touched her on the arm. She was semi-conscious, her stomach torn up. One of the sirens would belong to an ambulance. "We're going after the guy who did this."

Dottie said, "The medics will be here in two minutes," and kissed her on the forehead. "You're going to be okay. Don't argue with anybody. They know what they're doing."

Dottie stood. "Get what you need," she said to Brandi, "I'll meet you in the car."

Dottie packed the same kit she had taken when they'd gone after Tiny Bellows, including the SKS Soviet carbine, the

.22, a .38, and just in case, the 30–30 Winchester.

She pulled on an oversized black sweater and boots and met Brandi at the Caddy. They drove away just as two squad cars and an EMT truck from the North Hollywood FD turned onto Otsego.

Forty-five

. . .

FOR DOTTIE, TRYING to break into somebody's place at five in the morning was like advertising some masochistic need to be thrown in jail. People get up at five to work or go to the bathroom, or when any strange noise alerts them.

Dirk Bitteford lived in a complex of boxlike studios and one-bedroom apartments of Mediterranean design, lush with overhanging foliage and poorly built stucco walls, with a pool in the center. Apartments like these were usually occupied by struggling actors and writers hoping to hit it big.

Dottie parked the Caddy in the open underground garage of Tropez Gardens. She and Brandi, sluggish from lack of sleep, took their weapons and extra ammo clips, and handcuffs, and slid under the archway into the gardens themselves.

The only bright spot in this scenario was that they weren't going to the barrio or East L.A., where they could expect nasty neighbors with attitudes and firearms to back them up. Then again, with these actors, you never knew. And they knew nothing about Dirk Bitteford, who might have been the one who paid them a visit an hour ago.

They found Bitteford's apartment location on a map in the open air lobby. Dottie saw no Fed Ex or post office attempt-to-deliver-mail slips, no notes stuck to his mailbox.

They crossed the patio and wound through the foliage by the pool until they came to a sign with an arrow telling them that rooms 208 to 228 were this way. They climbed the stairs. The closer she got, the more difficult it was for Dottie to keep from thinking about the damage Ickes had done. She kept seeing the hypodermic sticking out of Myrna's forehead, Robin's bloody insides spilling out, and poor Bunny Mulcahe from Chatsworth, whose only desire had been to help. And then there was Ralph sitting in the Banana, turning the key, ready to take Brandi to work. Alive one moment, dead the next. Just like that. A hole in their lives where he had been yesterday, that morning, a few minutes before, and then nothing. And this miserable bastard who had taken his life.

"Mom?"

"It's okay, Brandi, just thinking."

"We passed it."

She stopped.

"His door. Two twenty-two. Are you zoning out again?"

"I'm over it. I'm on top of it."

Brandi searched her eyes, looking for the lie. "Okay, are you ready?"

"Let's do it."

This meant breaking into the apartment. Brandi was an expert lock picker, having learned her craft from Jimmy Wilson, one of Ralph's best baby bounty hunters. She could break into anything: apartments, safe-deposit boxes, safes of all kinds, vehicles. To Dottie's chagrin, she'd broken into cars and trucks and then taken them for drives, some of them long ones, across state lines.

On her key ring Brandi carried a tiny tool kit, which contained just about every device she needed to break into anything. Dirk Bitteford's was a lay-down.

Dottie watched Brandi's eyes, icy with determination, as she worked. In ten seconds she was through the lock and the door, and the two of them stood in Dirk Bitteford's murky apartment that reeked of liquor and stale smoke. And something else, a rank chemical odor, like formaldehyde, or ether.

Dottie almost couldn't stand the smell, almost didn't care if Dirk Bitteford was the man they were after if it meant she'd have to spent any more time in this pit.

Brandi, pinching her nose, whispered, "Breathe through your mouth."

Dottie followed her through the living room, strewn with clothes, liquor bottles and drug paraphernalia, to a closed door, presumably the bedroom.

Brandi turned the knob and pushed. The stench drove them back a step. Inside Dottie watched as a shower of dull red light saturated the room. On the bed and spilling over to the floor, in an eerie tableau, a half dozen naked, thick-muscled male bodies, slept. It was like a painting, almost beautiful for the way they lay there in erotic still life.

"What do you want?" A voice came to them from deep in the room. Dottie curled her trigger finger around the Stinger.

From out of the pile a musty body rose up like liquid. His dancer's body moved off the bed and glided across the floor toward them. He was tall and built like a god. And naked, his penis swinging trunklike across his thighs.

"Dirk Bitteford?" Brandi mumbled.

"Who's asking?" the man said, stopping short. The red light behind him outlined his perfect physique.

"We're here to ask him some questions."

"About what?"

"Who are you?" Brandi said.

"Dirk?" a voice called from the pile on the bed. "What's going on?"

"There's our answer." Dottie aimed the Stinger at his genitals. "Mind stepping into the other room so I can get a look at you?"

The man gave a low guttural chuckle. She couldn't see his face in the dark and she was damned if she was going to come all this way without getting a positive I.D.

He closed the door behind them and stepped into the living room. Brandi snapped on the light. The shock of seeing this perfectly formed naked man made Dottie blush. She saw immediately that he wasn't the security guard who had paid them a visit. Bitteford plucked a pair of chinos off the floor and drew a billfold out, handing it to her.

She caught a glimpse of Brandi, who was trying not to gawk but still be professional enough to keep an eye on him. Dottie found a picture I.D. that said that the naked man standing before them was in fact Dirk Bitteford, of this address.

"Sorry to bother you, Mr. Bitteford," Dottie said.

"What am I supposed to have done?"

"Nothing you'd be proud of," Brandi said, holstering the .38.

"Are you the police?"

"No."

Dottie kept the Stinger tucked under her sweater just in case.

"If you're not the police," Bitteford said, "maybe I should call them."

"Suit yourself." Dottie motioned to Brandi that they were leaving.

Bitteford followed them out. "See here, you can't just break in here without an explanation. I have the right as a citizen to . . ."

At the door Dottie said, "Be grateful you didn't commit these crimes, Mr. Bitteford. If you had, you'd be dead."

Bitteford's knees buckled slightly and his hands went to cover his groin, which was the way they left him.

In the car Brandi said wistfully, "Too bad all the pretty ones are arsonists or gay."

Ten minutes later, in the Bob's Big Boy parking lot off Ventura, Dottie called North Hollywood General and was told that Robin Ripley was in critical but stable condition and wasn't allowed visitors.

TO DOTTIE, THE Beverly Hills post office, keeper of one of the most sought-after zip codes in the world, looked like a lot of other Beverly Hills multi-million-dollar homes in the flats. She'd been here in the past and not once had she seen anyone famous. Brandi pointed out that at twenty-six she'd been played by a Hollywood star in a movie from Paramount Studios. How many people could say that?

Leaving Brandi in the car, Dottie went inside and approached a balding clerk of about forty-five, with the scarlet face and the small, frightened eyes of an alcoholic.

"Excuse me, sir," she said. "I have been told by the postmaster general's office to inquire about the money they stole from me."

On the word *stole* the man looked up from his work.

"I have been sending money to a company with a post office box here for a line of skin-care products and received nothing in return. Almost three hundred dollars. That's fraud."

The clerk waited.

"The postmaster general's office," Dottie repeated, "told me that I should get the address belonging to the post office box so that I can get some satisfaction."

"What's the box number?"

"Two-two-three-five-seven."

"Just a minute." He vanished into the back and returned with something for Dottie to sign. He handed her a duplicate with the address on it. "That'll be two dollars."

How simple, she thought. Of course, if Lloyd Battaglia could get a lifetime of information on you in under a minute, why shouldn't it be?

Forty-six

...

THE ADDRESS WAS on Mulholland Drive, where many of the rich and infamous lived. Brando. Nicholson. That crowd. Ten years ago Dottie had been up here with Ralph chasing down a mentally retarded ex-husband who had abducted his two children and hidden them in one of the small hillside enclaves along Mulholland. They had gotten the kids out alive, but not their father, who had shot himself to death.

Brandi tucked a leg under herself. "Mom, this Q. D. Reese is the one, isn't he?"

"He's the only one left, so I'd say it's a pretty safe assumption."

Dottie drove through the early-morning haze. Sunlight peeked through the tall firs lining Mulholland as it snaked along the ridge that separated Los Angeles proper from the Valley. Brandi had her head out the window, hair flying around her face, shouting numbers. "Two forty-five! Three eighteen!" And a little later: "Five ninety-seven! Seven forty-five and closing."

Dottie felt tension, like ropes, tightening around her. Had

she made a mistake in not calling Bill Sallie? Probably not, what with police red tape. Smart as he was, Ickes would smell cops coming, and find an escape hatch.

She told herself to stay calm, treat this as another case of going in, snatching the guy and hauling him downtown. Keeping it simple was what it was all about, right?

"Right?" she said aloud.

"Talking to yourself again, Mom?"

"I am not as old and decrepit as you think. Some people talk to themselves all the time."

"And live in the Camarillo nut ward on medication. It's okay. When you get older, things start to go."

"Like wiseass daughters."

"Be cool, Mom. Uh! Nine thirty-seven. We're here."

The house was a low-slung ranch dug into the side of the hill. Dottie passed by the tar driveway that sloped down into a two-car garage. All sorts of plants and trees she couldn't identify gave the place the feeling of a tropical rain forest. She wondered how Quentin Ickes, just out of prison, could afford such a place. If actors in B-movies and perverted maniac killers made enough to live here, why was she struggling to make ends meet?

There was no place to park on the narrow street. She pulled into the driveway next door and left a note under the windshield wiper. *Be right back. Police Business.*

Brandi spun the cylinder on the .38 and put the gun in her bag. She applied lipstick in the visor mirror.

"Want to borrow my eyeliner?" Dottie said.

"Funny."

"You don't have to come with me."

"Is that right?"

"What I mean is that this is probably just routine. I'll go in, get the drop on him, be back in five."

"Uh-huh." Brandi replaced the top of the lipstick and dropped it into her bag. "Ready?"

"What I mean—"

"I know what you mean, Mom, and the answer is no." She yanked the handle and climbed out. The road tapered off into scrub brush and in the distance a low morning smog hung shroudlike over the city.

From the trunk Dottie took out a couple of mace canisters and slid them into her pocket. "Got the cuffs?"

"Got 'em."

"Do we need anything else?"

"A SWAT team?"

Dottie went ahead. They spread out, twenty feet apart. Brandi had the .38 out, moving with caution, still as water. Dottie couldn't help but admire her cool and at the same time was worried to death.

They moved down the driveway to 957. Dottie motioned for Brandi to check the garage. The pane was so caked with grit she couldn't see a thing. Short of breaking the glass, they would have to move on.

On the deck, which stretched from one end of a glass-enclosed wall to the other, Dottie saw lounge chairs and hanging plants and curtains drawn across the windows.

The garden was exquisite—huge and more luscious than anything she'd seen since Mexico. This guy Q. D. Reese was into horticulture.

"Don't you remember?" Brandi said. "Quentin Ickes loved our garden in back of the house. He was always out there puttering around."

Dottie didn't know whether this was good news or bad. It certainly packed more anxiety into the moment. Brandi climbed the steps to the deck and tried to peek in the window. Dottie pulled her out of the way. "What are you doing?" she whispered.

"What does it look like?"

"Don't you know that's the easiest way to get your head blown off? What if he was behind there with a twelve-gauge?"

Brandi stepped back.

"What does your instinct say about him being in there?"

"Nothing." Though Dottie figured that if Ickes a.k.a. Q. D. Reese had been inside, he would have acted by now, she didn't want Brandi getting too complacent. Believe nothing until you see it had always been her motto, and she wasn't changing it now.

Brandi got out her lock-picking apparatus and silently jimmied the door open. Dottie, in a crouch, slid through the curtains and into the living room.

They spent the first few minutes on a cursory inspection of the place. Dottie checked the garage and found it empty. Gone, she figured, to Malibu and the movie set.

Brandi called for her and she hurried to the living room, where she found her on her knees in the corner, fixed on something. Closer in, Dottie saw a smattering of vaguely familiar photographs, some in frames, some torn in half, some pasted against cork board and scotch-taped to the wall.

She caught her breath when she realized that the face in a number of the photos belonged to Brandi. Brandi as a child, as a young woman, Brandi at eleven, Brandi at the house, Brandi with Ralph in the back yard. Dozens of them, some of which Dottie had taken herself. Some of them recently.

Dottie knelt down beside Brandi, who sat cross-legged in front of this gallery, and wrapped an arm over her shoulder.

"He's been in the house," Brandi said. "He took the snapshots from my dresser. And look there." Dottie followed her finger to a pile of clothes on the floor—blouses, underwear. "I wondered what'd happened to those, thought I'd lost them. I was mad at you, Mom, for misplacing them."

Dottie pulled her closer, and noticed that the face in other photos belonged to a blonde woman she had recently met . . . the late Sylvia Mulcahe. Bunny.

Brandi said, "That was the outfit Bunny wore at the mall. The same blouse, remember? After Ickes followed us, he went to her place and took these photos before he killed her." Ickes had scotch-taped the photos to the cork board: Bunny alive, scared to death. "And he took those"—shots of Bunny, splayed with blood—"*after* he killed her."

"Let's see what else he's got."

"Isn't this enough? He's the one."

In the other room Dottie called Fast Lane Productions, the company producing Quentin Ickes's movie that Lloyd had found for them.

A woman answered. Dottie said, "This is Valley Florists. I have a delivery for a Q. D. Reese."

"Hang on." The woman went away and returned a moment later. "He's working today."

"Could you give me directions, please?"

Brandi ambled in a moment later as Dottie hung up. "Who were you talking to?" she said.

Dottie's mind was racing at a hundred miles an hour. What she was about to do she might live to regret, but there was no time to think about it. "I was talking to Bill Sallie," Dottie lied. "I thought I'd call for some backup."

"Let's go, then."

"Well, now, in a minute. I'm not done here yet."

Dottie needed time to think about how she would do this. She reached again for the telephone.

"What the hell are you doing now?"

"Calling."

"Who?"

"Myrna, and then Robin."

"Mom, we've got this creep running around loose."

"Right now I need to know how they're doing, and so do you. We'll get this guy, don't you worry. The two of us, Brandikins." She dialed the hospital. Myrna was not available; resting, was the word. She had no luck getting through to Robin either, though Dottie couldn't let Brandi know that. She took a deep breath and said into the dead receiver: "Hello, Robin . . . No, Robin, it's me, Dottie . . . Brandi? Brandi's here, sweetheart . . . Now, Robin, don't you say that . . . Brandi would love to be there with you . . . Robin, please calm down . . ."

She glanced over at Brandi who mouthed, *"What?"*

Back into the receiver, Dottie said, "Robin? Hello? Robin? Oh, shit."

"What's the matter?" said Brandi.

"Robin sounded bad, honey, sounded in real bad shape. Damn. That's dangerous when you're in recovery—your spirit is the first thing to go." She looked at Brandi. "She was asking for you, sweetheart."

"Poor Robin. I'm gonna kill that no good Ickes when we get our hands on him."

"Ickes isn't going anywhere. Listen—we could swing by the hospital, just to check in with her, then meet up with Bill Sallie and go get Ickes together."

"I am not going to the hospital."

"C'mon, we're both going."

In the car, Brandi said, "I think you had better realign your priorities."

"Realign, really? I'll have you know that that's exactly what I've been doing. Robin's our *friend*, and friends come first."

It took them twenty minutes to reach the hospital's circular drive. She hated doing this to Brandi, but she was trying to save her life. It was like families who took separate airplane flights. In case one of the planes went down, at least somebody would be left. Better Brandi, who had her whole life ahead of her.

Dottie knew they'd be better off going after Ickes as a team, as they had with Tiny, but Ickes was another breed. You didn't know what door he was behind or what color he'd be wearing, coming out of which shadow. This small lie was necessary. Period. She had made up her mind.

She pulled in front of the hospital and said to Brandi, "Go up and see Robin. I'll park and call Bill Sallie to meet us with backup at the entrance to Malibu Canyon."

The minute Brandi vanished into the hospital, Dottie sped away. She felt guilty as hell and could imagine Brandi's expression when she realized she'd been duped. Dottie could not remember when she'd felt more alone, but she had to remind herself that this was the best—and only—way it could be. She passed phone booths along the way and came that close to calling Bill Sallie. The voice of reason told her this was the smart thing to do—get backup, seal off the exits, chase Ickes into the mountains if need be. The voice of experience, however, told her that Ickes would get away.

Get the job done, she told herself. *You have the tools, use them.* The voice of experience outshouted the voice of reason as she took the Calabasas exit and started her climb over Malibu Canyon toward the sea.

For Dottie there was little in that part of the universe that astonished her more than Malibu Canyon. A slender road wound through hard rock walls while, down below scrub and the depths of the lower canyon made her feel as if the Old West were not dead after all.

She followed the rough map she'd drawn from the production company woman's instructions. Turning off on Agoura Road, she reached a red silo, took the left fork and advanced higher still until the land leveled off. Up ahead she saw a fence guarding property on which many movies had been shot. She recognized the familiar mock-South Korean landscape from the opening helicopter sequence in the TV series "MASH."

Down a quarter mile, around a bend tucked into a kind of amphitheater, under a stand of oaks, she saw a cluster of trailers. On one of them a sign read Fast Lane Productions.

She pulled up and parked. She stayed behind the wheel for a few minutes, checking the Stinger's ammunition and the extra clip she transferred from the glove compartment to her jeans pocket. From under the seat she removed handcuffs and dropped them into her purse. She checked herself in the rearview mirror and took a moment to comb her hair. She was stalling, but what the hell.

On the way up here she had tried to come up with a cover. And like other situations, her thoughts didn't gel until the last minute. From the briefcase she took out a bailbond warrant form on which she filled out the necessary information, showing that she was empowered by the State of California, County of Los Angeles, to arrest and bring to justice one Q. D. Reese for jumping bail on an assault and battery/with intent to kill charge for which he had failed to appear in court. All phony, of course, but after years of filling these things out she could forge anything, scribble this name or that, make it so official that God wouldn't know the difference. She checked to see that her own papers were in order. Satisfied, she looked into the rearview mirror one last time and said, "Okay. Go get him."

She climbed out, closing the door behind her, and moved

across the rocky ground to the trailer. The door was open and she entered.

A man and a woman, healthy-looking movie people, just a little *too* good looking to be real, sat in directors' chairs before a bank of phones, Xerox and fax machines, and stacks of scripts.

When she came in they looked up sharply and gave her a who-are-you? look.

"Hi," Dottie said, smiling. "Fast Lane?"

"That's right," the woman said. She was about forty, in jeans and a work shirt, red hair, in good physical condition, rugged, with perfect movie teeth. The guy looked as if he came out of the same chic western-wear ad.

From the moment she walked through the door Dottie's calculations had begun: How to get them to lead her to Ickes without tipping him off; how to gauge what they would believe and what they wouldn't; how to accomplish this in little time with minimum fuss.

These people would not want to give up Ickes, who was playing a key part in the movie. Jail time translated into major dollar loss, production shutdown or shooting around him. What would work best? She was his sister, a friend? Should she muscle her way in?

"Q. D. Reese?" she said.

"What about him?" said the man.

She thought about saying: *He killed my husband, tried to kill my child, almost killed my best friend, did kill a young woman in Chatsworth and a pimp named Henry, shot up a young girl in my living room. For starters.*

She removed the papers and I.D. from her purse and laid them on the desk. "My name is Dottie Thorson, I'm a bounty hunter. I'm here to bring Quentin Ickes, a.k.a Q. D. Reese, in for jumping bail. He's wanted for the murders of Sylvia Mulcahe of Chatsworth and Henry Fowler of Los Angeles, and two assault counts." While they inspected the papers, she added, "I would very much appreciate your assistance on this. I'm also required to tell you that if you do not cooperate and Mr. Reese goes on to commit additional crimes, you will be charged as accessories. I'm sorry to be so blunt, but we're working against the clock here."

"How do we know you're who you say you are?" said the woman, probably thinking she was some crazed fan.

"Call five-six-four, four-one-four-one. That'll be the LAPD Valley Division. Ask for Commander Bill Sallie."

The guy snatched up the phone with typical macho and dialed. After a moment, when the Valley Division staffer had answered, the guy stammered, "Commander Bill Sallie, please . . . Who's calling? . . . my name? . . . Never mind." He replaced the receiver and looked at the woman, who said to Dottie, "We can't afford any trouble."

"Neither can I," Dottie said.

"Leave the trailer, turn right, at the tree line go left. You'll see it, a blue trailer, about half the size of this one. He should be in there; he was last time I looked."

Dottie returned the papers to her bag. "I'd suggest you stay in here and lock the door. Just in case."

They nodded.

Outside, Dottie followed the woman's directions. The stones made noise under her feet, her shoes squished in the damp grass, the fabric in her jeans rubbed together, combining to make what she imagined was a terrible racket. She was sure Quentin Ickes/Q. D. Reese had heard her approach and was waiting with his weapon of choice behind the trailer door.

She made it to the edge of a small clearing where the trailer, a blue rectangular box, stood, and considered the best approach. She heard nothing, saw no movement through the tiny windows.

She reached the front, where she found a small slide-in plate with a star that read Q. D. Reese. She could barely reach up and take hold of the knob, she was so nervous. She would have to take a step up to the trailer, which would put her off-balance and vulnerable to any sudden movement, like someone bolting through the door.

She held the Stinger in her right hand, at crotch level. With the fingers of her left hand, she turned the knob and pushed, eased it open, waited.

She took another step up and entered. The place was dark except for a night light above a fold-out table set against one wall. Down either side she saw shadowy pieces of furniture illuminated by dull morning light peeking through the curtains. The place felt empty, though there had been a presence here not long ago.

On the table she saw a ketchup bottle in the form of a clown's head and beneath it a piece of writing paper. She picked it up and read:

Think, Dottie. If you are here and I am not, where might I be? Exactly. Alas, dear girl, you'll never make it back in time.

Her face turned to fire. She stuffed the note into her pocket and hurried out of the trailer and back across the grass and stones to the car. She vaguely heard someone shout to her. In the car, she jammed the key into the ignition. Concentrate, she told herself.

She spun the Caddy around, kicking up so much dust she couldn't see out of the back window. In the Fast Lane trailer door she saw the woman and man looking out at her. She beeped the horn. They jumped back inside as she sped by. She prayed the road down the hill was clear because according to the speedometer she was doing fifty.

At the Malibu Canyon road she turned left and floored it. She remembered seeing phone booths at the foot of the road near the entrance to the Ventura Freeway. She estimated that the trip back would take maybe forty minutes to an hour in this traffic, not good. Don't think about it, she told herself, there's nothing you can do until you get there.

At the phone booths she dialed home: busy. She called the hospital and after the receptionist screwed around for a while, Robin was on the line, sounding loopy from the anaesthetic.

"Robin," Dottie said, trying to remain calm.

"Hey, Dottie. . . . What's up?"

"Where's Brandi?"

A pause. "Like you told her to, she went home . . . And is she pissed!"

"What do you mean, like I told her to?"

"The cop who called said you'd be at home. For Brandi to meet you there. She is so mad . . ."

"What cop?"

"The cop . . . guarding your house."

Oh, God, she thought. "How long ago?"

"How long ago?"

"How long ago did Brandi leave the hospital?"

"Jeez, I don't know . . . forty-five minutes, an hour."

"By what, bus?"

"Cab. I had to loan her the money. Twenty-five bucks."

It would take at least thirty minutes, which meant Brandi was already there and had been for . . . Dottie slammed the phone down and ran for the car.

Forty-seven

. . .

IT WAS ONE of those steaming hot days when all you wanted to do was sit under an air conditioner and read a mystery. The Caddy's air had needed freon and other minor adjustments for a long time. Dottie baked as she sped down the Ventura Freeway to the Hollywood Freeway and took the Lankersheim exit. She tried not to think of Brandi or what Quentin Ickes might be doing to her. And of course the harder she tried not to think about it, the more she did.

At Riverton she made a decision to park on the next street over, where she and Brandi had left Myrna's car on the Tiny Bellows job. She could then sneak in through the back yards, which of course Ickes would anticipate, having worked for Ralph and done it himself. He knew just about everything about the house, the escape hatch under the bathroom, the back exit, the nooks and crannies. He'd be waiting, to play out some grotesque climactic scene with the two of them.

She left the car on the street and followed the back yard path. She approached the fence that divided her property from the Kaharskis' and slid down along the fence, keeping her eye on the house.

It took her another few seconds to reach the back door and slip inside through the kitchen. The house was cool and dark in the shadows. She heard nothing but the whir of the refrigerator and normal household creaks.

The place was too still, like quiet water with a monster lurking below. Keeping the Stinger close to her, she checked the living room and office. Empty.

She stopped at the head of the hallway and listened. Her senses were so attuned that the atmosphere inside the house seemed sharply defined, crystal-clear.

She crept up to Brandi's bedroom door and looked inside. There she was, curled up on the covers, sleeping. Suspicious, Dottie crept into the room, keeping one eye on the door.

At the bed, Dottie knelt and reached for her when she saw it. A patch of duct tape stretched across her mouth. A dark stain under one eye. Blood trickling from her nose.

"Put the gun down, Dottie," the voice from behind her said, "or I'll be forced to shoot your daughter in the head . . . Now!"

Dottie placed the Stinger on the floor.

"Slide it back."

She did and watched as Ickes's hand came into her field of vision and grabbed the Stinger.

"Take the tape off her so we'll be able to have a civilized conversation, why don't you?"

Dottie slowly stripped the tape from Brandi's mouth. "Just a little more, honey," she said, feeling the pain herself, "that's it." She dabbed the blood from Brandi's upper lip and nose. Brandi opened one eye and stared at her, unblinking. Dottie held her stare and a flash of recognition passed between them: *We're going to be all right*, was the message. She didn't know where it came from, but she was grateful for it.

After a moment they were both sitting up in bed. Dottie took a look at Ickes. What she saw shocked her. This was not the same macho half-wit she remembered from ten years before. Instead she saw a hardened, evil-looking, even handsome man who had literally changed his appearance. He seemed taller, more lean, muscular, confident. And cruel. She was afraid of him and she was sure he saw the fear.

"Isn't this nice?" he said. "The three of us. Just like old times."

He wore a fashionable white polo shirt and khaki trousers, with a brown rope belt and matching shoes, no socks. Collegiate. He had slicked back his hair; a curl hung over his forehead. A gold earring dangled from his right lobe.

"You took that from my jewelry box," Brandi said.

Ickes flicked the earring with his index finger. "You've always been so observant, Brandi. Some things never change."

"Except you."

"Eight years in prison can do that to a man." He said this with a sinister ferocity that made Dottie shudder inside. "Which," he said directly to her, "your husband was responsible for. Lest we forget."

At this point Dottie thought better about saying anything. She sensed a storm bubbling beneath his surface, ready to blow.

"So what else did you steal from my room?" Brandi said.

"I was hoping your heart."

"Same old Quentin." She rubbed her hands together. "Always with the bullshit."

Dottie wanted to tell Brandi to cool it but held her tongue.

"Let me get this on tape," he said and reached behind him. He produced a camcorder, flicked the switch and a red light appeared. "Say something clever," he said, panning back and forth between them.

Dottie was certain that, given the right sequence of events, they could take him. That sequence, though, with his squatting just out of their reach, she would have to create.

Brandi stared defiantly at Ickes, then shot a glance in her mother's direction that said: *Whenever you're ready, Mom, go for it.*

"I wouldn't," he warned. "I can hear you two and, believe me, I wouldn't."

Suddenly, from between his white teeth, Dottie saw it, the circular flat bullet casing.

"Still chewing, huh?" Brandi said. Dottie noticed that she had slid back against the wall and tucked her legs under her body.

"One of these days," Ickes said, "this bullet is going to blow off the back of my head."

"Let's hope it's in the next few seconds."

"Still the sassy bitch, aren't we?"

"By the way, Quentin, we were up to your house . . ." Brandi said.

"Whose house *is* that?" Dottie asked.

"Did you notice how beautiful the garden was?" he said, recording everything on the camcorder.

"In fact," Dottie said, "I did."

"Isn't it amazing what human manure can bring to the care and management of flowers?"

"Who'd you bury?"

"The owner, a mama's boy who was given everything for doing nothing, and your friend Robin's pimp. He's there, too."

"By the way, Quentin," Brandi said, "speaking of mama's boys, was that *your* mama in those photos on the fireplace? She looked an awful lot like you."

Dottie watched Ickes's expression sour and wondered what Brandi hoped to accomplish by this.

"Let's not get too personal, little girl."

"I always thought you were a mama's boy, Quentin, with all your macho shit."

In an effortless move, Quentin reached over and slapped Brandi hard across the face. Her head snapped back. She brought her hand to her face and touched the red mark on her cheek. She sank further back on the bed and Dottie noticed that she had her right arm jammed into the space between the bed and the wall.

"This room has always meant so much to me," Ickes said. "When you were a girl, Brandi, do you remember when we would come in here together to be alone? You would sit where you are there and I would sit here and you'd tell me stories about why you wanted to be somebody else and I told you that I could help you?"

"I remember how mean you were, how you shot Pendergast because he talked to your girlfriend—"

"Talked? He fucked her! Bunny was mine!" The fierceness wore away into a kind of ugly smile. "But you two know—I should say *knew*—my Bunny. Feel guilty about that, do you? Well, you should, leading me right to her. On a certain level, we all killed her, a team hit. For which we'll all fry, but you a bit sooner than me. Gosh, I can't remember when I've had more fun, can you?"

"When my dog died," Brandi said.

"Brandi . . ." Dottie said.

"Hey, Mom, he's going to kill us anyway. Might as well have a few laughs before we go."

"Time's a-wasting." Ickes lay the camcorder down and from behind him produced a narrow thin-handled knife that looked made for cutting, both edges. Dottie flinched, remembering Bill Sallie's description of Bunny Mulcahe's mutilated remains.

Ickes said, "Put your hands out here, Dottie." When she made no move to obey him, he flicked the knife along her thigh, opening a six-inch gash in her jeans. She jumped at the pain. Blood flowed out of her leg and into the fabric. "Put them out here," he said.

She did and Ickes clamped handcuffs over her wrists. He then brought the knife up and pressed the tip against her nostril.

He's going to do this slowly, Dottie thought, and now with her hands cuffed she had little mobility.

"Eight years," Ickes said. "In a concrete-and-steel box, with thoughts of Bunny fucking other guys to keep me company. It's called self-destructive psychosis. You can't imagine the torment." He pressed the knife tip harder against her skin. "What was your husband thinking about when he put the word out on me? I worked for him, I cared for his family, I busted my ass for him."

"And now he's dead," Brandi said, "and you killed him."

"And that's supposed to bring back eight years of my life? If it had gone down the way it should have, if you, Brandikins, had taken the bomb, he would have had to suffer in life. I would have become his daily reminder. I could have watched his pain take shape."

Dottie saw Ickes's eyes turn inward, back into the darkness, searching for something. She felt a ripple of fear washing up her spine.

"I became," he said, "a kind of cartographer—map maker—in prison. I studied maps of the world, and drew them. Very elaborate, in color. I won awards. Best of show. Then I began to draw the maps on human bodies, like temporary tattoos. Lasted a few days. But they were so—what's the word?—ephemeral. I needed something permanent. Art should last."

Dottie watched him in his dreamy meandering; he was leading up to something.

"And so I began to experiment on myself." He removed his shirt and there, filling his chest and upper arms, Dottie saw strange intricate patterns. Scar tissue, done with a knife probably like this one, criss-crossing his body in a series of fleshy gutters.

"I had beautiful intentions, But it's not easy using your own body as the canvas for your art. So I used others, and lo and behold, art took shape. I even tried it on our friend Bunny the other day, but time was a factor and, you know, you just can't rush these things."

"What's your point?" Brandi said.

Ickes held the knife out before him, studying the gleaming tip. "I have dreamed of carving my likeness in you, Brandikins. I have designated you as my ultimate human canvas."

"I should be flattered?"

"But before I create my masterpiece on you . . ." He dropped to his knees and positioned himself in front of Dottie. "I thought I had better first let you see how it's done—on your dear mother."

Brandi pushed further back into the corner of the bed.

Ickes aimed the tip of the knife at the gash in Dottie's leg. "Since I've already begun the process, let's continue along this line. There's a pun. *Along this line*, get it? How come I'm the only one laughing?"

Dottie decided she had to make something happen. With

a little effort she thought she could distract Ickes long enough for Brandi to hop off the bed, leap over him and run. A long shot, but better than nothing.

She tried to catch Brandi's eye, but Brandi wasn't paying attention. Like Ickes, she was turned inward, as if something deep inside were commanding her focus.

All right, Dottie told herself, wait for an opportunity and go for it. Just then Brandi's eyes widened, as if she had heard her thoughts, and Dottie told herself the time was now.

Ickes was leaning forward, the knife poised over her leg. "The way to draw a likeness is to choose a central object— eyes, nose—and then draw, or in this case, etch, everything around it first, leaving the central object until the end. Get it?"

"I get it that you're boring me," said Dottie.

"Oh, really? Then let me wake you up."

He poked the knife into Dottie's leg. She jumped and let out a yelp and swung. Her hands, clamped together by the handcuffs, caught him against the side of his head. "Run," she shouted. "Run, Brandi!" At the same moment she felt his fist against the side of her head.

The air whooshed out of her. She tumbled over. A moment later she opened her eyes and found herself staring at the craters in Ickes's pock-marked face. Beyond his shoulder she saw Brandi, scrunched up against the wall. Dottie gave her a furious look, as if to say, *What's the matter with you!*

Ickes's breath smelled like cheap soap. "It's come to this, has it?" he said. "I'm pleased to say, Dottie dear, I have changed my mind. In the interest of time I'll be starting on your face." Ickes took her by the hair and pulled her head back so that she faced up at him.

She could see the tip of the blade as he angled it toward her eye. She thought she would pass out.

"Lights out, my sweet," he said quietly. Christ, she thought, he's going to blind me. She watched as he shifted the blade in his hand so that it was now just an inch from her. His face came into focus, his stained teeth. The stubble. The leer. She began to shake, as if a freezing wind had blown into the room.

Then, from far off, she heard a sound, a woman's voice shouting. She saw a flash, heard a crack. She saw Ickes's hand fly up to his neck, his head snap back. Then another flash and another crack and now Ickes reeling off to one side, his mouth an angry hole, shouting in pain.

Ickes tumbled off the bed and fell to the floor, writhing spasmodically.

Dottie looked down toward the foot of the bed, where she saw Brandi clutching a small-caliber pistol. Her eyes were clear as pools and resting on Ickes, who lay on the floor in a torrent of blood, eyes rolled back in his head, mouth hung open. Life departing him. He twitched once and then he lay still.

"Brandi?" Dottie whispered.

"Is he dead?" She was trembling.

"I don't know."

"He's not going to get up, is he?"

Dottie stuck her toe into Ickes, which proved nothing except that he wasn't responding. She said, "I'll call nine-one-one. If he moves, shoot him again."

"Don't worry."

Dottie climbed over Ickes's body and stumbled into the living room.

Moments later she was back in the room. "Where did you get the gun?" she asked.

"Remember when Daddy left a whole slew of them on the second bed? It was my birthday. I hid them in your room, all except this one, which I put in a hollowed-out part of my wall down here behind the bed. Look at it." She held the gun up, the pearl-handled .22 caliber pistol. "I'm surprised it even fired."

"Thank you, Ralph," Dottie said.

They peeked over the side of the bed to the floor where Ickes lay, curled up and bloody where the bullets had entered. Even with the holes in his neck where Brandi had shot him, he looked as if he might uncoil and spring at them.

Dottie felt Brandi shudder and wrapped an arm around her shoulders. "I love you, Brandikins."

"Ditto, Mom."

Epilogue

■ ■ ■

FOR DOTTIE IT was bad news and good news. Bad news
that Quentin Ickes a.k.a. Q. D. Reese had survived Brandi's
bullets. Good news that he was in a state mental ward under
psychiatric observation. Bad news that someday, though sen-
tenced to life imprisonment without benefit of parole, he
might still get out on a legal technicality to hunt them down
again. Unlikely, but who knew?

A month had passed. Dottie and Brandi were sitting in the
Otsego house with Myrna, who had been released from the
hospital and, as far as Dottie could tell, had not gone back
on junk. The bad news was that the cancer had returned and
Myrna had little time to live. She was spending most of her
days at the house and that was fine with Dottie.

Robin, as usual, was a wild card. Judge Ishi, who had
noticed a vast improvement in Robin's demeanor (which she
attributed to Dottie's influence), placed Robin on probation,
granting Dottie temporary custody until such time as Dottie
herself determined that Robin should be set free.

It was a Tuesday afternoon, a scalding summer day in the

Valley, and the four of them sat in front of fans, drinking lemonade.

The doorbell rang and Brandi went to get it. Dottie heard muffled conversation and then saw Brandi lead real-estate swindler Richard Levine into the room.

"Sit down, Mr. Levine," Dottie said. "Some lemonade?"

"I'm in a hurry, Dottie. What's this all about?"

"*Ms*. Thorson," Robin said.

"What's that?" Levine said.

"To you it's Ms. Thorson. Sit down."

He did as she said. The doorbell rang again, and again, Brandi answered it.

This time she returned with bailbondsman Paulie Dortmunder, who looked around the room, at the women, at Richard Levine.

"Hello, Paulie," said Dottie. "Lemonade?"

"What's going on, Dottie, what's this big deal you got for me?"

"I'd like you to meet Richard Levine. Mr. Levine, this is Paulie Dortmunder."

"Sit down, please," Robin said to Paulie.

"I'll stand."

"You heard her," said Brandi.

"Over here by me," Robin said. Paulie had adjusted his eyes to the light and now saw that it was a ravishing young girl who had made the offer and he took it.

"Here's the deal," Dottie said. "I want to continue living in this house. In order to do so, I need you, Paulie, to pay you, Mr. Levine, the sum of fifteen thousand dollars. Which happens to be the amount that you, Paulie, owe me for picking up Tiny Bellows."

"I owe you nothing—"

"Paulie," Brandi said, "shut up."

Dottie continued. "Which also happens to be the amount, you, Mr. Levine, paid my husband for this property."

"I paid him *one hundred* and fifteen . . ."

Dottie picked up a piece of paper from the table and handed it to him. "This is a signed affidavit from your real estate firm's comptroller stating otherwise."

Levine read it and placed it in his lap. "I'm listening."

"And Paulie," Dottie said, handing him a piece of paper, "you'll recognize this as a lien against the property on which your bailbond office sits. Unless I sign off on this by Friday, I'll own it."

"That's my fucking home!"

"Exactly." She got up and stood over them. "When we return in one hour I want this matter settled." She looked at her daughter and friends. "Ready, girls?"

Brandi, Robin and Myrna rose from their chairs and followed Dottie out of the room.

Paulie and Levine started protesting. At the door, Dottie turned back to them. "Work it out, gentlemen," she said and closed the door behind her.